# ASHLEY JUDD

# CRYING ON THE INSIDE

## BY JAMES L. DICKERSON

SCHIRMER
TRADE
BOOKS

NEW YORK/LONDON/PARIS/SYDNEY/COPENHAGEN/MADRID

Front cover photo: Armando Gallo/Retna Ltd. USA
Back cover photo: SWIRC/MPA Stills/Retna UK/Retna Ltd. USA

Copyright © 2002 by James L. Dickerson

This edition published 2002 by Schirmer Trade Books,
an imprint of the Music Sales Publishing Group

Order No. SCH 10111
International Standard Book Number: 0.8256.7273.2

Exclusive Distributors:
**Music Sales Corporation**
257 Park Avenue South, New York, NY 10010 USA
**Music Sales Limited**
8/9 Frith Street, London W1D 3JB England
**Music Sales Pty. Limited**
120 Rothschild Street, Rosebery, Sydney, NSW 2018, Australia

Printed in the United States of America by
Vicks Lithograph and Printing Corporation

# Contents

# Acknowledgements

I would like to thank the following people and institutions for their help with this book: Susan Abbott-Jamieson, Beverly Mirriam, Alan Mayor; my editor at Schirmer Trade Books, Larry Birnbaum; Marty Hunt, Louise Curnutte, the staff at the Williamson County Library, the Austin Film Office, Beverly Annas; the clerk's office, Williamson County Circuit Court; the clerk's office, Williamson County General Sessions Court, Grant Benedect; Rob Dollar, managing editor at Kentucky New Era, Victor Nunez; Julie Gordon at the Panama City Beach Film Commission, Carley Pender; Richard Warick, author of two excellent histories on Williamson County; Stewart Lippe, Marilyn Wall-Asse; Jean Dicie at Leiper's Fork Public Library, Robert Carnegie; Ralph Derickson, at the University of Kentucky, the staff at the Public Library of Nashville and Davidson County, and Valerie Zars at Archive Photos

*To Calvin and Ruby*

# Chapter One

## *The Early Years: Chaos in Motion*

Ashley Tyler Ciminella was not alone when she let out her first scream. The entire nation was screaming in chaotic harmony with her: 1968 was arguably one of the most violent and bewildering years in American history. The streets were filled with protesters opposed to the Vietnam War and with civil rights demonstrators demanding equal treatment under the law for African-Americans.

Early in the year, Dr. Martin Luther King, warning that guerrilla warfare was imminent in cities across America, made an effort to merge the antiwar and civil war movements. On March 31, in reaction to a growing swell of nationwide antiwar protests, President Lyndon Johnson went on television to announce a halt in the bombing of North Vietnam. He also announced that he was withdrawing from the presidential race.

Only a few days after Johnson's announcement, Dr. Martin Luther King was assassinated in Memphis, Tennessee, setting off rioting in 172 cities. Forty-three people were killed and over three thousand were injured in the violence that ensued.

On April 19, amid the chaos and violence in the streets, Diana Ciminella checked into the Holy Cross Hospital in Granada Hills, California, to give birth to her second child. Delivered by Cesarean section, Ashley had dark hair and dark eyes, and flashed an engaging smile that she would carry all the way into adulthood.

One of the things that set Ashley apart was the intense way she always made eye contact. When she looked someone in the eye, it was with an intensity that never wavered; she locked onto her target like radar and turned loose only when she was good and ready. It was not so much a stare as it was a probe, as if she were searching for something. Like her smile, it became part of her personality.

Ashley's four-year-old half-sister, Christina, was very much different. Her smile seemed more like a mask, a pleasantry she used to keep others at bay, and her eyes never lingered on someone's face

9

longer than was absolutely necessary to complete a social transaction. Despite the differences in the sisters, they bonded at a very early age and Christina sometimes seemed to think that she was Ashley's mother, not her sister. That may have been because the two girls just clicked emotionally—or it may have been because their mother always seemed so distracted by the complexities of life that they clung to each other as a form of self-defense.

Diana and Michael Ciminella had only been in California for a little over six months when Ashley was born. Michael had moved his family there after completing job training in Broadview, Illinois, for a sales position with Amphenol, a company that made parts for the aeronautics industry. They had only been in Illinois a few days when Diana learned she was pregnant with Ashley.

Michael's courtship of Diana had begun in Ashland, Kentucky, a small city of less than fifty thousand located on the high bank of the Ohio River about 125 miles southeast of Cincinnati, Ohio. Diana was only fourteen when she started dating Michael. He was two years older, but he did not attend the same school because his parents had enrolled him in a military school across the river in Virginia. She was impressed that he was only sixteen and had his own car. His parents had money and belonged to the country club. Her parents, Charles Glen and Pauline "Polly" Judd, supported themselves with the proceeds of a family owned gas station named Judd's Friendly Ashland Service. They had never even been invited to the country club.

By the summer of 1963, Diana and Michael's courtship had grown stale in her eyes, though he still had hopes of a future with her. By that time, he had graduated from the military school and enrolled in Georgia Tech. When that did not work out too well, he enrolled in Transylvania College in Lexington, Kentucky, about two hours away from Ashland. Diana liked his company but never felt a burning passion for him. Indeed, after three years of dating she remained a virgin. She just did not care for him in a sexual way.

Michael was still pressuring Diana to marry him that summer (he first asked her when she was fifteen) when a series of events occurred that forever affected both their lives. It began with a dinner table conversation, during which Diana noticed that there was a visible lump on the shoulder of her younger brother, Brian. He attributed it to the shoulder strap of his newspaper bag, but their mother was concerned enough to call the family doctor. After an initial examination, the doctor told them he thought the lump was cancerous. He suggested Brian be taken to a specialist in Columbus, Ohio.

Since Diana was seventeen and about to enter her senior year at Paul Blazer High School, Glen and Polly felt comfortable leaving her at home alone while they drove Brian to see the doctor in Columbus. It was the first time Diana had ever been left home alone. She laid out her clothes to wear the next morning, the first day of her senior year, and she neatly arranged her school supplies so that she would be certain not to forget anything. She felt good about starting school again; earlier in the year she had her braces removed, so she was, in effect, getting a fresh start with her peers.

That night she underwent a life changing experience. She had sexual intercourse for the first time. It was not with Michael and she has never disclosed the identity of her sexual partner, but any experienced social worker would look at the evidence—the fact that the sex was unplanned and was not with her steady boyfriend—and conclude that her partner was probably someone who had stopped by the house to console her over her brother's illness. Was it an older male, perhaps a family friend—or even a family member? Or was it a predatory schoolmate?

Diana was devastated by the experience. When her parents returned with Brian she learned that he had been diagnosed as having Hodgkin's disease. Her brother was going to die before he had ever lived! Guilt-ridden over both the sexual experience and the news of her brother's terminal illness (*Why Brian? she wondered—he wasn't the one who had defiled himself!*), she withdrew unto herself, unable to smile or carry on as a typical carefree teen with her whole life before her.

Just when she thought it could not possibly get any worse, it did: She learned she was pregnant. Now the whole world was going to know that she had engaged in filthy sex while her saintly brother was facing a death sentence with courage and dignity beyond his years. She pondered her possibilities and concluded she had none. Abortion was out of the question for religious reasons. It was during those dark hours that she concluded that suicide was the only way out for her.

"I wrote a poetic suicide note and was particularly nice to everyone that day," she confessed in her autobiography. "I selected a knife from the kitchen and locked myself in the bathroom. I sat on the toilet so I wouldn't make another mess for Mom and held the blade against my belly, pushing the dull point deep into the folds of flesh on my abdomen. I kept pushing and the blade went a little deeper, but it wasn't puncturing the skin." After a few awkward moments, she concluded that hari-kari was not the way to go. Undeterred, she decided to steal the keys to the family car and drive off a cliff. She was sneaking out the door at midnight, keys in hand, when she realized that was no good either because she did not know how to drive.

Afraid to tell her parents about her pregnancy, she confided in the only person she thought would be understanding, her best friend Linda McDonald. Linda advised Diana to tell Michael Ciminella, but Diana had not been returning his calls or answering his letters and she really did not want to discuss it with him. Although Linda promised she would keep her secret, according to Diana, she told both her mother and Michael.

Michael's reaction is interesting because it reflected no sense of jealousy or betrayal or anger toward a rival. Still very much in love with Diana, Michael wrote her a letter and offered to marry her, promising to raise the child as if it were his own.

Diana was relieved to receive the letter. She concluded that marriage was the only way out of a desperate situation. She hid the letter under her bed and went to school, only to return home and find her mother waiting for her, letter in hand. The secret was now out. After several heart-wrenching confrontations with her mother and father, it became apparent to her that marriage was her only real option.

Diana and Michael were too young to get married in Kentucky without parental permission—and Diana wanted to keep her parents out of what she called an "awful mess"—so they drove to Tennessee where they thought they could get married, but Diana was too young and they were turned away. Finally, they went to their parents and asked for help in getting married. Both families reluctantly agreed that marriage was the best solution. On January 3, 1964, Diana and Michael, along with both sets of parents, drove to Parisburg, Virginia, so that they could be pronounced man and wife in a proper Baptist church. Because of the scandalous nature of the situation, no one even considered going to the church in Ashland. No, this was a marriage that required stealth and as little ministerial dialogue as possible. Diana had secrets that she could share with no one but the Lord himself.

After the ceremony, Diana moved into Michael's attic bedroom at the Ciminella house. Since she was four months pregnant—and showing—the school agreed to send a tutor to the Ciminella house so that Diana could continue her studies and graduate on schedule. Polly's reaction to the marriage was curious. Once Diana was situated in the Ciminella house, Polly cleared out her bedroom, throwing many things away and moving the remaining items into the attic. As a wedding gift, she gave Diana an iron, perhaps a passive-aggressive symbol of the life of domesticity that she felt her daughter had chosen for herself.

On May 30, 1964, Diana gave birth to Christina Claire. She was born by C-section since the doctor had determined that the baby was too large to pass through Diana's birth canal. After a short stay in the hospital, Diana and Michael took Christina back to the Ciminella home, where a nursery had been prepared downstairs just off the kitchen. Their stay there was short-term and by fall they had moved to a small apartment in Lexington, where Michael was going to school.

Diana was unhappy but not really sure why. Sure, she was aware of the unhappiness that accompanied the birth of a baby at such a young age and the unhappiness of seeing that baby raised by a man who was not the child's father, but her unhappiness went much deeper than that. Even before that night of misplaced passion or abuse that produced her daughter, she had lived a fanciful life about her ultimate place in the universe. She had an instant bond with Christina, one that would supersede all future relationships in her life, but she could not help but wonder about the larger meaning of her secret. Did it mean she was destined for some sort of greatness, something that would justify and redeem the sinfulness of the secret? Or did it mean she was doomed to a lifetime of suffering for the actions of another person?

Diana enrolled for several courses at the University of Kentucky but dropped out after a couple of semesters when it became obvious that she could not be both a good mother and a good student. It was not long before that general sense of unhappiness transferred to her marriage. Michael helped out with the care of Christina, as he had promised, but Diana was disappointed that he never seemed to develop the deep bond that she shared with her daughter. But how could he? He was only an accomplice to the secret, not a participating player.

Of course, Diana was too young to understand the dynamics of such a complicated marital relationship. To her way of thinking, if Michael did not possess the same obsessive attachment to Christina as she did, then something must be wrong in the relationship. When he left school to enroll in a job-training program in Illinois, she was relieved to be leaving Kentucky and all the heartaches that living there had brought her, especially the death of her brother, Brian, whose last days and subsequent funeral brought her more pain than she knew existed in life. For her, there was something even worse than sexual abuse—the death of innocence.

By the time Ashley joined the Ciminella family, the emotional battle lines had pretty much been drawn. Michael was married to a woman who did not love him the way he loved her. Diana was at war with both the insecurities of low self-esteem over the secret she shared with Michael and the increasing belief that she was somehow destined for greatness. Under the best of circumstances, it is difficult to deal with either of those extremes; Diana's daily chore was to reconcile the two opposites in her life while raising two daughters and playing the role of a dutiful wife. Not surprisingly, Ashley frequently came up short as an equal member in the family.

Christina was having nightmares and suffering from asthma, and she was showing signs of aggressive behavior toward other children when Ashley came along, but there is no indication that she ever exhibited that behavior toward her sister. On the contrary, she smothered Ashley with attention, becoming, in effect, her substitute mother. As a result, Ashley's earliest memories focus on her relationship with Christina and not her mother.

When Christina started school, Ashley engaged in fantasies about her sister, a form of play-acting. "I must have been as young as two and a half, or maybe three, and I would go and pretend I was in school, because [Christina] was my hero and I wanted to be around her," she once told a reporter for the *Winnipeg Sun*. "It was kind of a mythic, otherworld place where she went, and she'd come back and tell me stories, and I think my memory of the way that I played at it was not unlike acting."

Diana had two lovely daughters and a husband who loved her, but it never seemed enough. She knew she was movie-star attractive, but it all seemed such a waste. She had fantasies of becoming a movie star. Unfortunately, living up in the hills offered few opportunities for advancement. Without telling Michael, she looked for a house in West Hollywood, a place where she could be closer to the action.

Once she found a house, she rented it on her own. They moved and tried to start their lives over again. By then it was pretty much too late. Diana and Michael no longer had a consistent sexual relationship—he often slept alone on the couch—and they seemed to argue over every little thing that arose.

Finally, Diana—new woman that she was trying to become—told Michael that he just didn't fit into their new hippie house. She asked him to leave—and he did. He moved in with a male friend who lived in Manhattan Beach. When he left, he took both the family Dodge and his company car, an action that Diana considered abandonment, even though it was she who demanded that he leave. At the time of the separation, Ashley was three and Christina was seven, old enough to feel the pain but not old enough to understand it. The only simple relationships they had were with each other.

With Michael out of her life, Diana struggled to find an identity of her own. She began that search in the classified-ad section of the local newspaper. One of the ads that caught her eye was for a receptionist at Mark Gordon Enterprises. Not until she arrived for the interview did she discover that Mark Gordon was the manager of a popular recording group, the Fifth Dimension. The group had enjoyed a long string of hits since 1967, including "Go Where You Wanna Go" and "Up, Up and Away." Gordon was, in fact, married to Florence LaRue, one of two women in the group. Diana left the interview with stars in her eyes, convinced that her luck was going to change.

Diana did not get the receptionist job—she later recalled that Gordon said he couldn't hire her because she was white, although the more likely scenario was that Florence did not want such an eager-eyed beauty working in the office—but Gordon did arrange for her to get a secretarial job with the group's booking agent. For a while, Diana's future looked promising. She spoke on the phone with famous songwriters and with recording artists who had business with the Fifth Dimension. Then, as abruptly as it began, it ended. The booking agent replaced her with his girlfriend.

For the next three years, Diana held a variety of jobs. She worked in a secretarial pool. She signed up with a modeling agency, though she swears she never posed nude. And she worked as a receptionist in a law office.

Life in the Ciminella household was a roller coaster. When Ashley and Christina were not hearing the latest bad news about their mother's employment situation, they were gleaning details of her relationships with other men. In 1972, Diana was only twenty-five, but it seemed to her as if she had endured a lifetime of bad relationships with men. One boyfriend, a sometimes-working actor named James, led her down a road of physical and emotional abuse that was difficult to hide from the children.

Throughout it all, Michael maintained a fatherly relationship with the girls. Christina was not his flesh and blood, but Ashley was and he felt that bond deeply and did his best to nurture that relationship. One of his favorite games with Ashley was hide-and-seek. She especially liked to play the game outdoors, especially if they were in a place not familiar to her. Once, while she was still in kindergarten, he took her out of school for a couple of weeks so that she could go on an adventure with him. "He was turning thirty, and he wanted to celebrate with a bunch of his wild, quasi-hippie friends, some of whom lived on government property in a domed tent," she explained to actress Salma Hayek for *Interview* magazine. "We played out there in the forests, and I was just thrilled and scared to death. I felt like I was the only person on the planet...there was one moment in particular I can remember where I didn't know where anybody was, and I was just standing in the forest alone."

That memory was more than just a reminiscence. It was symbolic of Ashley's position in the Ciminella family. As a child she was "standing in the forest alone"—not unloved, for both parents surely loved her, but devoid of an emotional core that assured her that she was not alone in the universe.

Although Ashley had been affected greatly by her parents' separation, the divorce itself had little meaning to her. Not so with Christina, who at eight years of age was old enough to understand the familial ramifications of the proceeding. "I was too young to understand what had happened to our family, but the divorce really affected [Christina]," Ashley told Louis B. Hobson of the *Calgary Sun*. "She was so angry and resentful."

Ashley was of a different emotional makeup than Christina, a fact that became apparent even at a very early age. When Christina felt emotionally bruised, she externalized her feelings by striking out physically or verbally. Ashley was just the opposite. She absorbed everything that came at her, keeping it all inside; the way she released it was through play-acting, by creating another world that she could inhabit with people of her own choosing.

Whenever Christina acted out with aggression, Diana responded because it was something she could see and hear (for example, when Christina started sleepwalking, she took her to a doctor to get advice), but whenever Ashley acted out, it was so subtle and so internalized that it flew right over Diana's head.

In many ways, Diana was a very immature adult, and considering the way she entered motherhood, that is not surprising. She loved her daughters dearly, but she falsely concluded that they would never be happy until she could provide them with the material things she thought they should have. Young mothers often decide that their children cannot possibly have happy lives until they have happy lives themselves, but that is seldom ever the case. Ashley and Christina needed Diana to put them at the center of her universe, but she could not do that until she found her own happiness as an adult. Diana knew that she was not providing her girls with a "normal" family life, but she rationalized it by convincing herself that it was simply a bumpy road she must travel until she arrived at a place where all three could live her version of a utopian family life.

Diana began a quest for love and financial security, but it was not what you could an orderly expedition. She was developing a pattern of short-term jobs and dead-end romances. She showed questionable judgment when it came to men, whether it involved work or romance. Was that poor judgment the reason why she began her young life with a secret? Or was it the result of the abuse she may have experienced conceiving the secret? The fact that she seemed to have lived a normal life prior to the night of that first sexual encounter lends credence to the belief that her life was spiraling out of control as a young adult as a result of that life-changing event. Some women, experiencing similar events, live a lifetime and never fully recover.

Almost always, the termination of both Diana's employment and her romances coincided with some traumatic and dramatic event associated with her job or her love life. Looking back, it is a wonder that she did not simply wander into a cave and refuse to come out. After one particularly unfortunate job experience—her boss paid her with checks that bounced and poisoned the work atmosphere with large amounts of cocaine, not to mention pimps and hookers— Christina came down with a severe kidney infection.

When the doctor told her that she would have to be admitted to the hospital, Diana panicked. She had no job and no health insurance. She swallowed her pride and called Michael, who by then had moved to Chicago, and she asked for his help. According to her reconstruction of that conversation, he told her she should have thought about that before she filed for divorce, then hung up.

Someone at the hospital suggested to Diana that she apply for assistance from the California Department of Social Services. As a single mother, she was eligible for financial assistance and, more importantly, she would have Christina's and Ashley's medical expenses covered by Medicaid. Typical for Diana, while she was standing in the welfare line, a man approached her and offered her five thousand dollars for a nude photo session. She turned down the offer but incorporated it into her increasingly feminist rationale for why she was having so much trouble in life.

Diana's next job was as a personal secretary to a wealthy financial consultant who, as a kung fu champion, sometimes worked as an adviser on martial arts movies. Diana worked in his house, paying his bills and overseeing the housekeeping and gardening. Sometimes she read scripts that were sent to him so that she could underline passages that had martial arts scenes.

Once she went with him to a martial arts exhibition, where she met an instructor named Mike Stone. Also there that day was Stone's new girlfriend, Priscilla Presley. The two women discovered they had several life experiences in common, including two daughters the same age, Lisa Marie and Ashley. It was during that brief encounter, Diana later recalled, that Priscilla confided in her that she had left Elvis for Stone.

That was heady stuff for Diana. Priscilla wasn't the king of rock 'n' roll, but she was a star in her own right. At long last Diana felt she was traveling in circles that would lead her into the dream world of her fantasies. Typical of her experience at that time, just as she was feeling a tinge of optimism over her future, something traumatic happened in her private life. Christina was walking home from elementary school one day when a man sitting in a car motioned her over to the window and exposed himself. Christina ran screaming away from the man and sought refuge at a playmate's house, where her friend's mother called police. Diana was notified of the incident while she was at work. She hurried home and held Christina on her lap while the child provided a description of the man to a police sketch artist. It turned out the man was a known pedophile.

As a result of the incident, Diana quit her job so that she could take a position in a health food store near her home. That way she would be in the neighborhood to keep an eye on her children. Unwilling to give up her dreams of becoming a movie star, she looked for part-time work that would allow her to leave the neighborhood for short periods of time. Maybe the best way to break into show business, she decided, was to just throw her face out there where her potential could be seen by a large audience.

She set her sights on the television game shows that were produced in Los Angeles. In 1973, she landed a spot as a contestant on *Hollywood Squares* and managed to get a full week's exposure. There followed two different appearances on the popular show *Password*. Word of the appearances made it back to Ashland. Diana was at last a star in her hometown. It wasn't much, but it was something.

In June 1974, Ashley and Christina were packed up and shipped off to Ashland to spend the summer with their grandparents. That was not a bad thing for them, for they spent time with both sets of grandparents and, for the most part, were able to live in a world that seemed to change little from year to year. What few tensions arose were over mundane issues, not child molesters, drug addicts, and haywire love affairs, as they were accustomed to in Hollywood. The Judds took them fishing and to visit relatives. The Ciminellas took them to fancy restaurants and to the country club.

With her children set for the summer, Diana quit her job—after six years in California she had lost track of how many—and loaded up her car to drive to Texas. One of her friends had spoken in a positive way about Austin and she figured she would give it a try. One never knew where one might find happiness. Why not Texas?

Diana stayed with a friend of a friend in Austin while she looked for work. She wanted something with a high profile. She interviewed for a job as a weather girl with a local television station (she didn't get the job) and she prowled the nightclub scene, soaking up the bluesy rock of the Fabulous Thunderbirds and Double Trouble with Lou Ann Barton. Perhaps music would be her vehicle to stardom, not the silver screen!

After a few weeks in Austin, she realized that it had turned into yet another dead-end dream. Texas was not the end of the rainbow and she found no bucket of gold with her name on it. She decided to return to California in search of a more practical dream. She had always been a compassionate person. Perhaps nursing was a profession in which she could make a name for herself.

While Ashley and Christina reveled in the love and affection of their grandparents, Diana headed off to northern California to investigate nursing possibilities. She had no training, but many hospitals had training programs and sometimes offered financial assistance to employees who wanted to pursue a degree.

Like so many other things she tried, that dream did not work out either. One day, while out driving, she stopped the car and walked out into a meadow. For the longest time she sat there, pondering her future. She was still sitting there, singing to herself, when a retired registered nurse named Dorothy Wells spotted her and took her home to the cattle ranch she operated with her husband, Henry. They took her into their home and gave her chores to do. In her spare time, she worked on a quilt for Christina and a backpack for Ashley. That sojourn lasted for about a month.

One morning Diana awoke and realized that it was almost time for school to start again. When she called Ashland to talk to the girls, Christina, who was then ten, suggested she return to Kentucky. That solution was so obvious that it had not occurred to Diana. She told Christina it was an excellent idea. She loaded up her car and drove from northern California to Ashland, where she thought she might regroup and re-examine that entire dream business. Maybe her happiness was in Kentucky after all!

On the way back, she got an idea. Michael had left his job in Chicago and returned to Lexington, where he got a job in a leather shop (at some point he decided that his true calling was as a leather craftsman; it was, after all, the mid-1970s, when such "dropping out" decisions were commonplace). He often slept in the back room of the leather shop, but he also had a fishing cabin on the outskirts of town.

Diana called Michael and offered him a deal. She would forget about the money he owed in child support if he would agree to let her live in the cabin with Ashley and Christina until she got back on her feet. It was the least he could do, she argued. Michael readily agreed.

The cabin turned out to be more rustic than she had imagined. Located at the end of a long dirt road, it was a wood-frame structure without indoor plumbing or heat. She spent the first couple of months getting the cabin in shape, then started investigating possibilities for nursing school. Although she had turned her back on the pretentious, glitzy ways of Hollywood, she could not shake her hippie indoctrination. She grew herbs and vegetables in a garden and kept wildflowers on the kitchen table, living a lifestyle that would be the envy of any flower-peddling hippie on the Sunset Strip.

"We had a really wonderful rural lifestyle there, " Ashley later told Bob Strauss of the *Boston Globe*. "There was no TV. We made our own soap and sometimes churned our own butter. My sister started to sing and I became captivated by books, absolutely rapt."

Only in the second grade that first year at the cabin, Ashley was already showing signs of becoming a serious reader. It was the perfect counterpoint to Christina's physicality and to her mother's emotional and fluctuating view of life (one moment, she was absorbed with the materialism of Hollywood, the next moment she was enamored of the simplicity and poverty of rural living). Why would Ashley *not* become an avid reader? It was the perfect escape to places that always had a beginning, a middle, and an end. To Ashley, books had an engaging reality to them, something that did not seem to exist in her real life.

In time, Christina found her own escape—music. When Michael visited the girls at the cabin, he sometimes brought along a guitar he had learned to play. Christina was instantly enthralled by the instrument, and Diana—who saw it as a means of self-entertainment, a replacement for television—encouraged her. Michael taught Christina to play three basic chords and she took it from there, spending all her free moments with the guitar, while Ashley spent her free time with books.

Almost without trying, Diana had fulfilled one of her dreams—self-entertaining daughters. Actually, she did not even know it was a dream until it happened, but she certainly knew a blessing when she saw one. Sometimes the Lord provided substitute blessings: Such was the serendipitous route of the Judd destiny.

In January 1975, immediately after the Christmas recess, all three of the Judds went off to school—Ashley to the first grade, Christina to the fifth grade, and Diana to nursing school at Eastern Kentucky University. That winter and spring, they each returned to their humble cabin with renewed purpose. Christina did her homework so that she could play her guitar. Diana did her housework so that she could delve into the mysteries of the human body. And Ashley, having no homework yet, turned to her books.

"She was a weird kid," Christina told *Us* magazine. "Most kids at that age are either Nintendo-ing or they're on the phone. Ashley was out creating villages for fairies and reading strange books." Sometimes, when she wasn't reading, Ashley gathered up empty cans and took them the supermarket to sell for spending money. Even at that early age, she was learning to survive in a parallel universe with her mother and sister.

"I always had an imaginary life," she explained to Ingrid Sischy for *Interview*. "I had fairies and built houses for them....I remember wanting to look at the world and experience things like the girl in the book that I was reading at the time did. I don't remember the title of it, I just remember that she was in a rather extraordinary circumstance, and I wanted to receive the world the way she would have. I'd look at a bush and wonder how would she feel when she looked at that bush."

It is not entirely surprising that Ashley lived such a fanciful life. Depending on her mother's point of reference, the reality of her own life changed from year to year. One year it might be important for everyone to be Hollywood glamorous. The next year Diana might proclaim that entirely wrong and say that everyone in the family should follow a hippie lifestyle. Now that they had moved to the cabin, it was important for them all to be frontier women. Diana cut the girls some slack on how they were allowed to dress, but she herself trudged off to school each morning wearing rubber gum boots, a grisly fur hat, and a tattered overcoat. The last thing she wanted to be at nursing school was some preppy ingénue in high heels.

Diana enrolled in a two-year program with the goal of receiving an associate degree in nursing so that she could become a licensed practical nurse. That first semester she took courses in English composition, nutrition, and basic human anatomy. Perhaps because she was still suffering from low self-esteem over her secret, she tried her best *not* to fit in with the younger students, many of whom were about the same age she was when she gave birth to Christina. She tried to look and act as little like them as possible.

Often Diana taunted her instructors with questions that challenged the philosophy or authority of the courses they taught. Diana tried so hard to be unlike everyone else that she ceased to be like herself. It was a fantasy world as rich as any traveled by Ashley in her books about fairies and adventuresome young girls.

That first semester of nursing school saw notable changes in the household. Michael came often to visit the girls, perhaps realizing that Ashley and Christina were more important to his life than he understood when they lived great distances apart. Sometimes he went rabbit hunting in the fields and woods near the cabin. Diana cooked the rabbits in stews that she fed to the family. Before one such meal, Diana recalled in her autobiography, Ashley was asked to say grace: "Hello God and Jesus. Tell Mr. Bunny Rabbit we're sorry we're gonna eat him. And I sure hope it doesn't make me choke and die, 'cause I'm too young to go—amen."

Of course, Diana, being a typical divorced mother, bitched when Michael did not visit the girls and then bitched again when he visited them too much. It was a no-win situation for him. He coped by moving into the cabin with them later that spring. Although he slept in one of the spare bedrooms, Diana was unhappy, to say the least. But what could she do? It was his cabin after all; he was the one who paid the rent. They fought often, and there are few things more unattractive to children than witnessing their divorced parents fight over issues that seem silly or incomprehensible.

Toward the end of the semester, Diana did what she always did when she felt trapped—she bolted. With only a month of school left, she rented a one-bedroom cabin in nearby Berea, a small town about twenty-five miles south of Richmond. She did not want to take the girls out of school, so she left them there with Michael.

On weekends, Diana kept the girls at her new cabin and together they explored the countryside to find a larger place to live. While this was going on, Diana received a note in her school mailbox from a faculty member at a local college who said she had a house that might interest her. Intrigued, Diana drove out to meet the woman, with the girls in tow. What they saw when they arrived alternately amazed, shocked, and delighted them. The mysterious letter writer turned out to be a wealthy music instructor who lived in a magnificent old house in Berea during the school terms and in Vermont during the summer months. Her daughter was married to Norman Vincent Peale's son and her son was editor of *Reader's Digest*. She offered Diana and the girls a second building on the estate, a completely furnished home that had a name—Chanticleer.

The four-bedroom house was filled with antique furniture and hand-braided rugs; it reeked of money and success and tradition. Diana said she could not possibly afford to rent such a house. With that, the woman offered her a deal she could not turn down: she would rent it to her for one hundred dollars a month.

For a mother and daughters who often seemed confused about where fantasy left off and reality began, it was confirmation of the practicality of their dreams. Ashley and Christina ran through the house like banshees, hardly bothered at all that it had neither a telephone nor a television. They moved in right away.

That first summer at Chanticleer was magical for the Ciminella women. Their new house was located in Morrill, a small community southeast of Berea in an area near the Daniel Boone National Forest. With school out for the summer, they had plenty of time to explore both the property and their rapidly changing relationships. It was that summer that Diana got serious about encouraging Christina's interest in music. She bought records at a second-hand store and suggested songs for her to learn to play. Perhaps *that* was the key to her identity!

As Diana and Christina paired off and spend countless hours making music, Ashley was left to her own devices. Why Diana did not include Ashley has never really been explained. Ashley attempted to learn to play the fiddle, but that quickly fell to the wayside because she was not encouraged to excel at it.

Diana never treated her daughters differently, not when it came to dispensing love, but there was a bond with Christina that did not exist with Ashley, and it became apparent that summer. There are a lot of reasons why that may have happened, but the most likely is that Ashley was never party to the shameful secret that Diana and Christina shared. Christina was never aware of that secret, of course, and did what any little girl would have done under those same circumstances—she took all the value-added attention that her mother heaped upon her and she ran with it, unconcerned about the fact that her sister was not receiving her share. Diana loved both her children; but, explained in male-female relationship terms, she was *in love* with Christina.

Ashley simply retreated further into her books, where her fictional heroes out-shined any music ever concocted by her mother and sister. Fortunately, she was born with a more introspective temperament than her mother and sister. When things did not go their way, mother and older daughter often lashed out at the world. Ashley did just the opposite. She internalized her frustrations and found fantasy outlets that accomplished the same goals.

Life at Chanticleer was everything Diana had hoped it would be. They got to know the neighbors and had picnics and informal get-togethers. Diana learned to make lye soap and she started carrying a pistol with her when she explored their two hundred-acre spread (ostensibly to kill the snakes that lurked in dark places).

That fall, Ashley enrolled in the second grade. It was her second school in two years. Sadly, it was a trend that would continue. During her twelve years of grammar and high school, she would end up attending thirteen different schools, more than enough to break the mind and spirit of a normal child. Of course, there was nothing normal about Ashley.

The Ciminellas had a spectacular summer, but bad things starting happening again shortly after they all returned to school in the fall of 1975. Eleven-year-old Christina began acting out in class. She refused to turn in homework and, unknown to Diana, she frequently skipped school altogether. Diana was called in to meet with her teachers. When Diana asked Christina for an explanation, she replied that her teachers all hated her. An irrational point of reference is not a point from which a mother and daughter can engage in a productive debate, so what developed was a series of confrontations, most ending in fierce arguments.

No sooner did the dust settle on those arguments than another crisis arose. On a visit with her mother and father, Diana learned that he was seeing another woman. Polly told her all the details, far more than she wanted to know. Diana was thirty years of age now, but news of serious marital problems between her parents hit hard, all the more so because her mother pleaded with her to testify against her father in the divorce proceedings.

Soon things started getting ugly at Chanticleer. Someone broke into the house and stole their record player and all Diana's costume jewelry. When she discovered the burglary, Diana rushed upstairs to get her pearl-handled Smith & Wesson revolver from her bedside table. To her horror, it, too, had been taken. She crammed the girls in the car and drove to a neighbor's house to call the police. Everyone said it was probably the hermit who lived on the edge of their property, but when the police searched his shed they found no incriminating evidence.

The next day, they all went to school. When they returned home, they found their cat dead on the front porch. Diana examined the pet and determined that all its bones had been broken. Soon after that, their dog disappeared. Neighbors said they thought they saw it nailed to the hermit's shed.

Later in the year, police told her that they had a man in custody who had confessed to being the hermit's accomplice in the burglary. The man was arrested and a trial date was set for a day near the end of the summer. Diana attempted to round up neighborhood witnesses to bolster the case, but everyone said the man was a bad actor and they were afraid to testify. The night before the trial, Diana and the girls were awakened by a series of gunshots outside the house. Assuming it was a warning not to testify, they fled to a neighbor's house and stayed there until it was time to go to the courthouse. To Diana's dismay, charges against the man were dismissed due to lack of evidence.

Soon after that, Diana sent Ashley and Christina to visit their grandmother Judd for a while. Alone in the house, Diana locked all the doors and windows and strapped on her new pistol. How much could a woman stand and stay sane? she wondered.

On August 4, 1976, she did the only thing she knew to do: She loaded up her car and struck out for California. She called her mother from the road and told her she was taking a little trip and would see her and the girls soon. That was a lie, of course, and it pained her to lie to her mother, but she had convinced herself that she was fighting for her life. She was determined to find her happiness, no matter what the cost.

On the road again, Diana seemed aimless at first. She wandered from city to city, making her way westward, pausing to talk to people and to sample conversations. She had a vision of herself as some sort of traveling troubadour whose mission and vision was to capture the pulse of America. At one point, using Christina's guitar, she paused to write a song while her car was being repaired.

Not until the mechanic told her it would cost five hundred dollars to repair her car did she call anyone to let them know that she was all right. She telephoned her father not long after midnight. He was shocked to hear that she was in Nebraska. He thought she was still at the cabin in Morrill. When she explained her predicament to him, he advised her to forget the repairs and get what she could for the car. The mechanic offered her one hundred and twenty-five dollars in cash and she took it. Soon she was on a plane to Marin County, California, just north of San Francisco.

Diana enrolled Ashley and Christina in school there, checked out the College of Marin nursing school, and rented an apartment in Marin City. Then she set out for Kentucky to retrieve her children, neither of whom had any idea what was in store for them. Glen Judd chose a U-Haul truck from his rental lot, packed up the girls, and drove to Morrill, where he met Diana. For the return trip to California, Diana, Christina, and Ashley discovered America in a U-Haul truck.

Once they were settled—Ashley began the third grade and Christina began the seventh grade—Diana enrolled in nursing school to complete her degree requirements. It was shortly after they arrived in California that Diana decided she wanted a new identity. At nursing school she began introducing herself as Naomi Judd. She later explained she chose that name because of its biblical references.

One can only imagine the effect that had on eight-year-old Ashley. She was in a new school (her third), she was removed from the emotional support of her father and her grandparents, and she was forced to reintroduce herself to a new set of children. On top of all that, her mother wanted to be called by a name she had never heard before, except in the Bible. What next? she must have wondered.

Naomi did not have a multiple personality, but she did have multiple identities. By day she was a hardworking if not slightly obsessive nursing student, and by night she was a musician in training. In between those two pursuits she was Ashley's and Christina's mother-with-a-new-name.

By that time, Naomi had decided, perhaps by elimination, that the secret to her happiness lay in music. She started dating a man who published a music magazine and had a financial interest in a makeshift recording studio located in a garage. She took harmonica lessons and she practiced on Christina's guitar. The trouble was she did not have a great singing voice and had little aptitude for the guitar or harmonica.

Luckily for Naomi, Christina had a great singing voice and had become an excellent rhythm guitarist. The secret to success might lie in a family group, Naomi concluded. For a while, she experimented with a concept she called Hillbilly Women. The idea was for Christina to move over to banjo, for Ashley to play the fiddle, and for her to play guitar and harmonica. For weeks they sat around the kitchen table, playing and singing, trying to forge a musical identity.

Hillbilly Women had several fatal flaws, the first of which was

Ashley's nondescript singing voice and the complexity of the fiddle (violins are more difficult to learn to play than guitars and there is no way to fake it by strumming chords). The second flaw was that there was no way that Christina could carry both her mother and her sister.

In later years, Naomi said that Ashley backed out of the group because she was not interested. There is probably a lot of truth in that. Ashley had always shown more interest in books than music. But even if that had not been the case, it would have been difficult for Ashley to fit into the group. She looked more like her mother than Christina did, and she had the same urge to please others, but she never had the bond that Christina had with their mother. It was a mystery to her. Naomi and Christina fought constantly, while she was always affectionate and eager to please. Ashley was an outsider in that family—and she knew it.

Once Ashley was cut from the group, Naomi pursued every opportunity to inject herself and Christina into the local music scene. When she learned that the college offered a course in studio engineering, she enrolled in the class and recorded a demo tape with Christina. At every opportunity she volunteered their services, free of charge, for background vocals recorded by other students.

In the winter of 1977, Naomi moved her family to a larger house. A couple of months later she graduated from the nursing program. It was around that time that she and Ashley were out riding around in her "new" 1957 Chevy when they were flagged down on the street by two young men who asked if they could rent her classic car for a George Lucas film titled *More American Graffiti.*

Naomi agreed to rent the car to them for three weeks for four hundred dollars. While she was signing the agreement with the production company she was offered work as a thirty-dollar-a-day extra in the film. How silly that must have seemed to Naomi. For nearly a decade she had been working night and day to become first a movie star and then a singing star, and there she was, driving along the street, when someone offered to put her in the movies!

*More American Graffiti* was a sequel to the 1973 hit and many of the stars of the first film had returned, including Ron Howard, Cindy Williams and Harrison Ford. Filmed in Freemont, California, the movie focused on life in the mid-1960s, by which time the wide-eyed optimism of 1962, when the first movie was set, had been corrupted by the evils of the Vietnam War. Ford reprised his role as Bob Falfa, who by then had become a San Francisco motorcycle cop. During one break in filming, he asked Naomi to go riding with him on the motorcycle, but she surprisingly declined.

After a few days of work as an extra—she played a convict on a prison bus with Cindy Williams—she was offered a job as a production secretary. It was sort of a glorified gofer's job in that her main duties were to run errands, but she was delighted with it because it put her in close contact with powerful people.

As she watched the film crew at work, she marveled at the creative process and she lobbied to get Christina hired as an extra so that she, too, could see firsthand what star power was all about. Finally, she got her hired for a scene that took place in a country-western nightclub. Why she got Christina—and not Ashley—a place in the movie has never been explained, and in retrospect it seems astonishingly callous. Christina had never showed an interest in movies or in any sort of fantasy world, but Ashley had been displaying interests along those lines for years.

Energized by her experiences on the movie set, Naomi pressed even harder in her efforts to find a career in music. She did not look for work as a nurse, the only thing in life she actually had training for; instead she worked as a waitress in a nightclub that featured live entertainment. In time, she and Christina performed at the restaurant.

Throughout this time, Christina was acting out in aggressive ways toward both Naomi and sweet Ashley. Naomi met with her teachers and even took her to a therapist, but nothing helped. By that point, their mother-daughter relationship was based on a routine of fighting and making up.

Finally, stressed out by her conflicts with Christina and her inability to get the big break they needed, she decided it was time to flee Marin City. She took out a loan, using her prized 1957 Chevy as collateral, and once again bolted for Ashland, her daughters in tow. This time her visit had a purpose. She had decided to leave Ashley with her father so that she and Christina could forge a new life as entertainers.

Shortly after Christmas 1978, Naomi and Christina said goodbye to Ashley and returned to California to box up all their belongings. That done, they packed just enough clothing to get by and headed east to Austin, Texas, where they hoped to be discovered as singing stars. Free of Ashley and hopefully free of any link to her old life, Naomi encouraged Christina to choose a new first name.

The name they came up with was Wynonna, taken from the song "Route 66," which made reference to a town named Winona. Naomi liked the way it sounded, plus it seemed to be a better match for Naomi than Christina.

One can only imagine the horror with which Ashley greeted that news when her mother told her over the telephone that her sister was now named Wynonna. It was the ultimate rejection, really. They were going to be Naomi and Wynonna Judd and she was going to remain Ashley Ciminella. It is one thing to be abandoned by your mother and sister, but for them to also change their names, drawing another boundary between them and you, would be incomprehensible to any child Ashley's age.

In later years, Naomi tried to sugarcoat her abandonment of Ashley by saying that she did it for her own good, but all the statements of good intentions in the world cannot change the fact that she chose one daughter over the other and left Ashley behind. It is the sort of decision that leaves deep scars that can last a lifetime.

While in Texas, Naomi took Wynonna to the Palomino Club to hear J. D. Sumner and the Stamps Quartet, a gospel group that became legendary in the 1950s and 1960s because of its association with Elvis Presley. One of the singers with the group was a tall, dark-haired bass named Larry Strickland. Naomi did not meet him that night, but he would later come to play an important role in her life.

The Texas adventure ultimately led them to Las Vegas, where Naomi had hopes of being cast in a television special with Lola Falana. When Naomi called her parents and the Ciminellas and told them that they were going to Nevada—and, by the way, she explained, it was going to be necessary for Wynonna to drop out of school for a semester—they expressed strong opposition and threatened to send a truant officer to to Las Vegas retrieve Wynonna.

Ashley wept when Naomi told her what was going to happen.

Now in the fifth grade, Ashley did everything possible to fit into her new surroundings. She did not want to be different from everyone else. She wanted to be popular, a member of the in crowd. She tried out for cheerleader and was accepted. "One of the great ambitions of my early life was to be a cheerleader," she confided to Gene Wyatt for the Nashville *Tennessean*. "We wore little, blue, silk pinafore outfits that were so cute. I also remember my shoes were not-so-cute Keds bought at a second-hand store."

Of course, the Las Vegas deal fell through—didn't they always? Jeff Thornton, the Nashville music executive who had put together the Las Vegas deal, told Naomi that when she returned to her apartment in California there would be two one-way tickets to Nashville waiting for her. Naomi believed him, even though he had not paid her anything thus far for her efforts. Before leaving Las Vegas, Naomi and Wynonna sent Ashley a postcard that said they hoped to see her soon.

When they arrived in California, the tickets were waiting for them as promised. They loaded all their possessions onto a moving van and trusted the mover to send their 1957 Chevy on the next van headed to Tennessee. Then they boarded a plane to begin a new chapter in their lives.

Throughout it all, eleven-year-old Ashley had only one question: "When are you coming to get me?"

# Chapter Two

## *From Kentucky with Love*

Despite their long quest for a break in the music business, Naomi and Wynonna had never visited Nashville, Tennessee, the self-made home of country music. It is especially odd when you consider that when they lived in Morrill, they were only a few hours drive from Nashville. The reason for that is obvious: Naomi had always envisioned herself a star of the Hollywood and Las Vegas variety. For the never-practical Naomi, Nashville was a last-chance roll of the dice.

When Naomi and Wynonna arrived at the Nashville airport on May 1, 1979, a driver sent by Jeff Thornton was there to pick them up. He drove a late-model car that he said Thornton was going to let them use until their car arrived. Naomi was not terribly impressed by the banged up land barge of a car, and she was even less thrilled by their accommodations at the Music City Motor Inn on the outskirts of town. If it had not been for the McDonald's located next door to the motel, Wynonna would have been miserable.

What Naomi saw when she peered out the motel door was a city just like every other Southern city she had ever seen. Rich neighborhoods and poor neighborhoods, chain restaurants and mom-and-pop cafes, upscale shopping malls in the suburbs and a run-down inner city. It was when she looked for country music that she really felt frustrated. Although Nashville—or Music City, as it likes to be called—is famous for country music, there was very little country music to be heard there in 1979 (or even now). There were several country music venues scattered about the city, but most of the nightclubs catered to audiences interested in blues or rock 'n' roll.

Try as she might, Naomi could not find any country music in Nashville. What she did not understand is that while all the major country music recording labels are in Nashville, along with most of the artists who record on those labels, Nashville is little more than a mailing address for country music.

When country music artists performed—and in 1979 the hottest stars were Dolly Parton, Barbara Mandrell, Kenny Rogers, and Willie Nelson—they did so in large venues in Los Angeles, Las Vegas, Michigan, and Texas. A country music fan could walk the streets of Nashville for twenty years and never see any of the stars perform, except at special promotional events sponsored by the record labels.

The next morning Naomi started work at her new job as a receptionist at Jeff Thornton's office. Since she did not want to leave Wynonna alone in the motel, she took her to work with her. Together they explored Music Row, the two streets that define the music industry, and when they returned to the motel they ate at McDonald's and then retreated to the motel bathroom to record songs on a cheap tape recorder.

In late May 1979, Naomi and Wynonna drove up to Kentucky to get Ashley. They had not seen each other in over five months. Accommodations in the motel were cramped for three people, but at least they were all together again and that was all that was important to Ashley. Naomi's job with Thornton paid only enough to cover the weekly motel rate and buy food at the corner store, so Naomi spent her evenings networking and developing ideas she pitched with little success.

Early in June they got a break when Naomi agreed to house-sit while the owner went to Colorado for a month. That got them out of the motel into a house near Franklin, a small town about a thirty-minute drive from Nashville. They were all ecstatic for a while, then Wynonna had an asthma attack and had to be hospitalized for several days in Franklin. Naomi was quite taken by the rustic charm of the town and decided that was where the girls needed to enroll in school.

When Wynonna recovered from her bout with asthma, Naomi sent the girls to Ashland to visit with their grandparents. That summer she located an inexpensive rental house in Franklin and investigated the school situation. She also began a romance with Larry Strickland, a relationship that would develop into the longest-running relationship of her life. It began when Jeff Thornton signed J. D. Sumner and the Stamps for representation. Naomi's job required her to be in frequent contact with the group, and from the day Strickland stepped foot in the office sparks flew between the two.

By the end of 1979, Naomi had quit her job with Jeff Thornton and found work as a nurse. Wynonna enrolled at Franklin High School and Ashley enrolled in the sixth grade at Grassland Elementary School. For the first time in years, the sisters had a mother with a regular job and a house they could live in together.

To all outward appearances, the Judds-plus-Ashley-Ciminella

were a normal family. Behind closed doors Wynonna and Naomi fought frequently, sometimes physically, but when the time came to face the world they always pulled themselves together and presented a united front. Ashley tended to withdraw from the fighting (there were always books to read), but when that was impossible she always had an ally in Wynonna. To the amazement of her mother, Ashley developed a cheerful, outgoing personality and made friends easily.

For the first time in years, Ashley felt safe and loved. Unfortunately, it was a state of being that came crashing down on her on May 25, 1982. After cheerleader practice that day, Naomi picked up the eighth grader and drove her to the neighborhood Wal-Mart to do some shopping. While at the front of the store, Naomi asked Ashley, then fourteen, to go to the rear of the building to see if the layaway department was open.

As Ashley made her way through the store she became aware of a man wearing a blue shirt and navy slacks who was following her. It did not concern her at first because he kept his distance. Suddenly, as she wove in and out of the displays, he closed in and reached out for her. It was then that she saw that his pants were unzipped and that he was touching himself in an obscene manner.

"You'd make a nice piece!" said the heavyset man as he grabbed her by the arm.

"No!" protested Ashley.

She struggled, but the man would not turn loose her arm. He continued to touch himself and to talk dirty to her. It was a young girl's worst nightmare.

Finally, Ashley screamed out "Mommy!"—and she pulled away from him.

As the man fled out the front of the store and into the parking lot, Naomi rushed to Ashley's aid. She was sobbing, saying over and over again, "That awful man," but despite being upset, she was able to give a description of the man. Naomi screamed for help and gave the description to the manager and several male clerks. The men rushed out of the store and tracked the suspect down in another store.

When they brought him back to Wal-Mart, he was apologetic to Naomi. "Please don't have me taken away," he said. "I'll apologize to your little girl. I'm sorry I did it. I don't know why I did it, and I'll tell her I'm sorry."

Neither Naomi nor Ashley was in a forgiving mood. When the police arrived, they stated they wanted to press charges against the man, later identified as Thomas Beard of Franklin. He was formally charged with sexual battery and ordered to undergo a pretrial psychological evaluation.

According to court records, Beard was an unemployed, twice-married veteran of the U.S. Army who began using marijuana while in the service. On the day of the incident he had gone to Wal-Mart to shop for furnishings for the mobile home he had recently moved into with his second wife. He had a daughter from his first marriage.

During the course of proceedings that lasted nearly a year and a half, Beard was ordered to undergo a psychological assessment. The examiner gave him the Minnesota Multiphasic Personality Inventory test, along with a Rorschach Psychodiagnostic Test and a Thematic Apperception Test, and conducted a clinical interview. In his report, the psychologist pointed out that Beard had attended several different schools growing up and had problems because he weighed 250 pounds in the seventh grade.

The psychologist's recommendations were largely positive. "It is the impression of the examiner that the incident in question was an isolated episode in Mr. Beard's life," said the report. "There is no evidence either from the test record or from the interview materials that Mr. Beard possesses enduring tendencies to act out harmfully sexually. It appears that he was under a great deal of pressure and experienced tensions both internal and real-world. Anger and frustration at his job loss, the unexpected pregnancy with the accompanying health problems of his wife, and the possible removal of his daughter from his immediate vicinity all were pressing on him."

Incredibly, the psychologist raised no issues over the possibility that there might have been a pathological association between the potential loss of his daughter and his attack on Ashley. Faced with such a positive report—and a guilty plea from Beard—the judge felt compelled to issue a light sentence of only sixty days.

Throughout the proceedings, Ashley strongly advocated a prison sentence. Surely she could be forgiven if, after the proceedings were over, she felt let down by the legal system. No one did a psychological evaluation on her to determine the extent of the damage she suffered. The court was interested in the fact that the accused had changed schools several times in his youth, but no one asked her how many times she had changed schools (it was eight at that point). The entire proceeding was geared toward the accused; no one was interested in the victim. In the eyes of the Tennessee justice system, it was no big deal for a man to make obscene gestures to a young girl.

Ashley was new in town, she had been separated from her mother and sister against her wishes, and she had not had time to feel safe in her new environment. The Wal-Mart attack was a traumatic event for a fourteen-year-old to experience and it affected her life for years to come, not only in relationships with men but from a career standpoint, as evidenced by the movie roles she later chose to play.

Despite one setback after another, Naomi worked as a nurse, fulfilled her duties as a mother to the girls, and maintained a relationship with Larry. In her off moments, she feverishly plotted ways to break into the music business. She and Wynonna sang on radio stations, they made tapes and gave them to anyone who would accept them, and they tried to make friends in an elusive music community that never met a stranger it liked.

Life in the Judd household was, at times, unbearable. "[Mother] would provoke me, like she did with Dad," Wynonna told Bruce Feiler. "The fights would often be about the three of us, with me being protective of Ashley. Mom was hard on her because Ashley was smart and popular and beautiful and everybody loved her."

When the fighting got to be too much for her, Naomi shipped Wynonna off to live with Michael for a while in Florida. Michael told her that she must quit playing music and prepare herself for college. To that end, he took her guitar away and refused to allow her to wear makeup. Wynonna responded by crashing Michael's car into a tree. It was a suicide attempt, she told Feiler: "Wouldn't you? I was being forced to go to college. To me, that was prison."

When Naomi decided Wynonna had been punished enough, she allowed her to return to Nashville. Naomi felt she was running out of options, both professionally and with her daughters. Even though Ashley never reacted physically, as Wynonna sometimes did, she had a sharp tongue and a biting wit that sometimes ran counter to the sweet smile on her face and that sometimes troubled Naomi as much as Wynonna's in-your-face outbursts. Besides that, Naomi was now entering her late thirties and the bloom of youth was beginning to fade, threatening to rob her of her most enduring asset, her beauty. How frustrating it must have been for her to watch Ashley blossom into a beautiful young woman, with her future all before her.

Just when the clock seemed to be ticking the loudest, Naomi and Wynonna got the break they had been dreaming about for three years, ever since their arrival in Nashville. It began in the summer of 1982, when Naomi learned that one of her nursing patients was the daughter of studio owner and producer Brent Maher. She met Maher one day while he visited his daughter in the hospital, and when the daughter was released Naomi went by the studio to slip Maher a tape that she and Wynonna had made on their "bathroom" recorder. It took a while for him to respond, so long that Naomi almost gave up hope, but when he did it was with good news. He thought they had talent, and he offered to work with them to take the rough edges off of their music.

While that was going on, Naomi met Woody Bowles, a public relations executive who invited her to come by his office with Wynonna to perform some of their songs. He was struck by the uniqueness of their sound and pledged his support in helping them find a record deal. He asked if they knew anyone in the music business, anyone at all that could help. Naomi told Bowles about Brent Maher and suggested he get in touch with him. Bowles and Maher ended up working together on the project.

There are only a handful of record labels in Nashville. Once would-be artists have run their music by the frontmen for the labels without success, they have to circumvent that process if they are to have any hopes of getting a record deal. One way to do that is to get signed by an independent label that has a deal with one of the major labels for the distribution of its product.

After Bowles and Maher struck out on Music Row with the Judds, Bowles decided to take their tapes to California and to pitch them to an independent label named Curb Records. The label was not well known in Nashville, but in California it had a very high profile, especially since its owner, Mike Curb, was the sitting lieutenant governor in the Jerry Brown administration. Since Brown was then involved in national politics and was often out of the state, Curb probably put in more time as governor than did Brown during his last year in office in 1983.

Curb was an unusual man, even by California standards. The son of a FBI agent and the grandson of a Baptist preacher, he formed a record label at the age of twenty and proceeded to release a long string of hit records, including Debby Boone's "You Light Up My Life" and the Osmonds' first chart-topper, "One Bad Apple." He disliked the hard-rock, hippie music being produced in California and built his label on songs that targeted the sentimental heartland of America.

Curb started dabbling in politics in 1976, when he became chairman of Ronald Reagan's presidential campaign in California. In 1978 he ran for lieutenant governor and was elected. Since Californians do not like their elected officials to stay involved in their private business interests once they take office, Curb left the day-to-day operations of the label in the hands of Dick Whitehead, though no one in the music business ever thought that the label ever signed acts that did not receive a thumbs up from the boss.

It was with Whitehead that Bowles met when he went to California. Whitehead was intrigued by the rough-cut demo he heard and flew to Nashville to hear Naomi and Wynonna audition live in his hotel room. Impressed, he bankrolled a professional demo in Maher's studio and, once he (and presumably Mike Curb) heard it, offered Naomi and Wynonna a recording contract that they accepted without delay.

As exciting as that deal was, there remained one final hurdle—and it was a big one. For any record produced by Curb Records to be a financial success, it would have to be jointly released by a major Nashville label. Curb Records had little experience with country acts and had no distribution system to get country records before the public.

A meeting was set up with the powerful head of RCA Nashville, Joe Galante. He was not interested in cementing a deal based solely on the demo tape; he wanted to hear the artists perform live, right there in his office. Galante was often like that. He had arrived in Nashville in the mid-seventies to take over operation of the record label at a time when country music's future seemed uncertain. It took him a while to adjust to Southern living and to the subtleties of country music, but once he did, he built RCA into a powerhouse with artists such as Waylon Jennings and Alabama. His only real competitor in Nashville at that time, insofar as the new wave was concerned, was CBS Records head Rick Blackburn. Both men were acutely aware of the global possibilities of country music, and they were primarily responsible for the success that it enjoyed worldwide in the 1980s and 1990s.

When Naomi and Wynonna walked into RCA for their audition, they were confronted by Galante and five other executives. In country music, that is about as intimidating as it gets. Most artists are signed based on their demos. If all artists had to go into the labels to sing live, there would be few people standing in line. Imagine getting a contract for a book based on how well you wrote while seated at a desk in front of the editor, with an egg timer ticking. That is the kind of pressure they faced.

Naomi and Wynonna did not know any better, or perhaps they understood it was their last chance and felt they had nothing to lose. "After several numbers, we remained perfectly still and looked to them for some sort of reaction," Naomi wrote in her autobiography. "The listeners sat with arms on their chairs, heads bowed, glancing over at whoever was next to them out of the corner of their eyes."

During that silence, Wynonna shocked Naomi by blurting out

that her mother had written a pretty good song. Naomi was horrified. It was not something they had planned to do. Trapped, she performed the song with Wynonna, then heard the dreaded silence again. After a moment, the men rose to their feet and asked Naomi and Wynonna to wait for them at a nearby restaurant. The two women had no appetite whatsoever and barely touched their food. After a while, the executives entered the restaurant and told them they had a deal. The Judds first album would be released by Curb/RCA.

Oddly, Naomi has never mentioned Mike Curb in her interviews as the man responsible for the Judds' success. His name does not even appear in her autobiography. Even so, there is no escaping the fact that Mike Curb made the Judds what they eventually became, even if he did so, in the beginning, in a clandestine manner from his office in the California state capitol.

As Naomi and Wynonna worked on their music, Ashley took a good look at herself in the mirror and decided she wanted to become a model. She read about a competition held by the Elite modeling agency in New York, and she persuaded Naomi to send her to a local photographer so that she could get some pictures to enter in the contest. To Naomi's surprise, fifteen-year-old Ashley won the competition and was sent to Japan in the summer of 1983 on a two-month modeling assignment. With the money she earned, according to Naomi, she opened a money market account and ordered a subscription to *Time* magazine. She was on her way, although the exact destination was still a mystery to everyone, Ashley included.

By then Naomi and Wynonna were recording their first album. The challenge was to find the right songs, never an easy task for new artists who don't write their own material. They ended up with a hodgepodge of self-penned, original, and previously recorded material. Naomi and Wynonna had a sound, but they did not yet have a direction. RCA executives did what they could to help.

Soon they faced the realities of the music business. Being signed to a recording contract does not mean you are suddenly rich. I don't know what their advance from RCA was, but let's say it was $50,000 (probably high for a country act in the early 1980s). The first thing the Judds would have learned is that the money was neither a gift nor a salary. The money was no more than a loan paid out of their royalty account. It would be deducted from their record sales, which means that if they sold fewer than fifty thousand albums, they would never make another penny from their recording contract. Their manager would take his ten or fifteen percent commission ($5,000 or $7,500);

then the studio in which they recorded the album would send them a bill for the album's production costs ($36,000, according to Naomi), and of course, the producer would have to be paid. From a $50,000 advance, the Judds would have been lucky to take home $5,000—and that would have to wait until all the other bills were paid.

Despite the euphoria of the moment, Naomi realized she would have to continue working at the hospital until they had an opportunity to go out on the road and play concerts. Wynonna had graduated from high school, but she had no work lined up. When someone suggested she get a job, she almost could not believe her ears. "A job!" she gasped, horrified at the thought.

As mother and daughter alternated between their new dreamland and the realities of everyday life, Ashley lived in a world apart. In 1983, while the Judds's first album was being put together, Ashley was a student at Franklin High School, a one-story brick structure on the outskirts of town. That summer, she went from her freshman to her sophomore year. Her class photo shows her wearing a light colored sweater, with hair touching her shoulders.

Ashley's freshman year she was a cheerleader for the football team, named, appropriately enough, the Rebels (in the annual picture, she is shown with an upperclassman standing on her hips and back). She also was treasurer of the Rebel Council, the name of the elected student body organization.

Photos of her in the school annual always show her smiling or laughing, the very picture of a well-adjusted teen. Well, that was not entirely true. She had her moments of frustration. "I got into trouble and was in hall probation," she told Stephen Schaefer for the entertainment website Mr. Showbiz. "We were the last ones to get lunch, and we had a 10-minute break. I wasn't supposed to wander, and I went to the girls' room. I was in there when this teacher came in looking for me—and she sent a note to my mom. There was just no way I could convince this woman I was innocent. She had me written off as a bad kid."

Naomi did not yell at her as she did with Wynonna, but she let her know in not-so-subtle ways that she was disappointed in her. Mothers have an instinct not only for knowing how to love their children but for knowing how to hurt them. Cold disappointment was the worst thing Naomi could show to Ashley because she was so self-motivated to achieve. A psychologist could argue that her motivation to achieve was the result of a desire to please her mother so that she would not abandon her again. By showing cold disappointment, Naomi was silently threatening the very abandonment that Ashley feared. Emotionally, it was a vicious circle for mother and daughter. In time, Ashley's defense would assume all the physical characteristics of her mother's offense—a sweet, smiling face that belied the fact that she was crying buckets on the inside.

In late 1983, the Judds' first single, "Had a Dream," was shipped to radio. Realizing that a large part of the duo's appeal was visual, RCA sent them out on the road, traveling from radio station to radio station to promote the single. They were an instant hit with radio: their music was different, they were fun to interview live, and the concept of a mother-daughter act ran counter to the rhinestone-studded, overproduced artists then dominating the market.

Despite their success with radio, the big unknown was how they would do in concert. They found that out on March 20, 1984, when they went to Omaha, Nebraska, to open for the Statler Brothers, at that time one of the top country acts in the nation. Naomi and Wynonna panicked before going on stage, especially when they peered out into the crowd of ten thousand people, but years of rejection gave them the motivation to dash out onto the stage. To their surprise, they were warmly embraced by the audience, even though they had bought tickets to see the Statler Brothers. The following day, the *Omaha World-Herald* gave them a rave review: "Once the hubbub dies down about the youthfulness of the mother, folks will doubtless start talking about her song-writing ability, their musical appeal and the almost certain stardom in store for the Judds."

Encouraged by reaction to the first single and the reception at the Omaha concert, RCA went all out on behalf of the Judds. Already they had the top acts in country music—Dolly Parton, Kenny Rogers, Alabama, Ronnie Milsap, and Vince Gill, to name a few—but label executives saw a window of opportunity for the Judds.

Four years later, when the Judds were at their peak, RCA boss Joe Galante put it this way: "One of the things we always have been is an innovator, and I see that continuing, whether it is done through music or through the way we take music to the marketplace....It's always in developing the act. I've got bunches of gold and platinum albums and the ones that I have hanging on the walls are the first gold and the first platinum albums I received. It's always going to be the firsts and watching the artists grow."

In the mid-1980s, Galante was in an expansive mood. That first year with the Judds, he brought in a new public relations manager named Pam Lewis. She had only been out of college for a short time and had attracted Galante's attention while working for MTV. Galante was correct about her talent—she later became Garth Brooks's co-manager and was responsible to a great degree for the enormous success he achieved—but he was mistaken in his belief that he would be able to work closely with her.

What Lewis brought to RCA was a MTV mentality that envisioned recording artists as multidimensional products that could be sold visually as well as on the radio. The Judds benefited greatly from Lewis's vision of the future, for of all the acts on the RCA roster, it was the Judds who had the most visual sales potential. Lewis was with RCA for only about a year—Galante ended up firing her over what she described as her brashness—but it was long enough to fire up the new-wave techno-machine that made stars of the Judds. For all the talk about the Judds' Kentucky roots and sweet harmonies, it was television that enabled them to turn the corner.

For the next year, the Judds were on the road constantly. For Wynonna, it was a real test of her desire for stardom. "I was on a bus forty feet long, eight feet wide with a woman who is very much a perfectionist...much is given, much is required," she explained to Matt Lauer for MSNBC's *Headliners and Legends*.

For Ashley, it was a test of her inner strength. Not willing to leave her seventeen-year-old daughter at home alone, Naomi did what she always did when her youngest daughter got in the way: She sent her away.

Ashley was enrolled in the Sayre School, a private, coeducational college preparatory school located in downtown Lexington. The three years she had spent at schools in Franklin was the longest stretch she ever had, and packing up and moving again was not easy for her. She was popular in Franklin and she had many friends who appreciated her for her enthusiasm and her wit. Once again, she was asked to forge a new path among a new group of strangers.

One can well imagine the pain she felt leaving home again. Ashley was happy for her mother and her sister, she truly was, for they had no bigger fan, but it is difficult to balance happiness for loved ones with sadness over one's own less fortunate predicament. Why did their success have to come at her expense? Why was she always on the outside looking in?

Ashley spent her junior year at Sayre, where she was unhappy living alone and much too independent to surrender to the inane rules and regulations that private schools promulgate in order to be different from their public school competitors.

The most notable thing that happened to her during that school term was that her father confided in her about Wynonna's birth. Swearing her to secrecy, Michael told Ashley that he was not Wynonna's father. She was his only child. That came as a shock to Ashley, who never had any reason to doubt Wynonna's paternity. Why, she must have wondered, had her mother forsaken her to shower attention on a half-sister? For years to come, Michael, Naomi, and Ashley shared that secret, never letting on to Wynonna that her entire life thus far had been a lie.

In the summer of 1985 Ashley joined Naomi and Wynonna on the road. They allowed her to travel on the bus with them, but only on condition that she clean the bus every day. For her services they agreed to pay the modern-day Cinderella ten dollars a day. Most daughters would have been humiliated by the experience. Not Ashley. She was just happy to be included as a family member. They were earning thousands of dollars a day and paying her only ten to be their maid, but Ashley did not create a scene or suggest that she was being mistreated. Instead, she dove into the books that she carried with her everywhere and she walked among gentle giants in a make-believe world that recognized her as being worthy of attention.

When summer ended, Naomi decided to send Ashley to Ashland to live with Polly. She had remarried after her divorce from Glen (he died in 1984) and she was happy to have Ashley live with her and go to school. Before starting school, Ashley pleaded to spend more time with the tour (that ten dollars a day added up and she knew she would need extra money when she started school).

In mid-September 1985, the Judds' tour bus took them to Memphis, Tennessee, where they were booked at the Mid-South Coliseum. Coincidentally, the biggest single recording session in Memphis history was taking place that week at Sam Phillips's old Sun Studio and Chips Moman's old American Recording Studios.

For the historic session, Moman had brought in Johnny Cash, Carl Perkins, Jerry Lee Lewis, and Roy Orbison for an album titled *Class of '55*. There, documenting the session with a television crew, was Dick Clark's production company. The crew said it was the first time in history that a recording session had been videotaped from start to finish.

The session was also important because it was linked to Moman's return to Memphis from Nashville. Before moving to Nashville in 1973 he had produced an incredible string of hits, including Elvis Presley's 1969 hit album *From Elvis in Memphis*, Neil Diamond's "Sweet Caroline," Dusty Springfield's "Son of a Preacher Man," and B. J. Thomas's "Hooked on a Feeling." The year he left Memphis he had "eighty to ninety" records, he recalls, that made the charts. While in Nashville, he worked with Cash, Waylon Jennings, Willie Nelson, and others, revolutionizing country music as he injected the rock-and-blues-based Memphis sound into what had by then become a tired and uninspired country format.

Because of the history involved and the public interest in Cash, Perkins, Orbison, and Lewis, the national media had descended upon Memphis to cover the week-long session. The initial tracks were recorded at the Sun Studio, but the final tracks were laid down at the old American Recording Studio. For the last song, Moman chose John Fogerty's "Big Train (from Memphis)." The idea was for all four stars to sing on the song together. Unknown to the stars, invitations to attend the session went out to a select few individuals, including John Fogerty, Rick Nelson, Sun Records founder Sam Phillips, saxman Ace Cannon, and British record producer Dave Edmunds. This writer was also in attendance.

Late that evening, just as the session was about to begin, in walked Naomi and Wynonna, still dressed in the flashy pantsuits they had worn for their last number at the Mid-South Coliseum. Someone in Moman's organization, probably the well-meaning Herb O. Mell, had invited the Judds to sing in the final jam.

When Moman spotted the Judds, he was perplexed. He approached me and asked if I knew who they were. He said he had never heard of them. I explained that they were a new RCA act that was having success on country radio.

"This ain't a country record," he said.

Moman gazed at the Judds a moment, then asked me a question.

"Should I let them stay?"

I gave him a thumbs-up.

On "Big Train (from Memphis)," Naomi and Wynonna sang at a microphone alongside June Carter Cash and Moman's wife, Toni Wine, while at two other microphones adjacent to them gathered Johnny Cash, Roy Orbison, Jerry Lee Lewis, Carl Perkins, John Fogerty, Dave Edmunds, Rick Nelson, Sam Phillips, Jack Clement—a veritable who's who of rock 'n' roll.

The Judds benefited greatly from that session, not so much because they sang on "Big Train" or appeared in the Dick Clark documentary but because of the exposure they received with the national music media. Everyone assumed that if the who's who of rock 'n' roll thought the Judds were important, they must be someone to watch. Of course, no one at the session had a clue about who the Judds were, but that did not matter in the end, because music writers liked what they saw in the Judds and gave them the exposure they needed to be successful on the pop charts.

Naomi never understood what happened that night, and when she wrote about the session in her autobiography, she mistakenly wrote that she had gone to the Sun Studio, and she garbled the title of the album. Even if her brain was not working that night, her emotions were, because when she returned to the hotel after the session, she was "too jazzed to sleep."

I was at the session that night, but I do not recall seeing Ashley there. She may have been on the tour bus, cleaning up after her mother and sister (every ten dollars counts when you are being banished to Kentucky!).

For her senior year, Ashley enrolled about two weeks late at Blazer High School, the same institution attended by her mother. Naomi had graduated in disgrace. Ashley hoped to do better. If possible, she would redeem the family name.

"She never made any kind of notion that she was anyone special," recalled her math teacher Dixie Johnson. "We all knew who Naomi and Wynonna were, but I don't know if we knew there was an Ashley."

English teacher Louise Curnutte recalled the day Ashley first walked into her classroom. "She was a star before she ever was a star," she said. "She was a star when she walked into the door of my classroom. She had the bearing and that appearance. I don't think she was even aware of it. She must have known she was pretty. I've seen her when she's not made up and she looks like any other girl, but she's so gorgeous when she's gorgeous."

Curnutte was struck by Ashley's intelligence and writing ability, and the gift she had for making friends. "In six weeks time, there was a homecoming dance and she was elected one of the homecoming attendants," she said. "You know, when pretty, senior high-school girls move to a new school, they are usually not accepted. She was incredible. I think she left a mark on everybody that she met. She was sweet and kind, not what you would expect from a pretty girl of her intelligence."

About her intelligence, the English teacher said: "Ashley was always way ahead of everyone else on having read novels. Usually any novel I assigned, she had already read. She was a voracious reader."

Typically, Ashley sat on the front row in class and asked a lot of questions. Other students soon learned about her famous mother and sister, but Ashley never played off of their country music success. On the contrary, she sometimes complained to other students that

Naomi and Wynonna sometimes overdid their country roots routine.

Shortly after enrolling in the school, she started dating a boy named Bill McKinney. He was not the super-jock type. He had sandy, reddish hair and freckles, and he sometimes reminded people of a *Tom Sawyer* character. Everyone seemed surprised that Ashley would be interested in a plain Joe like that, but Ashley apparently was intrigued by his intelligence and his sense of humor. He made her laugh and that was one of the things Ashley most needed out of life.

Ashley was constantly surprising her classmates and teachers. "She bought her dresses for homecoming and special dances at secondhand stores," said Mrs. Johnson. "A lot of people did it because they had to, but she would do it and talk about it. She would say, 'I got this at the thrift store.' She was full of confidence. Not cocky, but mature. It was her way of saying, 'I'm not special.' She didn't wear tacky clothes. She just showed she didn't have to go out and spend thousands on clothes. She was making a statement that she was not special."

Of course, Ashley's openness about shopping at a thrift store was defensive in nature. The other students had no way of knowing that Ashley's status with her mother and sister the summer before school began was as a ten-dollar-a-day maid on their bus tour. Ashley shopped at the thrift stores because she did not exactly have a star's budget for homecoming gowns. True, she would probably have shopped at thrift stores even if she had plenty of money, but in this case she did what Ashley does best: she twisted wart-nosed reality into something noble and beautiful.

In spite of all her personal travails with her family, Ashley had a big heart, one that she displayed when it was least expected. A lot of the boys in Blazer High considered Ashley crush-worthy, but aside from Bill McKinney, it was a special education student that touched her heart the most.

"He was really in love with her," said Mrs. Johnson, who thinks the boy may have had Down syndrome. "He had such a crush on her. She was so kind to him. The whole year, it was so cute the way she treated him. She really made that year special for him. The other senior girls would not have done that. She didn't lead him on so that it was dangerous, but she was very nice to him."

After graduating near the top of her class from Blazer High School in 1986, Ashley again joined Naomi and Wynonna out on the road. Although she was only a part-time Judd, she was enthusiastic about the success being realized by her mother and sister. She was their biggest fan, no question about it.

No one seemed to know what Ashley wanted to do with her life, primarily because no one had ever asked. That changed in August 1986, when the Judds' tour bus pulled into Hopkinsville, Kentucky, for a concert at the Western Kentucky State Fair, where they were billed as the headliners.

When reporter Rob Dollar, sent by the *Kentucky New Era* newspaper to interview the Judds, arrived at the venue to conduct the pre-arranged interview, he was told the Judds were having some problems with their equipment and would be unavailable. "Someone pointed out Ashley to me and said there's the other daughter, the one who is in high school," Dollar later recalled. "I was sort of looking for a story and that was the best I could do." Dollar strode over to where Ashley was sitting and asked her for an interview. "She seemed pretty thrilled about it, and she was very, very nice to spend some time with us."

Dollar asked if she felt she was living in the shadow of the fame enjoyed by her mother and sister. "I don't feel as though I'm in the shadow because the music is something I enjoy, but it's not my life—it's not my forte," Ashley explained. "I have always been included in an intimate way. I was in the studio. I was with them the first time we heard the songs on the radio. I think I missed one number, one party and that was it. I'm very involved. I don't produce the music and I don't have anything to do with the creative control, but still I'm part of it."

Dollar naturally asked her if she had a good singing voice.

"Whether I have a capacity for singing, I don't know," she answered. "I can sincerely say that there is no way in the world I, or anyone else, could sing as my sister does. I think very highly of her talent. I think she's an extraordinarily gifted person" She paused, then teasingly added: "I do have a low speaking voice and an even lower singing voice. Like I can sing the French national anthem and not disgrace anyone, including myself."

Dollar asked how she thought her mother and sister were handling the "grueling" schedule associated with country music success. "Wynonna gets so sick of the bus sometimes she could throw up and then two weeks later, she's crying she misses it so badly," said Ashley. "But they treat the road as a way of life. Humor is important as an ingredient for happiness. Mom loves to laugh. We all do, but that's not to say we're slap-happy."

It was the first interview Ashley had ever given and she handled herself beautifully. "I was struck by the fact that she was so young and yet was so mature," said Dollar. "She seemed really intelligent and head and shoulders above most high-school-age kids. She was articulate, someone who made a pretty good impression."

During the interview, Ashley told him that she would start classes at the University of Kentucky the following month. The university was not necessarily her first choice. "Actually mother did not let me apply to any schools outside of a certain geographical region because she wanted me to be close to Nashville," she said. "When they're on the road and they are finally home, she wanted me to be accessible."

When Dollar asked her about what she wanted to do with her life, she said that she had appeared as a "perturbed wife" in the Judds' video for the song "Grandpa" and was thinking about pursuing an acting career. "I hate to even say 'going Hollywood.' That's such a cliché. I've never really said that before, but film does interest me."

When Naomi read the newspaper article, she was shocked to learn that her daughter wanted to become an actress. It was the first she had heard about it. Writing about the newspaper article in her autobiography (and misspelling Dollar's first name), Naomi said she "shuddered even to think of her going to Hollywood."

Years later, Dollar, who is now managing editor of the *New Era*, said he did not mind that Naomi called him Bob instead of Rob. "I got a kick when her mother put me in her book," he said, adding that being the first person to interview Ashley and the first to talk to her about her hopes of a film career was a pleasure. "I would like to meet Ashley again to see if she remembers the interview."

By 1986, the Judds' career seemed unstoppable. America was nostalgic, not only for a different time but also for a different feeling. The Judds gave America what it wanted. They sang music that sounded old-fashioned even though it was not, and they projected a middle-American persona that bombarded music lovers with homey images that made everyone feel all warm and cozy inside.

In an 1984 review in the *Washington Post,* Joe Sasfy wrote: "Their first full-length album, *Why Not Me,* continues to set the seamless, flowing harmonies of this mother-daughter duo in a warm tapestry of acoustic instrumentation that recalls the duo's Kentucky heritage while remaining absolutely contemporary in its sparkling clarity." In his review, he echoed the general feeling among critics that the Judds were "much more than country singers."

Gordon Stoker, who, as a member of the Jordanaires, provided background vocals for Elvis Presley during the length of his career, told the Associated Press that Wynonna reminded him of the King. "She's a female Elvis," he explained. "She has the same feel, the same heart that Elvis had originally. Elvis put a lot of feeling in everything and she does, too. She has a lot of heart and soul."

No one could ever quite figure out what Naomi's role was—she sang gentle harmonies and danced around the stage in a frilly frock, while Wynonna manned the microphone—but everyone was too taken by the duo to ask embarrassing questions and simply accepted the Judds at face value.

Naomi turned on the down-home charm at every opportunity. On their first trip to New York City, they stayed at the St. Moritz Hotel and had dinner at Windows on the World in the World Trade Center. Puffy-eyed from lack of sleep, Naomi complained to *Philadelphia Inquirer* writer Steven Rea about the noise. "I could not sleep with this traffic last night. I am used to mountains and hills and meadows. All there is here is concrete and glass. I am used to wide-open spaces. All there is here is crowds. I'm also used to clean air and fresh water....So I'm ready to go home."

The Judds scored one hit after another, including "Why Not Me," "Grandpa (Tell Me About the Good Ole Days)," and "I Know Where I'm Going" (they had twelve number one hits that subsequently were offered on a single album). They were awarded five Grammys, eight Country Music Association Awards, and eight American Country Music Awards.

Their party looked like it would go on forever, but even as the Judds reached their zenith in the late 1980s, fickle Nashville was already looking for the next big thing. Recording acts typically have a shelf life of five years if they are lucky, and by late 1987 and early 1988 the Judds were deemed to be on the endangered list, not so much for the music they were making but because recording executives had decided the Nashville sound should be edgier.

"Anyone who sits on their rear end and says, 'I've got Alabama, I've got the Judds,' is going to be unemployed in a few years," RCA Records head Joe Galante told me in 1988. "Record executives, like artists, have a life span."

Rick Blackburn, Galante's competitor at CBS Records and one of the true visionaries of country music, did not mince words. "There's a clear signal coming back from the marketplace, from the fans, that simply says, 'I like country music as well as I did five years ago, but give me something new, fresh and exciting; I'm tired of the sameness,'" he said in late 1987. "That's a clear signal. If you ignore the signal, you will have serious problems."

Usually the stars are the last to know, but even as the Judds were at their zenith, a chubby, baby-faced crooner from Oklahoma named

Garth Brooks was nervously waiting in the wings, getting ready to make sweet harmonies and petticoat nostalgia obsolete.

Like many universities and colleges in the South, the University of Kentucky was created in the aftermath of the Civil War, when it became apparent that education would be the foundation of the new social and economic order. In the beginning, the University of Kentucky was an agricultural college, but in the decades since then it has evolved into a highly regarded institution of higher learning, with nearly one hundred degree programs that lead to bachelor's degrees and more than sixty doctorate programs.

When Ashley entered the University of Kentucky in 1986 (it was not her first choice: higher up the list were Georgetown, the University of California at Berkeley, Duke University, and the University of Virginia), she was not certain exactly which degree program she wanted to pursue. She had many interests. By the process of elimination, she decided to seek a major in French and minors in anthropology, art history, acting, and women's studies.

"At UK I learned a lot about my own strength and self-reliance," she told *Interview* magazine. "Instead of simply reacting to curve balls, I was throwing some really nice pitches."

For the first time in her life, she was allowed to make plans and to look ahead. As the only school she would attend for more than two years, it provided her with a sense of identity and a power over her own destiny that she had never imagined possible. If no one else in her family thought she was important, she did—and she set out to prove it.

Ashley decided that her mind was more important than her popularity. She threw herself into her studies. Blessed with a good memory, the ability to mimic others, and a real longing for knowledge, she developed every facet of her intellect, except one—her ability to make critical assessments. It was a shortcoming that would come back to haunt her as an adult, affecting major decisions throughout her career.

Once asked by *Ampersand,* the university's alumni review, why she chose a liberal arts education, she replied: "Well, the fact is that one's imagination is critically important, and if you have had your imagination stimulated by what is basically a variety of subjects, you are much more amenable to accepting, to understanding and interacting with the realities of the world....Your eyes are already open and you are more ready to believe and have awe at the wonders of humanity."

According to Dr. Susan Abbott-Jamieson, one of her

anthropology professors, Ashley was very active in classroom discussions and was involved in her course work. "I think she considered going on to do graduate work in anthropology," she said. "Ashley is a very bright person and she could have done many different things. I will be interested to see if she grows in her [acting] craft to see what she does as she matures."

To Dr. Jamieson's surprise, Ashley donated fifty thousand dollars to the anthropology department in 2001 to create a scholarship for what she requested be called the Susan Abbott-Jamieson Dissertation Research Fund (the state matched that grant, thus endowing the fund with a one-hundred-thousand-dollar base).

"I am delighted that Kentucky is matching my donation, dollar for dollar, thus doubling the size of the endowment and exponentially increasing its impact on talented students who wish to pursue their doctorate in anthropology," Ashley said in a press release. "Knowing of the government's matching campaign, I hope others will be enticed to give."

Dr. Jamieson, who is now retired, said Ashley called her and asked if she could name the fund after her. "I was delighted," she said. "I was honored that she felt enough about my teaching that she wanted to name it for me."

Of course, Ashley was not all studies at the university. She joined a social sorority named Kappa Kappa Gamma and she socialized with the other students. Her mother approved of that, for Naomi was very much a social animal, but Ashley developed a social and political consciousness during her university years that made Naomi cringe.

Ashley became a compassionate liberal. Naomi had shared many of those same opinions during her "hippie" years, but now that she had become a high-profile symbol of right-wing America, her daughter's opinions caused her problems. When Ashley returned to Nashville for visits, dinner table conversation invariably became spirited.

Ashley's finest hour at UK, at least in this writer's opinion, came when former Governor A. B. "Happy" Chandler allegedly made a public comment about the "niggers" in Zimbabwe. Since Chandler was a member of the university's board of trustees, Ashley and other students staged a vociferous protest in an effort to have him removed. Ironically, Chandler's granddaughter, Ann, was one of Ashley's closest friends.

"I went to a couple of meetings that the African-American students held to talk about what had happened, and we teamed up and there was a walkout of classes in protest of the administration not requiring [Chandler's] resignation," Ashley told Ingrid Sischy for *Interview* magazine. "I'm very glad I did it....Some of my sorority sisters were looking at me like I had aliens living with me in my room. They just couldn't believe what I was doing. But what had occurred was just not acceptable to me."

Ashley had always been a free spirit, but she kept those feelings to herself. Now she wanted to express herself. University life made her want to explore her emotions and her intellect, and, not surprisingly, the world itself.

In the summer of 1989, Ashley signed on for a student trip to France. She had a romantic notion of the language and wanted to experience its roots. She traveled to Brussels, where she, four other students, and a professor from the university French department rented a Volkswagen minibus and drove into France.

It was an economical trip (the entire cost to each student was just twelve hundred dollars), but it was packed with adventure as they toured Paris and the French countryside. In between the points of interest, as they tooled about in the minibus, Ashley listened to American music on a Sony Walkman.

One of the stops important to the professor was Omaha Beach, where many American soldiers who died in World War II are buried and honored. The professor thought that seeing it was important to understand America's role in French history. At first the students refused to go, but when the professor insisted, they relented and accompanied him on the trip, though with a certain amount of pouting. Their attitudes changed radically, however, when they arrived at Omaha Beach and saw the American flag and row after row of grave markers flashing pristine white in the sun. Before they left the memorial, they were all in tears, overwhelmed by the scope of the loss.

In Paris they stayed at the International Student Center. While in the city they toured the Louvre Museum and Versailles, and experienced the sidewalk cafes. After one full day of touring, they headed back to the International Student Center at two in the morning, walking because there was no subway. Abruptly, Ashley broke away from the group, saying she needed to make a telephone call. The professor yelled at her to return, explaining that there were no phone booths in the city. When she ignored his pleas, he dashed after her, tripping over a metal grating that left a nasty gash in his leg. Seeing the injury, Ashley returned to the group.

When the fall semester began, Ashley, perhaps feeling that she had been held back by the needs of the group, dropped out of school for a short time to travel to France a second time, only this time she went alone.

Ashley's lowest point at UK was probably later that fall, when she was involved in a homecoming queen scandal. There was no nudity or alcohol or marijuana involved, but it did cause quite a stir on campus. The trouble began when Ashley was nominated by her sorority for the elected position of homecoming queen.

Since she did not feel that she was well-known enough on campus to be a good competitor, Ashley's supporters placed a paid advertisement in the student newspaper, the *Kentucky Kernel*, that extolled her qualifications to be homecoming queen.

What she did not understand was that it was against the rules to run such an ad. The Student Activities Board responded quickly by booting Ashley off the ballot. In a page-one story that bore the headline "Queen proves to be a royal pain for campus," the *Kentucky Kernel* gave prominent play to what quickly became a nasty catfight.

"I'm a victim of circumstance," Ashley told reporters. "I don't see how someone having placed an ad in the *Kernel* would have caused a spot on the contest. I don't think the rule was unfair, I think it's unfair someone told the [sorority] to go ahead and put the ad in the paper."

The newspaper backed Ashley, saying that no one had told them not to run ads related to homecoming. "Although technically Judd's sponsor may have broken the rules, the personal [ad] probably did little to affect the outcome of the voting," editorialized the *Kernel*. "After all, if Judd really wanted to advertise, she could have used the clout that her celebrity name carries with many country western music fans on campus."

Bloodied but not bowed, Ashley went to Nashville for the Christmas recess. While there, she came down with a bad case of the flu. Not wanting to send her back to school in that shape, Naomi took her to see the family doctor so that she could get a blood test. Feeling tired and rundown, Naomi asked the nurse to give her a blood test as well.

The following day, after Naomi sent Ashley back to school, she returned to the doctor's office to inquire about her lab results. To her surprise, the doctor told her that she was very ill with a stealth virus known as hepatitis C.

Naomi was devastated. With her knowledge of medicine, she knew the disease was often a death sentence. There was no cure. Since the virus is passed on mostly through contact with infected blood, Naomi was at a loss to explain how she got it. She finally determined that she had picked it up while working as a nurse; perhaps it came from a pinprick from an infected needle that she never even noticed at the time.

Ashley went home often during the next few months. The illness was more than a family tragedy, it was a musical upheaval, for it meant that Naomi would have to retire, terminating the Judds' recording and touring career. If there was a blessing involved, it may have been that before Naomi's illness was diagnosed, rumors circulated around Nashville that RCA Records might not renew the Judds' recording contract. If true, the illness provided Naomi with a graceful exit, a blessing cloaked in adversity.

Ashley was attentive to her mother, but by the time school was out, Naomi's illness seemed manageable. The Judds were still touring, still playing concerts. Although she had been nominated for Phi Beta Kappa, Ashley did not graduate with honors. In fact, she did not graduate at all. She was three hours short of fulfilling her degree requirements. She had attended university for four years and then walked away with nothing except what she had learned. To her, that was plenty. "I got an absolutely fabulous education at UK," she later explained to *Kentucky Monthly*. "And it helped me get my tendrils into the Kentucky soil. It was very much consistent with my childhood."

At that point in her life, Ashley felt she had three options: She could return to school and get her degree and then enroll in graduate school, with a goal of getting her doctorate in anthropology; she could join the Peace Corps and help save the world (she was passionate about the cause); or she could strike out for Hollywood to see if she had what it took to become an actress.

After a few sleepless nights, she loaded up the U-Haul in the summer of 1990 and drove west to the bright lights of Hollywood. More than anything else, Naomi had wanted to be a movie star. Perhaps Ashley could make that dream come true through her own efforts. What better gift could there be for a dying mother?

One other thing she did that year: she changed her name to Judd.

# Chapter
# Three

## *Ashley in Paradise*

Before setting out for Los Angeles, Ashley contacted one of her best friends from the University of Kentucky, Erin Chandler, the granddaughter of former Kentucky governor Happy Chandler. Erin had preceded Ashley to California and enrolled in acting classes. Erin, who subsequently became an actress herself—she had roles in *Dead Connection* and *You're Killing Me*—invited her to stay with her until she found a place of her own. She also suggested that Ashley enroll in acting classes at the same place where she was receiving instruction, Playhouse West.

Ashley took Erin's advice and enrolled in the school. She also got a job as a waitress at The Ivy, an expensive Beverly Hills restaurant, and she volunteered to work as an intern at a powerful management agency. Even though she was fresh out of college and reeling from news of her mother's illness, Ashley had the presence of mind to devise an intelligent plan of attack in her quest to become an actress.

Volunteering to be a gofer at the management agency was brilliant, for it allowed her not only to learn about the entertainment business but also to make friends in high places. She never told them who she was and she never mentioned to the agency that she wanted to become an actress.

Most would-be actresses her age would have scoffed at the idea, refusing to do anything that did not pay them for their time. Ashley swallowed her pride to work as a waitress for low wages and to work at the agency for no wages. She made up her mind early on that she would do whatever it took to get her name up in lights.

This was not sibling rivalry. Ashley's motivation ran much deeper than that. Actually, Wynonna was a big supporter of Ashley's dream. "Wy knew me," Ashley once explained to *Orbit*. "Acting was a way for me to lose myself into other characters, even at a pretty young age. I knew it was acting, though. I wasn't exactly sure what to label it. But I knew I could enjoy the same pleasurable, enlightening experience I'd found in books—and thankfully, no one tried to sew me in."

Ever since she was a small child, Ashley wanted her mother to be proud of her. Later, when she saw the way Wynonna's success brought tears of joy to her mother, she knew she had to do something equally dazzling. Naomi's illness brought an urgency to the situation. How sad would it be for everyone involved, Wynonna included, if Naomi died before Ashley achieved her goals?

Playhouse West was probably the best choice Ashley could have made for an acting school, though there is no evidence that she understood why at the time (some of her good fortune has simply been old-fashioned good luck). Playhouse West was founded in the early 1980s by Robert Carnegie, a devotee of the Meisner technique of acting. It was devised by noted acting coach Sanford Meisner in the 1930s.

Unlike Method acting, which encourages actors to reach back into their lives to past events to find a source of emotion, the Meisner method employs a moment-to-moment approach based on the premise that an actor's success is derived from being able to connect with his or her fellow actors in a particular scene.

Robert Carnegie, who today remains the director of the school, explained it this way: "We define acting as living truthfully under imaginary circumstances and that is quite a different thing than what is thought of as the Method, where various psychological efforts are employed to arrive at emotion. In our approach, the emotion and the experience come spontaneously from just living out the thing when you do it."

It is interesting to speculate about Ashley's future as an actress if her friend Erin had been a student at a Method acting school. It is unlikely, considering her temperament and her past experiences, that Ashley would have survived such an introspective examination of her family life. Truthfully, Ashley almost did not survive Playhouse West.

In the beginning, Ashley made no impression whatsoever on Carnegie. "She was nondescript and really bore no relationship to what she has become," said Carnegie. "She was self-effacing. She did not dress particularly well. You would not even notice her."

At one point, one of the students asked Carnegie if he was aware of Ashley's music business lineage. "I was not a fan of country music at that time and I only vaguely knew the name," he said. "She was like anyone else. She gave no indication through her presence that she would become the great achiever that she became. If anything, you might have got the impression that she suffered from an inferiority complex."

Ashley's performance in class was so off the mark, according to

Carnegie, that the students set up a secret betting pool, whereby everyone put in money and guessed when Ashley was going to quit. The winner would take home all the money.

"She had great deal of difficulty with the work that we do and I was constantly finding fault with her and she had great difficulty arriving at what we wanted to do," said Carnegie. "But she never did quit. She was trying terribly, terribly hard to make an impression and to be good and there is nothing more destructive in acting than trying to do that. It is like comedy. The harder you try to be funny, the less funny you are, and the harder you try to be good when you act, the worse you are, and that was pretty much her situation."

Under the system set up at Playhouse West, students sometimes attend classes for as long a six months without ever acting out a scene. Instead, they are encouraged to learn to act through exercises designed to help the student react to the other students.

"Ashley was not so much interested in working off the other person," Carnegie said with a laugh. "She was more interested in talking a lot. She would get up on stage and you couldn't shut her up. She would talk and talk and talk. And it had nothing to do with the other person. We have a route the actors take in response with the other person. That was her difficulty."

No one realized it at the time, not even Ashley, but she was desperate for approval from her ailing mother. Under those circumstance, she would have died rather than walk out of those acting classes, for they represented her only hope for the level of fame and fortune achieved by her mother and sister. She "talked and talked and talked" because she felt the hot breath of an imagined beast behind her, gaining ground. Time was everything to her. When you add that sense of urgency with overpowering self-doubt, you get a woman-in-the-making whose only comfort is the sound of her own voice.

Ashley's career as an actress might have ended there on the drawing board of the Playhouse West theater were it not for a fortuitous event that brought her plight to Carnegie's attention. Despite the dire prognosis of Naomi's illness, the Judds continued to do concerts. When Ashley learned that they would be performing at the Universal Amphitheater in Los Angeles, which is only about two blocks from the school, she offered Carnegie free tickets for himself and his wife. Although a native Virginian, Carnegie did not know much about country music (it never made the A-list in Hollywood acting circles), but he took his wife to the concert, partly out of curiosity and partly as a show of support for his student.

After the concert, Ashley invited Carnegie and his wife backstage to meet her mother. Naomi was in a wheelchair. "She was extremely concerned about Ashley and about the direction she was headed," recalled Carnegie. "I think she wanted to find out who she was involved with and what she was doing. She was really checking us out. But my wife is from Oregon and I'm from Virginia and we are not the normal Hollywood people, so we got along famously with the mother. She was very ill. She had to be wheelchaired back and forth to the stage. I sat there [and listened] and it wasn't hard for me to pick up that this was a mother concerned for her daughter, that she was afraid she would not be there for the daughter too much longer and wanted to know that whatever she was doing was going to be OK. I was extremely touched by the concern for Ashley that her mother displayed. I was very moved by that. I took on a real responsibility toward Ashley. I wanted to see her do well for the sake of the mother. I was so worried about her."

Over the next few days, Carnegie devised a plan to help Ashley realize her full potential. He did things for her that he had never done for other students. He invited her over to his house now and then (that had never happened with other students) and he took her to a party to meet Sanford Meisner. Academically, he restructured her academic program. He asked her to come in for two additional classes each week (without charge) and he put her in a play, "Welcome Home Soldier," so that she could get firsthand acting experience.

"She had no dialogue, but there is a cast of about forty and the idea was to put her in a play with all my top students—and there were some incredible people in that play—just for her to work with them every week, to let it rub off on her," he said. "Although there are parts in the play where you don't say anything, you're still on stage and interacting for forty or fifty minutes, so she had plenty to do."

Ashley labored for months over her studies at Playhouse West, well into 1991, yet there still seemed to be something missing in her development. Carnegie was perplexed. "Then it dawned on me what was going on with her and why she was trying so hard," he said. "I felt it was because, whether she knew it or not, she was in competition with her mother and sister. When I met them that time, it was very obvious. There was Wynonna and there was Mom and they were getting enormous attention and there was Ashley and she was a nobody. What she was trying to do was to come into her own and show that she was someone, too. But the problem was that she was working too hard at it. I took her aside after class one day. I talked a little about her family and I explained to her that I understood how she wanted to become someone also, but that how she was doing it all wrong. That she wasn't going to become someone by trying so hard to be good. She would have to relax into her own truth and accept whoever she was and learn to live with that and maybe, perhaps, if she does that, it will be good enough and she will achieve something. But I told her she would have to stop competing with her family."

After their conversation, Carnegie saw an improvement in Ashley's work. "She did relax and she started to respond to the other person and found her own sense of truth," he said. "From that point on, she just grew and developed gradually, the way most actors do. It is a very gradual process of learning to bring your real self to the material rather than what so many think acting is, pretending to be something you are not for the sake of the material."

On October 17, 1990, several months after Ashley moved to California, Naomi and Wynonna held a press conference to announce that Naomi was retiring, thus bringing to an end the recording career of the Judds. Weeping, Naomi said it was the "most difficult day of my life." It was also announced, though Naomi did not say the actual words herself, that Wynonna would release her first solo album on Curb/MCA.

Ashley was at the press conference to support her mother and sister.

Afterward, Naomi, Wynonna, Ashley, and Larry Strickland drove in two separate cars to a Franklin restaurant. As they sat there in the parking lot, listening to the radio, they heard news of the breakup. It was an emotional moment for them, hearing someone announce the end of their long dream, and, as Naomi relates in her autobiography, she sent Larry and Ashley into the restaurant so that she could comfort Wynonna, who said, "I feel like I'm dying, Mommy."

It was a critical moment for the Judd family and Naomi, once again, pushed Ashley out the door. By then, Larry was officially a family member—he and Naomi had finally married in 1989—but for Naomi to equate Larry and Ashley as one level of family members and Wynonna as another was yet another rejection of her youngest daughter. In healthy families, the members grieve together when they suffer a loss. Naomi's insistence that she and Wynonna be left alone in their moment of grief offered validation to Ashley, psychologically speaking, that she was still the outsider in the family. It must have broken her heart.

Those expecting the Judds to go quietly into history were

mistaken. Naomi and Wynonna decided to have a farewell tour in order to say goodbye to their fans. At first, people thought, how nice: as sick as Naomi is, she still wants to perform. Everyone figured that the Judds would do two or three concerts, then call it quits. Naomi would go home and, well, pass over into that great country music jamboree in the sky. It would be a romantic end to a successful career.

It did not happen exactly that way.

The Judds' farewell tour began in February 1991 and ended on December 4, 1991—ten long months. They performed in 116 cities across North America and they took in over twenty-one million dollars. It was the longest goodbye in history. Some people wondered how a woman that ill could do so many concerts, but for the most part, people kept those thoughts to themselves. No one wanted to slam a dying woman, especially one who had provided so much joy to her fans.

Russ DeVault, a staff writer for the *Atlanta Constitution*, talked to Naomi about her health in late July, about ten months after her retirement announcement. "I went to the Mayo Clinic last month for a full checkup and then my doctor called me into his office, shut his door, took his phone off the hook and asked me how I was doing this [touring]," Naomi said, breaking into a giggle. "I just pointed up at the ceiling. All I can really do is stay prayerful and realize that I'm a child of God."

Naomi told the reporter that she did not know whether the breakup of the Judds was tougher on her or her daughter. "Wynonna has been so tuned-in to me that we're having problems disentangling," Naomi explained. "She hasn't really been away from me for twenty-seven years and I've had to fight for her from the minute she was conceived."

When the tour reached the West Coast, Naomi made time for a visit with Ashley. They rented a car and drove north to explore their old neighborhood in Marin County. It was one of the few times in recent years that Ashley and Naomi had spent time alone together. As always, Ashley was supportive of her mother. She gave her a pep talk, telling her that she was certain she could beat the illness.

One of their stops was at the restaurant where Naomi had worked while she was going to nursing school. They slipped quietly into the restaurant, with Naomi wearing a hat and sunglasses, but they were recognized—or at least Naomi was recognized—by a young employee. As they sat there, a song Naomi had written while they lived in Marin came on the jukebox. "It was a unique feeling of closure for me," Naomi wrote in her autobiography. "I put my arm around Ashley, reminding her how, although it seemed preposterous at the time, I'd vowed that someday we'd be on that very jukebox."

Of course, "we" were not on the jukebox. "They" were on the jukebox. Unfazed, Ashley, who was unselfish sometimes to the extreme, took her solitary moments with her mother as she could get them. By that point in her life, she had an almost biblical devotion to her mother and sister. Whatever the strength of her contradictory feelings, she pushed them deep inside of herself.

The Judds' final farewell concert was on December 4, 1991. It was held at Middle Tennessee State University in Murfreesboro, Tennessee, less than an hour's drive from their home. Unlike their other concerts, this one was broadcast on a three-hour pay-per-view show that was offered to fans on cable television for twenty-five dollars. There was a sellout crowd at the venue itself and more than six million fans paid twenty-five dollars each for the cable show, generating revenues of 150 million dollars. If it was money Mama Judd wanted to celebrate her career, she took it in by the buckets.

The concert itself was vintage Judds entertainment. They sang their biggest hits and they played to the live audience, with Wynonna standing stoically at the microphone and Naomi moving about the stage to engage the audience.

Thirty minutes into the concert, Naomi got serious. "I think Wynonna and I love country music more right this minute than the day we discovered it, because you have allowed us for the last eight years to heal our relationship and become best friends, and you quite possibly may have saved my life."

Sitting in the audience was Ashley, her face streaked with tears. Also moved were the other country stars that came to pay tribute to the Judds. Sitting in the audience were Brenda Lee, Reba McEntire, Kathy Mattea, Larry Gatlin, and Emmylou Harris. They did not go to the concert necessarily to hear the Judds sing. They went to say goodbye to a friend and colleague they thought was dying.

By the time the concert ended, everyone was in tears, except for a pay-per-view fan in Chicago who later sued the Judds because they failed to deliver a full three hours of entertainment. Lawyers for the fan told reporters that he intended to seek reimbursement of the "ticket" price, plus punitive damages. Most critics were kind to the duo, all the more so since they thought it was a death march.

As usual, Naomi was wrestling with her feelings about her career and her relationship with her daughters. Before the concert Naomi told David Zimmerman of *USA Today* that she now realized it was time to "disentangle" from Wynonna: "I told her last night I'm going to form a support group for post-traumatic stress disorder for mothers with hepatitis who break up with red-headed daughters."

The dynamics of the Judd family were changing drastically. When Ashley returned to Tennessee for the final concert, she and Wynonna left Naomi for a moment to go into Wynonna's bedroom. They closed the door, but Naomi could hear the muffled sounds of a song Wynonna had recorded for her upcoming solo album. "It was just a weird experience to hear anybody besides Mom here sing harmony on Wynonna," Naomi told Zimmerman. "Yet for her to be that sensitive means everything to me. Of course, I went into the room and said, 'That's a killer song.'"

That reaction was typical of Naomi. She assumed the private conference in Wynonna's bedroom was meant to exclude her. Perhaps. But another more likely possibility was that Wynonna simply wanted to share something intensely private with Ashley—the only song she had ever recorded without her mother looking over her shoulder. Naomi assumed it was about her and she assumed that it was done to spare her feelings. Whatever the reality, by barging in on her daughters' private moment, she reasserted her dominance at the expense of their budding self-actualization as sisters.

Clearly, Naomi would not go quietly into the night.

During the course of the excruciatingly long farewell tour, Ashley increased the pressure on herself to succeed. She pushed herself harder in class and she pushed herself harder on her homework assignments. The curriculum at Playhouse West required her to read books and write reports on what she read. By that point, Robert Carnegie estimated, she was reading seven thousand pages a month.

"People get the wrong idea about Ashley," said Carnegie. "They think that her mother and sister had something to do with where she is and that is just not the case. There is nobody in Hollywood that is going to give someone a job because they are related to country and western stars. She had a master plan that was based on the work ethic. This girl worked as hard and was as dedicated as anybody I have ever seen at the school and we have had some impressive students at the school [that list includes Jim Carrey, Jeff Goldblum, and James Franco, to name a few]. The way to success is not by being born into the right family but by being willing to work, and Ashley did that. She came to four classes a week and she rehearsed twice as much as everyone else, plus she was in that play, which she did every Saturday night religiously, where you got there at five and did not get out until eleven at night. There is nothing accidental about her rise to fame."

Meanwhile, Ashley networked at the management agency where she volunteered her time. When she thought she was ready, she shared her dream of an acting career with the executives there and asked them if they would send her out on an audition. They sent her to audition for the part of the Tool Time Girl on the television show *Home Improvement.* Ashley did not get the job—it went to ex-Playmate Pamela Anderson, who parlayed the role into a multi-million dollar "tool girl" empire—but the director did offer to create a role for her as Tim Allen's sister. Ashley told him she would think about it. She walked up and down the beach, pondering the pluses and minuses. On the plus side, of course, was the money it would pay. On the minus side was the fact that she really saw herself as a serious actress. She questioned whether being in a sitcom would be a good career move for her. She thanked the director, nicely of course, but said no.

Since the management agency received positive feedback from the director, they sent Ashley out on another audition. This time it was for a movie titled *Hero Wanted* (later changed to *Kuffs*). Director and writer Bruce Evans already had Christian Slater on board to play the male lead and he was searching for a female love interest to play opposite Slater. By that point in his career, the then-twenty-two-year-old actor had twenty major television and theatrical movies to his credit, including *Young Guns II, Mobsters,* and *Robin Hood: Prince of Thieves,* in which he played the role of Will Scarlett. This was several years before his run-ins with the law and he was considered an up-and-coming leading man. *Kuffs,* it was thought, could be his breakout role.

In the movie, Slater plays the part of George Kuffs, a twenty-one-year-old screw-up who abandons his pregnant girlfriend and moves to San Francisco to get financial help from his big brother (played by Bruce Boxleitner), who is the head of what the movie refers to as Patrol Specials—special police districts that are privately owned. Residents and business leaders pay the Specials for police protection. It is a silly idea, but that was the concept on which the script was based.

Shortly after Kuffs arrives in town, his brother is murdered, making him the new owner of the district. The movie is about both his experiences learning to operate the district as an untrained cop and his attempts to avenge his brother's death.

Ashley was offered the role of Slater's girlfriend, but after a little soul-searching she turned it down because the script required her to show her breasts. "Good luck with your movie," she told the casting agents, according to the *Philadelphia Inquirer.* "My mother hasn't worked her butt off so that I can take off my clothes in my first film." She was not a prude; she just felt that it would be a shock to her dying mother. Instead, she accepted a non-speaking role as the wife of a paint-store owner who is being strong-armed to sell his business. Ashley appears early in the movie and her scene lasts only a few seconds.

Hired to play the role of Slater's girlfriend was Ukrainian-born model Milla Jovovich, the daughter of Russian stage actress Gallina Loginova. Jovovich was just sixteen at the time and was not intimidated by doing a nude scene. Two years earlier, at the age of fourteen, she was filmed bare-breasted for *Return to the Blue Lagoon.* As it turned out, the nude scene for *Kuffs* was either filmed and then cut or simply never filmed, for when the movie was released in 1992 there was no nudity and it had a PG-13 rating. Even so, the highlight of the entire movie was a sexy scene in which Jovovich danced about in her underwear.

When the movie was released, critics jumped on it with claws bared—and with good reason, since it was one of the worst films of 1991. "*Kuffs* is krap," wrote *Washington Post* critic Richard Harrington. "The most offensive thing about *Kuffs,* however, is not its lack of substance or absence of achievement, but its PG-13 rating, suggesting it is suitable for children. That rating and the previews highlight the movie's zany and perhaps edgy aspects, but do not at all suggest its level of violence."

Critic Leonard Maltin called the movie "unbearably flip." John Hartl, in a review for film.com, wrote that the movie was a "pure act of self-destruction. Slater did have a few accomplices, chief among them first-time director Evans, who clutters the movie with look-ma-I'm-directing touches: cutely bleeped obscenities, characters who materialize like ghosts, sub titles to interpret what Slater's saying when his mouth is covered." Luckily for Ashley, no one noticed she was even in the movie.

After *Kuffs,* Ashley landed a small role as Gwen Fox in the made-for-television movie, *Till Death Us Do Part,* starring Treat Williams, Arliss Howard, and Rebecca Freeman. The R-rated movie, based on Vincent Bugliosi's book of the same name, was about a Los Angeles district attorney who is obsessed with prosecuting a renegade police officer. The movie went to video the same year it was aired.

Next for Ashley was a role as Ensign Mussler on television's *Star Trek: The Next Generation.* Naomi and Wynonna taped the show and watched it over and over again, finally learning the lines so that they could recite them in harmony with Ashley. Naomi cried every time she watched it. She was amazed at the transformation Ashley made on screen. It was the same Ashley, but she was oh so different in so many different ways!

In 1991, Ashley was twenty-three, but she had the poise of an older woman and the presence of a veteran actress. On screen, she was cool, self-assured, and capable of weaving a characterization out of little more than a smile and an expectant glint in her eyes. She showed an instinct for knowing what she could make the viewer believe.

Ashley's next break was a role on NBC-television's hour-long drama *Sisters*. The show starred Swoozie Kurtz as Alex Reed, Patricia Kalember as Georgie Reed, Julianne Phillips as Frankie Reed, and Sela Ward as Teddy Reed, all sisters who dealt each week with their changing lives and expectations for the future. It was the television equivalent of a "chick flick," which is to say that it was laced with estrogen and wrong-headed men such as Detective James Falconer, played by George Clooney.

Ashley was given the role of Kurtz's strong-willed daughter, Reid. To everyone's surprise, Ashley's character glowed whenever she appeared on screen. Although she was playing opposite some strong women actresses, Ashley stole scenes more than once. "I was amazed at how well she carried herself," Kurtz told *Biography* magazine. "She has always been wise beyond her years."

Ashley stayed with the series for three years, but she sought movie roles the entire time. She found the role neither inspiring nor gratifying. Cast members would often see her in her trailer between takes, reading movie scripts that had been sent to her.

During that year of the farewell tour, while Ashley spread her acting wings and Naomi bravely faced her impending death, Wynonna worked on her first solo album for Curb/MCA Records. Released in 1992, it was titled simply *Wynonna*.

To record the album, Wynonna had to make some major changes in her professional life. Since MCA executive Tony Brown wanted to produce the album, Wynonna was forced to fire Brent Maher as her producer. He took the termination of their relationship with good grace, but he would not have been human if he had not harbored some resentment, since it was he who had produced the albums that had made Wynonna and Naomi household names.

Reaction to the album was better than anyone expected. Critically, it was heralded as the next big thing in country music. The

*New York Times* said it was "faultless," without "an extraneous note or languid moment." *Rolling Stone* said *Wynonna* was "the most important release by a country artist this decade."

Music fans had a similar reaction. The album ended up selling over three million copies, making it one of the hottest-selling albums ever recorded by a female country artist. Her second solo album, *Tell Me Why*, released in 1993, also went platinum (an industry term that signifies albums that have sold in excess of one million units).

No one was more surprised than Wynonna. Always plagued by self-doubt, she felt doubly pressured when the time came to tour in support of the album. She insisted that Naomi travel with her, which she did for the first six concert dates. Naomi boosted her daughter's confidence and tried to keep her calm. Finally, she stole away after the sixth concert, leaving a note behind to explain her departure. Wynonna was devastated. On the outside, she seemed fine—her concerts were energy packed—but on the inside she was in pain. Over the years, she had desperately wanted to be free of her mother's influence, but now that she was, she felt a void in her life.

"Going through this year without [Naomi] has been really hard," she told *Us* magazine. "My mother has always been the focus of what the Judds did. While she would be the cheerleader onstage, I would hide behind the drums, acting goofy. Now I don't have Mom anymore to cut up my meat. It's scary when you go, 'Oh, my God, I have to use my mind.'"

Several years after Wynonna launched her solo career, Jane Pauley asked her during a *NBC Dateline* interview how it felt the first time the bus pulled away without her mother. "I felt very alone, but all of a sudden, my next thought was…'OK, now what do I do?' I was definitely in the moment of the pain and sorrow," Wynonna explained. "I grieved. But then I got up off my butt, quit complaining, and went back out there and did exactly what I've been doing my whole life, which is surviving and singing."

That is true as far as it goes, but doing and feeling are two separate things. She did what she had to do, but the hole inside her never went away. In time, she tried to fill the void with food. She had never been as slender as Ashley, but now she was eating everything in sight and ballooning out like something out of a monster movie. When food did not assuage her pain, she looked for love, as the song says, in all the wrong places. She got pregnant during an affair with Nashville businessman Arch Kelley III, but refused to marry him. The child, Elijah, was born out of wedlock on December 23, 1994. It was not until she got pregnant a second time, this time with Grace

Pauline, born on June 21, 1996, that she decided to marry the children's father.

When Elijah was born it both delighted and horrified her fans. Some of those who rejoiced did so because they had begun to wonder if Wynonna might not have lesbian tendencies. Those fears had swelled not as the result of anything she had ever done, but because of the butchy attitude she had taken once she launched her solo career. Those fans who were horrified had difficulty reconciling Wynonna's out-of-wedlock pregnancy with traditional country values. Wasn't Wynonna doing something that the Bible frowned upon? they wondered.

Fans worked hard to give her the benefit of the doubt, but it was not always easy because most of the time Wynonna behaved as if she did not care what her fans thought. That was not the way she really felt, of course. Over the years, her outward behavior seldom reflected her inner feelings. There were times when she appeared to be happy and talkative when she was actually frightened and depressed, her anger screaming and clawing on the inside like a wounded animal. That was when she and Naomi fought the hardest, and when the unwavering love of her sister was her only grounding.

By the mid-1980s, Florida filmmaker Victor Nunez had two feature films to his credit—*Gal Young 'Un*, a 1979 drama that tells the story of widowed Florida woman and her husband's girlfriend, and *Flash of Green*, a mystery about a newspaper reporter who investigates a crooked land deal in a small Florida coastal town. Prior to that, the talented Peruvian-born, Florida-raised director had spent the 1970s making a series of short fictional films, most of which received critical acclaim.

Content to live and work in Florida, Nunez sometimes goes for years without making a film. That is because he essentially views himself as a Southern filmmaker, and snagging the right story to tell requires a certain amount of patience. "It's a very naïve, very romantic notion," he said, explaining his concept of Southern filmmaking to John Rogers of Associated Press. "And I'm not sure I've even answered it. Because it's sort of made me the exception that proves the fool."

After completing *Flash of Green* in 1984, Nunez decided the time had come for him to write his own Southern story. The resulting script, titled *Ruby in Paradise*, was set in a Florida coastal town, just the type of place he visited as a teen while growing up in Tallahassee. Unfortunately, when he began shopping the script in an effort to obtain a financing and distribution deal, he found that Hollywood was in no mood for another sensitive coming-of-age story.

"I couldn't get anyone interested in the movie," he said without even a hint of bitterness in his voice. "They said, 'Who cares about a shop clerk in the middle of nowhere? If you want to have a whore on Fifty-second Street doing drugs, we'll talk.'"

For nearly ten years, he made the rounds with his script. He made no other feature films during that time. He was totally devoted to *Ruby in Paradise*. Just when it seemed he had run out of doors on which to knock, good fortune shined on him.

Nunez's great aunt, his grandfather's sister, had never met Victor, but when she died he received a call from her bank saying that she had left him four hundred thousand dollars. At first, he thought he would invest the money so that he would have a nest egg for his old age. Then he underwent an epiphany: "I woke at three in the morning and thought, 'You know you're just supposed to take that and make this movie.'"

In late 1991, he decided to use the inheritance to finance the film. It was a gutsy decision, but one that clearly demonstrated the intensity of his feelings about the project. Nunez's first and most important task was to cast the female lead. Since this was a coming-of-age story about a young woman from Tennessee who drove to Florida in search of herself, the believability of the story depended on the believability of the actress. Everything depended on his choice.

Nunez went through numerous interviews in his search. Their credentials mattered less than their ability to convince him of their passion for the role. But even more than that was required. Nunez took Polaroid photos of each actress he interviewed. Motion pictures are a visual medium. If, once the interview was over, Nunez could look at the Polaroid and still see what he perceived when he was face-to-face with an actress, then he knew he had the right person for the role.

On the way to the audition, Ashley nearly wrecked her car. "I was so intense and emotional, and thinking, 'Ohmagosh!' If I get this part, it validates the dream and interpretation I've had of myself since I was in the third grade,'" she told Glenn Lovell of the *San Jose Mercury News*. "[The script] was like listening to an album and one song grips you and becomes an anthem for your whole life. From the first three sentences, I knew it was written for me."

By the time Nunez got to Ashley he had gone through most of the actresses who had responded to the audition. Nothing had clicked. At least nothing that you would want to wrap an inheritance around.

There was something about the half-charming, half-charging-buffalo way Ashley had stormed into his office and demanded his attention.

"I was pushing people out of the way so I could get to him and say, 'I understand your movie,'" Ashley told Lovell. "Other people said the same thing, but there was something about my conveyance which was genuine and resonated within him."

Nunez was not sure exactly what he was looking for. He just figured he would know it when he saw it. That is the way it happened with Ashley. "We had seen twenty to twenty-five people before Ashley," said Nunez. "She had been out of town and came in midway through the project. Even though I am from the South, I did not know who the Judds were. She told me when she came into the office and I acted dutifully impressed, but I did not know who they were."

Ashley immediately went to the top of the list, but not because of her famous mother and sister. "I got the feeling that she had an intuitive understanding of Ruby and the core center of her life, which was not let life pass her by—and that was critical to the character," he said. "She had done some work on *Star Trek* and *Sisters*, but to be honest, neither of those things, when they sent them over, impressed me very much."

Nunez was urged to go with an actress with more experience, but he had a gut feeling about Ashley. "I can remember driving from the casting office across the valley over into Hollywood all by myself in my rental car, and I remember thinking that I have always tried to work from what I perceived inside the characters and I would rather feel that that core was there instead of some certainty that someone had done ten movies....Of course, you go with Ashley. I have never regretted that decision."

Nunez offered the part to her, and when she asked why, perhaps seeking validation for her good fortune, he explained that the others were "too Tennessee Williams and not enough Tennessee."

Actually, Ashley did have stiff competition from an actress with a similar background. "She had gone to Japan and stayed longer [than Ashley] and she clearly had been to the edge of something that it was not apparent she would be able to come back from," Nunez said. "It was very alarming—not to say that Ashley went anywhere near that place—but she was like a lot of young actresses. It would scare a lot of men to know the kinds of experiences they have had by the age of twenty-one."

Once Ashley accepted—was there ever any doubt she would?—Nunez shared his discovery with members of his production team. Marilyn Wall-Asse, who was in charge of makeup and costumes, had never heard of Ashley Judd, but she could see the excitement on Nunez's face: "He showed me a little Polaroid of her and said this is an actress that had a tremendous potential and talent. He said she was a Judd and he thought she would be great." To Stewart Lippe, the production manager, Nunez laughingly said, "People will remember this as Ashley's first film, not my third film."

Ashley subsequently told people that she got the part based solely on her own initiative, adding that being a Judd had nothing to do with it. Ashley believed that, but it was not entirely true. A Hollywood casting director named Judy Courtney screened the actresses before they were sent to interview with Nunez. Courtney knew all about Naomi Judd, indeed she considered her to be a very interesting woman, and she felt that the mother's notoriety might be an asset to Ashley's public image. While that consideration shaped her decision as a screener, she did not pass it along to Nunez.

Thrilled to get the part, Ashley took the script in to Playhouse West to show to Robert Carnegie. "That was her first opportunity to do anything of substantial worth in a movie," said Carnegie. "It was a movie that was going to be made on a very low budget, but it was a part that was extremely right for her. I remember very clearly what I told her, because all she knew was what we did in the classes, she had not been polluted by anything else. I told her that when she went off to do the picture there would probably be difficulties with the director if she sticks to what she has learned with us, but she had to stick with what she had learned. Because by this point she was very good. I didn't want her to go off and do a movie and give up the base she had."

*Ruby in Paradise* began production in March 1992 at Panama City Beach, Florida. In addition to Ashley, Nunez had cast Todd Field as Mike McCaslin, Ruby's love interest, Bentley Mitchum as Ricky Chambers, Ruby's hate interest, and Allison Dean as Rochelle Bridges, Ruby's best friend. Ashley was not the only actor of celebrity parentage in the film: Bentley Mitchum is son of Christopher Mitchum and the grandson of Hollywood legend Robert Mitchum. Prior to signing on for *Ruby*, he had appeared in six motion pictures, including *Meatballs 4* and *Man in the Moon*.

The story begins with Ashley running away from her home in Manning, Tennessee, to find her happiness in Florida. Says Ruby in the movie, "I got out of Manning without getting pregnant or beat up. That's saying something."

Prior to filming, Ashley flew to Nashville and borrowed her mother's car so that she could research the role. Nunez thought it was a brilliant strategic move on her part. "She drove south and literally made Ruby's journey down, and as she did, she shed her L.A. mannerisms, so that when she showed up she was perfect."

Prior to filming on location in Florida, Nunez, Ashley, and a skeleton crew went to North Carolina so that Ashley could be filmed actually driving to Florida. Nunez, who always acts as his own cameraman, went along and filmed Ashley from the passenger seat of the car as she drove south through the mountains of North Carolina into South Carolina and Georgia.

"We had shot the scene early, when it was properly exposed," said Nunez, "but it just didn't feel right, so I said, 'Ashley, let's just go down the road one more time.'" The result was the scene that appears in the movie. It shows Ashley's profile as she drives into the dusk, perfectly capturing the emotion of her journey into the great unknown. "It was a special moment," said Nunez. "It was just the two of us."

Marilyn Wall-Asse, like everyone else in the crew, was eager to meet Nunez's discovery. The entire project depended on Ashley and everyone was more interested than usual because they knew Nunez had bankrolled the project with his inheritance. Everyone on the crew had worked with him before—they were like a family—and they wanted the movie to be a success for his sake.

"When I met Ashley, I was with the crew, maybe twenty-five people, eating dinner in this hotel room," explained Wall-Asse. "And she comes in. She had on this blue calico cotton dress, sort of torn up, cowboy boots, a baseball hat, a retainer in her mouth, and she was holding a little rabbit. She said hello to the crew. Everyone said, 'Here's our actress,' so we all smiled. I did a fitting on her that night and we started shooting the next day."

Wall-Asse was surprised at how well Ashley did when solo scenes were called for. "A lot of actors are not comfortable alone, but Ashley was really comfortable during her solo moments on camera. The camera just loved her and her face. She has this depth of what her face can do. You hold a camera on her and it says ten different things."

*Ruby in Paradise* begins with Ruby making her escape from Tennessee. She is not certain what she wants out of life, only that it does not exist in Tennessee. She chose Florida because she had visited with her parents when she was ten and felt there was something special about the Gulf Coast. It is winter when she arrives, so the beaches are pretty much deserted. The first thing she does is rent a beach cottage.

Since it is the off-season, it is difficult to find a job. Eventually, she gets a job in a tourist shop in a strip mall, not because of her qualifications (she had no real experience), but because of her personality. The shop owner, Mildred Chambers, played by Dorothy Lyman, takes a liking to her and hires her even though she knows she will not need help in the store until students hit the beach during spring break.

Despite warnings from the shop owner, Ashley goes out with her son Ricky, played by Mitchum, and ends up in bed with him. The sex scene is without words. Ruby talks with her eyes, watching Ricky with curiosity, not affection. The next day, he gives her a CD player as a gift. On their next date, they have sex at his place and Ruby looks in his dresser drawer and sees that he has several identical CD players, all decorated with the same red ribbon.

At first, Ruby's only true friend is her diary. "Are there any real reasons for living right anyway?" she asks herself in the diary. "Mama always thought so and they held her like a moth to the light with the hopes of earning everlasting peace and glory. There's life in the next world, she used to say. It was all a bloody, mean trick. I don't want none of it."

On her days off from the shop, Ruby explores the beach and works to get her cottage just the way she wants it. On a trip to a nursery to buy a plant, she meets an employee named Mike McCaslin (played by Todd Field). She is cool to him at first, but he perseveres and she agrees to have dinner with him.

The scene of Ruby eating a raw oyster on a cracker, while smiling at the same time, is one of the visual highlights of the film. In fact, all of Ashley's scenes with Field are dazzling to watch. She is not acting during those moments, she is *living* the life of her character. Ruby battles with changing herself to accommodate Field, who is more intellectual, more cynical in a quirky sort of way, but less feeling about life in general.

"Ashley is an incredibly complex person, as all actors are," Nunez said in explaining her effectiveness. "I have a theory about actors. When they are performing and it is right, it is a truth that is as powerful and articulate as any philosopher or writer or song could ever be. That is what we love about a wonderful performance, because we feel like we can see into their soul."

One night, while Ruby is involved with Field, Ricky shows up at Ruby's cottage. She lets him in reluctantly and then pays the price for not listening to her heart. He tries to rape her. When she resists, he fires her from her job.

Devastated, she looks for a new job. It was while they were filming her job search that Nunez realized just how perfect Ashley was for the part. "There is a scene when she is looking for work. She walks out of the building and goes up to the car and starts to cry. She just nailed it. I almost dropped the camera I was so amazed. I went over to her and I said, 'Wherever you were in that scene, that was Ruby."

After a series of rejections, Ruby considers topless dancing for a moment. "Impressive stuff," she thinks, while sitting in her car outside the club. "To flaunt it in front of paying customers. The ultimate merchandise. Maybe that's all there is. We're all selling. Forget what's inside."

The remainder of the film deals with Ruby's sensitive journey into a sort of tentative womanhood. It is a quiet story that stalks the viewer's emotions from a distance. Ruby emerges from her journey with a better understanding of the world in which she lives, and the viewer is left with an intimate glimpse into a young woman's life.

The film only took six weeks to shoot, but it was an exciting, event-filled time for Ashley. Throughout that time she insisted that her rabbit be allowed to live with her in her hotel room. "Ashley loved her room to be in great order," recalled Wall-Asse. "But she had this little bunny hopping around. It was like a little puppy."

All movies have at least one incident that makes them memorable for reasons that have nothing to do with the actual filming. In the case of *Ruby in Paradise*, it was the Great Bunny Caper. One day, while directing a scene, Nunez noticed a mark on Ashley's nose and asked Marilyn if she could take care of it.

Ashley, who had worn a nose ring in college, apparently had successfully covered the scar during her screen test. When Wall-Asse asked her about it, she said the bunny had scratched her on the nose. Said Wall-Asse, "We had to deal all through *Ruby* with covering up that scratch."

For the duration of the filming, while Wall-Asse worked with Ashley to cover up the "bunny scratch," Nunez suspected a nose ring the entire time. "They blamed it on the rabbit," said Nunez. "But once I realized they were going to go to the rabbit, I said, 'You don't need to go there.'" Later, in what can only be attributed to an act of lagomorph revenge, the bunny took out its frustrations on Nunez. "Somehow my shoes got left in some communal place at rehearsal and the rabbit was roaming around and found them. It chewed through my shoe laces and I only had one pair of shoes and I had to rush out before we shot that day to get new shoelaces."

It would take ten years for him to finally solve the mystery associated with the Great Bunny Caper. Told in 2002 that Ashley wore a nose ring in college, he sighed with satisfaction. All along he just *knew* it had been a nose ring.

Another eccentricity Ashley displayed was a penchant for wearing only pajamas. When they were not shooting—and she was not required to be in costume—she changed into her pajamas. "One time, while we were doing the lighting, she jumped out of the Winnebago and jogged about in her pajamas," laughed Wall-Asse. It was things like that that endeared Ashley to the crew. Wall-Asse recalled one occasion when it rained for three days and they could not work. Ashley showed up early one of those mornings and cooked breakfast for the crew. Not cereal and sliced fruit, mind you—hot biscuits and gravy, the type of breakfast she cherished when she visited her mother. Then, as everyone sat around in stunned silence, Ashley served up what she had cooked, treating the crew members as if they were the closest of family.

Ashley usually traveled from the hotel to the set with Wall-Asse in her Winnebego. On one occasion, after they had completed a scene on the beach, they headed back to the hotel in the Winnebego. As Wall-Asse drove, Ashley reached up and grabbed an overhead bar in the lumbering vehicle, lifted herself, and, overcome with emotion, screamed out, "God, I love to work!"

Since those Winnebago rides were a daily occurrence, sometimes lasting up to an hour at a time, Ashley brought along her own entertainment. Wynonna's second solo album, *Tell Me Why*, had just been released and Ashley carried it with her in the truck. "We would play that full blast and listen to it and Ashley would sing along with the songs," said Wall-Asse. "She sat there with her feet propped up on the dashboard and sang along. She can sing—boy, at the top of her lungs!"

When they were not driving around in the Winnebago singing, they talked about Ashley's dreams. Each morning Ashley would tell Wall-Asse about the dream she had the night before, and as they drove they talked about the dream, trying to interpret it.

Professionally, Ashley was full of surprises. One scene called for her to wake up one morning and look out her window and see an Indian family outside. Ashley thought the wonderment of that experience could be better captured if she slept on the set. Nunez thought that was a good idea and he had a crew member stay in the house with her to make certain she would be safe. The next morning, while Ashley slept, Nunez crept into the cottage so that he could film her actually awakening and looking out the window. That is the cut that remained in the film.

"Ruby was a much more simple person than Ashley is," said Wall-Asse. "Ashley spent a lot of time trying to understand her. I thought she gave the character this wonderful simplicity and dignity. Victor seems to write these amazing scripts about women. He gives redemption to ordinary people. I think Ashley saw that when she read the script."

Stewart Lippe, the production manager, was impressed with how well Ashley took direction. "I think she had an intuitive feel for the script because Victor knows exactly what he wants and he talks pretty in-depth with the actors explaining exactly what he wants, and I think she executed it very effectively. There were some rehearsals, but not a lot. He would make suggestions and recommendations that she spread out the moment."

That "spreading out of the moment," of course, is at the heart of the artistic vision of the film. "Some people don't get that the movie makes a commitment to the moments in between things," said Nunez. "It was not a lazy choice. In terms of the number of shots, there were a lot—about eight hundred. You cannot make an actor be something they are not. What you can do is weed the garden and clear some space where their soul has been neglected. In Ashley's case, all of that was her own. The resonance, those moments, was not contrived. It was just a matter of creating the scene and trusting that it was worth telling."

In real life, Ashley is very much unlike Ruby. Ashley's reaction time is faster, her interactions with other people more complex, and her speaking rhythm more exotic. It is a measure of Ashley's talent and Nunez's direction that the character of Ruby is so believable on the screen. It is also a testament to Ashley's fledgling professionalism that she never let on to anyone in the crew that she was having some problems with the direction. Her acting coach, Robert Carnegie, realized that when she returned home after the shooting. Said Carnegie: "She told me that for the first two weeks there were difficulties, because what she was doing was so simple, you know, that it wasn't immediately recognizable what it was from watching it."

Julie Gordon, the 2001 head of the Panama City Beach Film Commission, was in high school when the film was made, but she recalls how excited local residents were to have another film-company in town. At that time, *Ruby in Paradise* was only the second feature film to be shot in the Panama City area (the first was an eminently forgettable movie titled *Frogs*). She said: "When they shot *Ruby*, they used Holiday Lodge as a casting area [for extras] and they literally, for almost a week, had lines pouring out of the inn, people dying to be in the movie. Business owners love for them to film here."

One of the extras who signed on for the movie was Carley Pender. He and a female friend were asked to be diners in one of the restaurant scenes. He had never seen a movie being made and he was surprised that they were asked to fake acting naturally.

"The place was packed with imitation guests," he recalled. "We were just sitting there moving our lips, saying whatever, but nothing was coming out since they didn't want any background noise. We were never able to eat out of our plates. Basically, we sat there for three hours and pretended like we were having conversations with the people we were with."

Beverly Mirriam was a real waitress in the restaurant. It was her day off, but she went to work anyway so that she could watch. "It was exciting," she said. "What surprised me was that they changed it into an Italian restaurant. We were just a restaurant where you could get burgers and breakfast. We had to go get these fancy wine glasses. We had to take our own glasses down and put tableclothes on the tables. I thought, 'Why did they go to all that trouble?' It would have been cooler to leave it the way it was." Mirriam was asked to be a waitress in the movie, but she said no. "I chickened out," she said. "Everyone told me that I was stupid."

The last scene filmed was one in which Ruby runs out into the ocean. They saved it for last in hopes that the water would be warmer. "Ashley was so funny," said Wall-Asse. "She was worried, saying she had to wear something that her mama would approve of. It was freezing that day, but she held her breath and ran out into the ocean screaming."

Before the film was released, Nunez took Ashley and some crew members to France, where he introduced the film at the Cannes Film Festival. The film was warmly embraced, but reaction to the film was nothing compared to the reaction to Ashley. Said Lippe: "My favorite memory of making the film was at Cannes, just watching Ashley totally seduce that entire audience with her charm and graciousness. She gave a short speech and thanked the audience in perfect French. The audience was sort of drooling, standing and applauding wildly, because she was very eloquent in French." Interviewed in 2001, Lippe said, "It is amazing—people come up to me all the time and tell me how *Ruby in Paradise* was such an important film to them—Ashley is a very charismatic individual."

When *Ruby in Paradise* was released in 1993, *Chicago Sun-Times* movie critic Roger Ebert gave it four stars and said Ashley gave one of the best performances of the year: "*Ruby in Paradise* is a breathtaking movie about a young woman who opens the book of her life to a fresh page, and begins to write." When Ashley read Ebert's review, she was speechless—well, almost. She told a reporter: "I thought, 'Who is he talking about?'"

Writing in the *Atlanta Constitution*, Eleanor Ringel said it was "a movie as rare and wonderful in its own gentle, unassuming way as a perfectly formed seashell you might happen upon at the beach...you find yourself slowing down to its quieter pace, slipping into its simpler point of view. And when you leave the theater, it's the strangest thing—you feel like going out and being nice to people."

*Washington Post* critic Rita Kempley was impressed by the movie's intelligence and its tip of the hat to introspective female writers such as Flannery O'Connor and Marjorie Kinnan Rawlings. Writes Kempley: "Nunez fills [Ruby's] head and her journal with thoughtful observations on the nature of morality, men and occasionally the environment. It all sounds politically correct and cosmic, which it is, yet it's leavened mightily with Ruby's common sense and country girl's humor. 'Driving on the road once,' she says, 'I swerved to keep from hitting a rabbit and ran over a skunk.' Hey, that's life."

Encouraged by public reaction to the film, Nunez sent Ashley out on a twenty-city promotional tour. She could hardly believe her good fortune. Now it was *she* who was out on tour while Naomi sat at home wondering what was happening in her daughter's life. Ashley was enthusiastic about promoting the film, but the relentless schedule sometimes made her a tad cranky. To the surprise and amusement of reporters, she would sometimes be catty and semi-insulting to the reporters who interviewed her, then turn around and smother them with Southern charm, using the same honey-coated platitudes she had heard her mother use so many times.

At an interview in Atlanta, she refused to pose for a photograph because she had not brushed her hair and had not put on makeup. An executive from October Films, the distributor, called and pleaded with her to do it. She relented and did the photograph, but she was not happy about it.

"I actually started to cry when we got off the phone because people want so (expletive) much, they never give in," she explained to Steve Murray of the *Atlanta Constitution*. "What more can I give you, what more can I possibly give you, what more can I possibly do, how much more accommodating can I be?"

That attitude was not typical of Ashley—and it only flared up when she was very tired—but it is indicative of the contradictory feelings she had about fame and fortune, even at that early stage of her career. She wants to be adored by the public, but she wants that interchange to occur from a distance. It is a contradiction she sees in herself. She once explained it this way to Carrie Rickey of the *Philadelphia Inquirer:* "It's mysterious to me how I have all these opinions about needing my privacy, but not only will I talk about it, I'll talk about it at length."

Ashley was out on the road promoting the film when she learned that Naomi's life-threatening illness had gone into remission. Doctors said they had never seen anything like it, since there is no cure for hepatitis C—it simply went away. Ashley told Rickey: "Tell your readers that Mom is in full clinical remission, inexplicable by medical standards."

Ashley limped into San Francisco stunned by the news of her mother's recovery (she telephoned her four times a day while out on the road) and weary of the media attention, which she found exhausting, only to learn that the Malibu cottage she shared with her two cats, Charlotte and Emily, was in the path of a raging forest fire. "Maybe there is some extraordinarily small chance that the fire hopscotched my house," she said during an interview with Glenn Lovell of the *San Jose Mercury News*. "But, by all reports, it's completely gone."

The only bright spot in her life at that precise moment, she said, was that a man had asked her out on a date. "I'm very excited," she told Lovell. "A boy actually asked me out. We're going for sushi. You know how long it's been since I've laid eyes on anybody I would want to ask me out? We're talking a really long time."

At that point she pushed out her bottom lip into a pout and recited a line from a B. B. King song, "Nobody loves me 'cept my mama." She did not recite the second line, but it goes, "and I'm not too sure about her!"

When Ashley returned to Malibu, she learned that her home had burned to the ground, along with the diaries she had kept for years and a collection of Wynonna's favorite albums. Fortunately, her two cats escaped the fire without a scratch or singe. There was joy in that discovery, but the reality of her situation stung her to the core. Here she was, finally, a successful actress, with reporters hanging on her every word—and aside from her mother and sister, and that one extraordinarily lucky suitor in San Francisco, she was totally alone in life. On top of that, she was now homeless.

The Natchez Trace stretches over four hundred miles from

Natchez, Mississippi, to Nashville, Tennessee. Originally trod by buffalo, the eight thousand-year-old trail was subsequently traveled by Native Americans, European trappers and traders, and finally missionaries intent on taking the word of God into the wilderness. Early French and Spanish maps of the Trace date back to the 1700s.

By the 1800s, it had become a major trade route, with ships and riverboats going upstream on the Mississippi River to dock at Natchez to unload cargoes for overland shipment on the Trace into what was then the heartland of America—Tennessee, Kentucky, Virginia, and North Carolina.

Because of the large volume of trade that occurred on the Trace, it became a natural haven for outlaws and bandits. Travelers were routinely robbed and killed by bandits who could carry out their foul deeds and then blend back into the dense foliage. For that reason, it took courage to travel the Trace in the 1800s. There were only twenty rest stops—then called stands—along the route, and nights spent in the wilderness were subject to interruptions by wild animals, bandits, and hostile Chickasaw and Choctaw Indians who considered it part of their sacred domain. Today the Trace is a federal parkway and is maintained by the National Park Service. Each year millions of travelers visit the Trace and travel the two-lane highway with little fear of bandits.

Punctuated by rolling hills, dark forests, and moss-covered trees, the Trace has a long history of mystery associated with it. It was on the Trace that Meriwether Lewis, the revered member of the Lewis and Clark expedition, died about fifty miles south of Nashville while en route to Washington, D.C. There is no mystery about how he died. It was from gunshot wounds. But to this date, it is unknown whether he died of self-inflicted wounds or was murdered.

Aside from the beauty and mystery of the Trace, there is a strong element of spirituality attached to it. Some people believe that it is the most spiritual stretch of land in America. There are several reasons for that. Existing burial mounds along the Trace date as far back as 100 B.C. While Jesus Christ was walking the earth on the other side of the globe, Native Americans were walking the Trace in search of their spiritual identities. Even today, one cannot walk the Trace alone without feeling the presence of the spirits that still inhabit it, lost and found souls on the move. Whatever your religion, there is no better place in America to find God.

A second reason that many people believe in the spirituality of the Trace is its long history as an incubator for artistic talent. It is a fact that some of America's most creative and innovative writers, musicians, and media personalities were born on the Trace, or within a one-hundred-mile radius. That list includes Elvis Presley, Oprah Winfrey, William Faulkner, Richard Wright, Robert Penn Warren, Tammy Wynette, Tennessee Williams, Eudora Welty, Beth Henley, Elizabeth Spencer, B.B. King, Robert Johnson, Muddy Waters, Howlin' Wolf, and Sun Records founder Sam Phillips, to name a few. What those individuals have in common, aside from their creativity, is a strong spiritual sense of self-identity. They may express it in different ways, but it lies at the core of their work and it typically infiltrates their conversation and writings.

When Naomi Judd made enough money from her music to purchase a house, she was drawn inexplicably to the Natchez Trace community of Leiper's Fork, Tennessee, located about fifteen miles southwest of Nashville.

Naomi did not know the spiritual history of the Trace, nor was she aware of its curative powers, when she purchased her home in the mid-1980s. All she knew was that the land made her feel different inside. It made her feel calmer, more at peace with the universe. In time, Wynonna bought a home and adjoining land about a half-mile from Naomi. Together they acquired about one thousand acres of prime pasture and farmland. The Natchez Trace cuts through the Judd fiefdom like a meandering riverbed.

In November 1993, when Wynonna learned that Ashley's Malibu cottage had burned to the ground, her heartfelt response was immediate—come home, Ashley! Ashley explained that she could not do that because she was a Hollywood actress now. No problem, Wynonna countered: Nashville has a fine airport and you can get helicopter service right to your back door! Ashley wavered, but Wynonna sealed the deal by giving her a house on the property known to locals as the Old Meacham Place.

The two-story red-brick house was built in the 1850s by Matthew Meacham, one of Franklin County's most successful farmers and cattlemen. According to Richard Warick, who has written two histories on Franklin County and the surrounding area, the house was once rebuilt after it was hit by a tornado.

Meacham's son, Harold, lived in the house after his father passed away and carried on the Meacham tradition. Harold was a bank director, as was his father, and he was once appointed to the Federal Reserve Board. In addition, Harold was a country court magistrate and had the authority to hold court right there in the house. "Locals would come there to get married, or if there was a dispute or if a constable arrested someone," said Warick. "They went there and judgment could be rendered right there on the spot. Mr. Harold said there were a lot of marriages in the front hall."

Ashley was enthusiastic about accepting the house. It needed some work done on it, but that was fine with her. "I'm modeling it after C. S. Lewis's *Chronicles of Narnia*," she explained to David Hochman of *Us* magazine, "with cubbyholes and secret passageways, old gun cabinets and medicine chests built of chestnut, all because it was the first book that was ever read to me as a child and my house needs to be a magical place."

The house, with its heavily shaded front yard, is almost flush against the road, so one of the first things she had to do was add a fence and a security gate to keep out the curious. The house is not built into a hillside, but it is close enough to a hillside to have some protection from northerly and westerly winds. Across the road from the house are a barn and a pasture filled with grazing llamas.

At first glance, you wonder why Ashley would want to live in the Old Meacham Place. Then, after you have gazed at the house for a while—no one advertises it, but you can see Ashley's house from the Natchez Trace parkway—you know exactly why Ashley feels so much at home there. It's secluded, romantic, rustic, historic, and close enough to both Naomi and Wynonna to enable them to circle their wagons if the need should ever arise. And, based on the house's colorful history, it affords Judge Ashley the moral authority to marry or hang anyone who ventures into her entrance hall. Who in their right mind would turn her back on all those perks?

As if starring in her first feature film and receiving rave reviews, having her home burn to the ground, and learning that her dying mother was not dying after all were not enough excitement for one year, fate dealt Ashley another major adrenaline rush in 1993: Naomi published her autobiography. Titled *Love Can Build a Bridge*, it was a chatty, folksy family history that heaped praise on her friends and disdain on her enemies.

The *Chicago Tribune* called the book an "explosive autobiography...outrageous, breathless, voluble, fast-moving, funny...and always mercilessly candid." *USA Today* described it as not "quite the dust-off-your-Bible Cinderella story fans might have expected. There's more than a little sin, occasional gunplay and thousands of U-Haul miles."

*Love Can Build a Bridge* was all that and more. There were only a few things seriously wrong with the book: it contained misspelled names, garbled facts, questionable interpretations of events, and a self-righteous attitude that was, at times, unkind to those who loved

Naomi the most—her daughters.

Both Ashley and Wynonna were horrified by the book.

"My mother remembered things a bit differently than I did and that hurt," Ashley told Louis Hobson of the *Calgary Sun*. "We haven't resolved everything by a long stretch, but my mom and I have at least agreed to disagree." To Bob Morris of *Elle* magazine, she said, "[Mother] just has her own kind of reality. Sister says she's going to write her own version of Mom's autobiography someday, and it's going to be called *The Truth*."

# Chapter
# Four

## *Where There's Smoke There's Heat*

Whatever doubts Ashley had about living near Naomi and Wynonna were addressed in late 1993 when she broke her right ankle in a fall from one of her mother's horses. She was hospitalized for nearly a week in a hospital that also had as a patient country music legend Tammy Wynette. The singer had been hospitalized because of serious stomach problems. When Naomi was not hovering over Ashley's hospital bed, she went to the intensive care unit to visit with Wynette, who had a respirator in her throat. Since Wynette could not do much talking, Naomi had a captive audience.

When Ashley left the hospital and returned to the farm, her mobility was curtailed. In a way, she, too, was hooked up to a life support system—her mother! Ashley's speech was not impeded by her injury, but no longer could she jump up and dash out of the room whenever Naomi took their conversation in directions she did not want to go. As a result, Ashley and her mother spoke, really communicated, for the first time in many years. As Ashley's ankle healed, so did the long-standing rift between the two of them. It was at that point, during the healing of her ankle injury, that Ashley decided that accepting the house from Wynonna had been a good idea.

In some respects, the relationships between Naomi and her daughters were changing, however slightly. Now it was Ashley who pondered the possible benefits of a closer relationship with her mother, while Wynonna tried to escape her smothering influence. There were days when she must have thought that never would happen.

Nineteen ninety-four began with a reunion of the Judds at Super Bowl XXVIII in Atlanta, Georgia. Naomi and Wynonna performed their hit "Love Can Build a Bridge" during halftime before nearly one hundred thousand football fans. Actually, they did not sing it; they lip-synched a shortened, prerecorded version.

Fans wondered if the appearance meant that the Judds were going to reunite for a new album and tour. Not much chance of that, mother and daughter explained to the media. Wynonna was out on tour promoting her second solo album and Naomi was still doing book tours to promote her autobiography.

Actually, personal gain was not the reason for the Super Bowl appearance, Naomi explained to Russ DeVault of the *Atlanta Constitution*: "I wrote the song, 'Love Can Build a Bridge,' because I'd been on the road for eight years and I had seen the trouble and violence that America was sinking into. I was trying to say that hope has always been my constant companion. It's the theme of my book, too."

Wynonna had mixed feelings about performing with her mother. On one hand, it diminished her talent (in her eyes only) and made her feel trapped, not just personally but musically as well. On the other hand, it took pressure off her on stage to have Naomi prissing about in her frilly skirts, diverting attention away from her own increasingly bulky frame. Wynonna loved the adulation of the audience, for it stoked her creativity, but she hated for them to look at her so intently because she was not comfortable with herself. If she could have performed behind a screen she would have done so gladly.

As it turned out, the Super Bowl performance marked yet another turning point for the Judds, all of them. Unknown to Naomi, Wynonna had invited Michael Ciminella to the football game. She thought it would be a thrill for him to see the sporting event from a backstage perspective. Also, she wanted him to ride back to Nashville with her in the bus so that they could get caught up on everything.

While Wynonna was in her dressing room getting ready to go on stage—and wondering why she had not heard yet from her father—she learned that Michael was being held by security guards at Naomi's request. She saw to it that Michael was released, and that night after the game, they rode back to Nashville together on the bus.

The next morning Wynonna received a call for her therapist asking her to come into her office that afternoon. When she arrived at the therapist's office, she saw Ashley's and Naomi's cars in the parking lot. She knew something was wrong, but not until they all were seated in the therapist's office together did she learn exactly what.

Wynonna, at the age of twenty-nine, was told that Michael was not her real father. Naomi explained that she had lied to her—indeed, to the entire world—to protect her from the truth. Ashley confessed that she had known for years and had joined in the deception to keep her sister from being hurt.

Once the words were spoken, Naomi retreated to a nearby window to cry. Wynonna sat there, unable to move. As bad as things had gotten at times in the family, never had she imagined any deceit could be as large as this one.

"Of course, my whole life was passing before me," Wynonna told author Bruce Feiler for his book *Dreaming Out Loud*. "No wonder Dad was never allowed on that stage. No wonder he was never allowed on the bus. Mom was afraid she was going to tell me. I 'get it.' It put everything in its proper place. Each piece of the puzzle went in. Like the year he told me that he always felt a greater connection with Ashley than with me. 'Now I get it. Now I see.'"

Wynonna's reaction surprised everyone. Instead of getting angry with her mother and her sister, she was drawn closer to them. That day, Ashley wrapped Wynonna in her arms and, weeping uncontrollably, told her that she loved her, that it did not matter that they were only half sisters. Wynonna forgave everyone on the spot, even Michael. Not long after the encounter in the therapist's office, the tabloids identified a Kentucky man as her natural father. Wynonna even forgave him, even though there was no proof that he actually was her father. To this day, there is no public proof of Wynonna's paternal parentage.

The only person Wynonna could not forgive was herself. She was gracious and forgiving on the outside, but on the inside she was coming apart. Typically, the time in a teenager's life that she is most likely to get pregnant is when her self-esteem is at its lowest. Wynonna was no teenager, not in chronological years, but emotionally she was a teenager, and news of the deception about her parentage sent her self-esteem to its lowest point ever. In the months after the confrontation in the therapist's office, she reacted to the news of her own confused parentage by getting pregnant with her first child. That spring, the tabloids, not yet apprised of her pregnancy, reported that Wynonna had gained so much weight that it had caused her serious back problems. The *Star* blamed her problems on the cowboy boots she wore during her concerts.

In some ways, the confrontation in the therapist's office was as hard on Ashley as it was on Wynonna. Ashley liked to think of herself as the anti-Naomi. Her mother's political opinions were conservative, so she adopted a liberal perspective. Her mother was the epitome of frilliness, so she wore jeans and T-shirts and, for a time at least, wore a nose ring and refused to shave her underarms. Her mother was deceitful and calculating, so she programmed herself to be honest and straightforward.

The Wynonna deception showed Ashley a side of herself she did not want to acknowledge. How open could she be if she had deceived her sister for so many years? For the first time in her life, Ashley began to take a close look at herself.

It was against that emotional backdrop, following a winter of discontent, that Ashley dyed her hair blonde and went to New York in the spring of 1994 to star in a Broadway production of William Inge's Pulitzer Prize–winning play, *Picnic*. Prior to leaving for New York, she made a career-altering decision involving *Sisters*. Her role as the daughter of one of the primary stars left little room for advancement.

After three years on the show, she did not feel particularly inspired by her character. She decided it was time to move on, so she notified the show's producers that the 1993–1994 season would be her last. The producers thought it would be interesting to have Naomi appear on Ashley's final show, so they wrote a small part for her. The show was aired in May 1994, during sweeps week, a time when the networks compete for revenue-boosting ratings. Ashley's character was written out of the show for the next year, but then she was reintroduced the following season, with Noelle Parker playing the role Ashley had originated.

To Ashley's way of thinking, a starring role in *Picnic* was a step up from a recurring minor role in a television drama. In *Picnic*, she played the role of Madge, a small-town girl whose only options are working at the dime store or marrying a rich but unexciting local boy. The rest of her life seems predictable, but then enters Hal, a shirtless drifter, played by Kyle Chandler, who sets her soul on fire.

Reviews of her performance were mixed. David Richards of the *New York Times* wrote that "the luminous Ms. Judd looks the part. The trouble is, she can't act it." Linda Winer of *Newsday* said that Ashley was a "beauty," but she added that she "needs to be doing more than competently reading lines." Howard Kissel of the New York *Daily News* was kinder, with his description of her performance as "passionately eloquent." Despite the mixed reviews, Ashley was nominated for an Outer Critics Circle Award in the category of Outstanding Debut of an Actress.

Excited by the prospect of a former University of Kentucky student making good on Broadway, the *Lexington Herald-Leader* sent reporter Kevin Nance to New York to talk to Ashley about the play. He found her at her Manhattan apartment wearing no makeup, with "wispy and tangled" hair. "I'm a—what would you call it?—an actaholic? [*sic*]" she told him. "I wake up and there's this secret I have with myself: I know that sometime during the day, I get to go do this thing that I love to do. The reward isn't fame. The reward is to keep acting."

Nance also spoke to director Scott Ellis, who suggested that Ashley was having problems sustaining her character through long periods in which she had no lines. "Her experience has been mostly on television and film, where you're there for the moment and then the camera cuts away," he explained. "Onstage, there is no cutting away, and once you begin, you must fill every moment as it goes. It's a very different type of thing for her, but she's one of the hardest-working actresses I've ever worked with."

Nance returned to Lexington with a story that was favorable to Ashley, but probably not the story that he—or she in her yearning for hometown recognition—had envisioned. *Picnic* made it clear that while Ashley was an actress of great beauty and talent, the Broadway stage was not quite her cup of tea.

*Picnic* was not a total failure on Ashley's part—and one can only speculate on how her house burning to the ground, breaking her ankle, and her confession to Wynonna had affected her performance and her ability to stay focused—but the Broadway experiment was nonetheless a disappointment, and nothing grates on her nerves so much as reaching for the brass ring and grabbing a fistful of air.

Ashley went back to her farmhouse determined to do better next time.

At first glance, movie producer and director Oliver Stone would seem to be a good match, cinematically speaking, for Ashley Judd. Their family backgrounds were similar in that Stone was raised by nannies (his mother frequently took vacations in Europe without him and his father was a successful stockbroker who never saw himself as a stay-at-home dad), causing Stone to grow up with more than his share of parental alienation. Educated at Yale University, he won the Bronze Star for valor in Vietnam, then was arrested for a drug-related offense when he returned to the States.

Stone did not find himself until he enrolled in the film school at New York University. Between 1974, when he did his first feature, and 1993, when he started filming *Natural Born Killers*, he had amassed an amazing body of work, including the screenplay for *Scarface*, director credit for *Born on the Fourth of July*, and producer credits for *JFK*, *Nixon*, and *The People vs. Larry Flynt*.

Like Ashley, Stone's childhood and early adulthood had made him semi-crazy, though in a good way that illuminated his creative vision. Ashley was thrilled when she learned she had received a small part in *Natural Born Killers*. The movie was a dark comedy that told the story of Mickey and Mallory Knox (played by Woody Harrelson and Juliette Lewis), mass murderers who became media celebrities as a result of their bloody, psychotic killing sprees. Ashley was asked to play the part of seventeen-year-old Grace Mulberry, the only surviving witness to the couple's rampage.

Ashley is first seen being brought to the courthouse where Harrelson and Lewis are on trial for their crimes. There is a mob outside, only it is not there to lynch the crime couple, it is there to pay tribute to them. "We want Mallory!" goes the chant. True to the film's dark vision of the way the media has made celebrities of Americans who commit heinous crimes, there is a surreal, carnival atmosphere outside the courtroom.

Americans like their heroes to be killers, whether in wartime, when those who do the most killing are given medals, or in peacetime, when those who do the most killing are celebrated in books and movies, and made wealthy beyond their wildest dreams. Or so goes the creative vision of *Natural Born Killers*.

Inside the courtroom, Ashley is questioned on the witness stand by Harrelson, who acts as his own attorney. He asks her if she wants to be there and she answers no. He asks her about her brother Tim, whom he had murdered. She explained to the court that he was a martial arts expert. Harrelson raises questions about how he could possibly kill a man so well trained in martial arts. As he speaks, he picks up the knife from the evidence table and approaches the witness stand. But before he reaches Ashley, the judge orders the knife taken away from him.

Harrelson continues to press her with questions. As a parody of lawyers, especially the television variety, the scene is superb. At one point, when he approaches the witness stand, Ashley spits on him. Unfazed, he wipes the spit from his forehead and continues his questioning. As he does so, he taps a pencil against the witness stand.

"You're not human!" Ashley cries out.

Harrelson laughs at her display of emotion and says he has one last question: "Do you believe in fate?" As she gazes at him, he stabs her repeatedly with the pencil, murdering her on the witness stand in full view of the court.

For some reason, Ashley seemed out of sync in her performance. She did well when she had to summon emotion to deliver her lines (she was an A-list screamer from day one), but she seemed wooden when she tried to keep pace with Harrelson during the slow, rhythmic dialogue that Stone had injected as a parody of the legal system. Ashley played it straight when she should have played a comic playing it straight. Her earnestness took the edge off of the scene.

Ashley spent a week filming her scenes (the entire movie took only fifty-six days to shoot) in a Chicago courthouse. "I cried and passed out a lot because it was so emotionally exhausting," she told Glenn Lovell of the *San Jose Mercury News*. "It was the highlight of my summer."

When the movie was released in 1994, Ashley learned, to her disappointment, that her entire contribution to the movie had been left on the cutting room floor. The movie she had enthusiastically promoted with family and friends did not have a single scene with her in it. The only thing more depressing than not getting a coveted role is getting it and then losing it in editing after the performance has been given. Ashley learned that she had been cut from the film in August 1994, shortly after the failure of *Picnic*.

Not until 2001, when the director's cut of the film was released on video, was the public able to see Ashley's performance. In a taped interview that accompanied the video, Stone explained why he cut Ashley from the movie.

"After shooting it and cutting it, it was the wrong scene for this movie because it really reverses the flow of the movie in the sense that in the present version, Mickey and Mallory, after their sojourn in the desert when they murdered the Indian shaman, seemed to be influenced by this, especially Mallory," he explained. "In a sense her behavior in the courtroom and the way they gratuitously kill Ashley Judd is a throwback to the earlier Mickey and Mallory, the desensitized ones in their killing spree. It was a tough cut to make, because I think people would have enjoyed the scene, but it was the wrong direction for the movie to take."

When the original version was released, reaction was predictable. The public stood in line to see it, while the critics who understood it heaped praise on Stone and those who did not snarled and bared their teeth. Wrote Hal Hinson for the *Washington Post*: "Our culture may be drifting toward the sort of calamity that Stone describes in *Natural Born Killers*, but the hysteria he depicts seems to come from within him. His soul is in turmoil and so he keeps trying to convince us that we're sick."

Marjorie Baumgarten wrote in the *Austin Chronicle*: "visually and thematically, NBK is the most audacious movie to come out of Hollywood in a long time and it may also rank as the best conceived and executed movie of Oliver Stone's career."

Passions ran so high over the movie that when an Oklahoma couple went on a killing spree in 1995 after viewing *Natural Born Killers*, Oliver Stone was sued for damages by the victims of the crime. In a bizarre twist, Mississippi novelist John Grisham took sides in the case because he knew one of the victims, a cotton gin manager in Hernando, Mississippi. Writing in the *Oxford American*, a magazine he publishes, Grisham said: "Think of a movie as a product, something created and brought to market, not too dissimilar from... Ford Pintos. If something goes wrong with the product, whether by design or defect, and injury ensues, its makers are held responsible."

It was a ludicrous argument. The only "product"-makers in America protected by the Constitution are writers, those who exercise freedom of speech. Motion pictures certainly come under that protection. An individual may not like the views expressed by writers or filmmakers, but the health of the republic depends on their freedom to state those views in any format they choose.

When the matter went to court, philosophically speaking (Grisham, a lawyer, did not try the case), it was a battle of the titans—the convictions of the best-selling novelist in America versus the convictions of one of the country's most successful filmmakers. As the case wound its way through the courts, Grisham softened his position somewhat, telling *Entertainment Weekly* in 2000 that he may have been "too emotionally involved to pick that fight." To the surprise of no one, the judge in the case eventually dismissed it on First Amendment grounds. The United States Supreme Court subsequently upheld that decision in 2001.

The true irony of the controversy was that Grisham, through his popular crime novels, had created a fictional world that focused attention on criminals and the lawyers who defended them. There is no evidence that Stone or Quentin Tarantino, who contributed the original story for the script, had Grisham's work in mind as a subject of parody, but it is obvious that the intent of the movie was to hold a mirror up to those in the media, including novelists, who routinely subject the public to images of violence and terror without ever questioning their own motivations.

Ashley had endured some bad years in her life, but the twelve months between November 1993 and the end of October 1994 seemed to fall in the award-winning category. The fire at her Malibu house, the broken ankle, the confession to Wynonna, the failure of *Picnic*, and perhaps worst of all, being deleted from *Natural Born Killers*, all added up to a year of almost unbelievable heartache and trauma.

On edge, Ashley gave an interview to Frank Bruni of the *Detroit*

*Free Press* in which she blasted director Robert Altman, who showed up at a Manhattan party given in her honor and then addressed her as "Leslie" as he was leaving. She also lashed out at movies that she felt offered only violent titillation. "Why are we so preoccupied with the moment of explosion or the moment of decapitation?" she asked. "I don't get it. Your mind grows what you sow...and if you plant this kind of filth in your mind, it's what our life will be about. I swear to God, I don't know if I'm going to have children."

Adding to her frustration level were a slate of tabloid stories, the most annoying of which suggested a romantic link between her and country singer Lyle Lovett, a married man. She denied the relationship, but it did little good. It seemed plausible—if Julia Roberts would *do* Lovett, why wouldn't Ashley?—so people believed what they wanted to believe.

Is it any wonder that Ashley fell in love with her Tennessee farm? Farms are like dogs in that they will love you no matter what. The bigger the pounding on her still-evolving sensibilities, the closer she cuddled to her farm, even though that meant dealing with a complex and sometimes hurtful relationship with her mother and sister.

Watching Ashley's career from a distance was Rob Dollar, the reporter at the *Kentucky New Era* who had conducted the first interview with her and noted her first public statements about wanting a career as an actress. He had followed her career, noting with a Kentucky newsman's pride her success in *Sisters* and *Ruby in Paradise*.

In 1994, spurred by the reporting of the tabloids, Dollar decided to revisit his interview with Ashley by writing a newspaper column for the *New Era*. "I never gave much thought to my interview with the Judd that wasn't famous until she became famous," he wrote. "The *National Enquirer* put her on its cover with Oprah, Lyle Lovett and Julia Roberts a few months ago. That's when I knew for sure that Ashley Judd had truly arrived on the Hollywood scene." Dollar wondered aloud if Ashley remembered the "kind, sensitive, dashing reporter who put her on the front page for the first time."

If Ashley did remember him, she never made an effort to contact him again, a gesture that would have been appreciated by the reporter. Perhaps influenced by the same tabloid stories that had re-inspired Dollar, Ashley made what in retrospect seems like a reckless grab for recognition and self-validation. She signed on for three movies, all of which were scheduled for release in 1995.

*Smoke*, the first of those movies, was a script-driven story directed by Wayne Wang and written by novelist Paul Auster. Starring Harvey

Keitel, William Hurt, Forest Whitaker, and Stockard Channing, it told the story of a Brooklyn cigar-store owner who accidentally ends up spending Christmas with a thief's blind grandmother. Auster originally wrote the story for the *New York Times* as an inspirational piece. Wang read it and contacted Auster, and they decided to work on the film together.

The story takes place in the summer of 1990 and revolves around the characters that come into Harvey Keitel's cigar store to load up on smokes and gossip. One of them is a novelist, played by William Hurt, who has lived alone in his apartment since the death of his wife. Lonely and curious about a culture he does not fully understand, he takes in a seventeen-year-old homeless black youth (played by Harold Perrineau).

As the story of Perrineau's homelessness plays out, Keitel is visited in his store by an old flame (played by Stockard Channing), who informs him that he has a daughter he never knew existed. Channing is there to ask for financial help for the girl who ran away from home, only to get pregnant and strung out on crack cocaine.

Resistant at first, Keitel finally agrees to meet the girl (played by Ashley Judd), although he insists that she could not possibly be his daughter. Ashley, dressed in a housecoat, goes to the door with a cigarette in her hand. Right away she informs her mother that she had an abortion two days earlier. "Bye, bye, baby," she says sullenly.

Keitel says he has seen enough; he is ready to leave.

"That's right," Ashley snarls. "You better go."

Ashley tells her mother that her boyfriend is a "real man," not some "scuzzy dickhead you picked out of last month's garbage." She tells them to get out of her apartment before her boyfriend comes back. "He'll chop Mr. Dad here into little pieces. Kick the living shit out of him."

As Keitel and Channing leave the apartment, Ashley's tortured face radiates uncertainty and regret. It is her only scene in the movie, but she handles it masterfully, giving the character an explosive rage that the moviegoer can recognize as a cover for self-loathing. Ashley's character is filled with alternating feelings of pain and anger, but she despises no one more than she does herself. The scene is a good example of what Ashley learned at Playhouse West about interacting with the other actors. Considering everything that had happened to her the previous year, she probably did not have to reach too far to find the pain and anger the character required.

Critics were impressed by her performance. "In her brief, explosive cameo, Ashley Judd tears into the mellow mood with acetylene-torch force (the film needs her boost of rage)," wrote Peter Rainer in the *Los Angeles Times*. He goes on to write that the movie was "as illusory as a smoke screen and just about as wispy....It's a sweet, forlorn little snapshot." Zachary Woodruff, writing in the *Tucson Weekly*, noted Ashley's "impressive cameo" and depicted her character as a "young addict whose self-denial has left her with only one form of expression: a sooty, black smoke called cruelty."

*Smoke* was not a blockbuster movie, and Ashley had only a brief scene in it, but it was well received by the critics and that gave her tender ego a massage when she perhaps needed it the most. Unfortunately, she turned right around and squandered that emotional capital on a movie that, by any standards, was one of the worst of 1995.

When Ashley read the script for *The Passion of Darkly Noon*, written by respected English novelist Philip Ridley, she saw a story that dealt with serious issues such as religious persecution, insanity, and dysfunctional relationships. It looked like something that she could really sink her teeth into.

Ashley also was impressed that Ridley had signed on to direct the film, even though he had only one previous directing credit, for 1990's *Reflecting Skin*. Also attracting her to the script was the fact that she would play the female lead opposite Canadian actor Brendan Fraser, who at that point had appeared in more than a dozen feature films and television movies, including *Encino Man, Now and Then,* and *Younger and Younger*. Not since *Ruby in Paradise* had she had a costarring role.

*The Passion of Darkly Noon* begins, fittingly enough, with a man named Darkly Noon (Brandon Fraser) stumbling out of the forest and collapsing on a country road. He is picked up by a man who is on his way to deliver supplies to a remote cabin inhabited by Ashley and her boyfriend, played by Viggo Mortensen. Even though Ashley's boyfriend is not at home, she takes Fraser into the house and cares for him until he regains consciousness.

When he awakens, he explains that he belongs to a religious cult but had to flee because townspeople murdered his parents. Ashley gives him a job on the farm and makes a place for him in the barn. She tells him he can stay as long as he wishes.

The movie was billed as an erotic thriller, but despite Ashley's considerable sex appeal, it never manages to fit either niche. Ashley wears short dresses and cutoffs, but she does not appear nude. Fraser, on the other hand, does a nude scene, although it is tastefully shot from the rear. There is one scene that offers possibilities for eroticism, when Ashley takes Fraser with her to bathe in a spring, but Ashley pretty much destroys the scene's potential sexuality by repeatedly flashing her unshaven armpits.

Ashley delivers a credible performance, but whatever gains she makes developing her character are taken away by Fraser's over-the-top acting style, obviously based on the mistaken premise that the insane typically are manic and overexpressive. Fraser makes his character so crazy that he seems humorous, and that is not the way you want to go in an erotic thriller. The most interesting thing about Ashley's performance is that she seems to have based her character on Naomi. She walks like Naomi and she moves like her, slow and deliberate to the extreme, oozing flirtatious possibilities.

Of course, Ashley's kindness to Fraser backfires, and the remainder of the movie is about Fraser's descent into madness and violence. Since the movie was written and directed by an Englishman and filmed in Europe, primarily in Germany, it has a typical European ending, with circus performers, an elephant, and nonsensical symbolism.

The problem with the movie is that it is supposed to be an American story, about American religious fundamentalists and backwoods hermits, perhaps along the lines of James Dickey's *Deliverance*, but it is so European in design and execution that it never rises about the level of self-parody.

The movie was the first serious mistake Ashley made as an actress, but it was not the last, and there is a reason for that. As intelligent as Ashley is, and as passionate as she is about words and social issues, there is one aspect of her development that she has failed to realize, and that is her ability to do critical assessments. According to one college professor, who asked not to be identified by name, one of her biggest problems as a student was the inability to think in a critical manner. Oddly enough, she does not make those mistakes in her acting, only in her reading.

When *The Passion of Darkly Noon* was released in Europe in 1995, its reception was predictably positive. Movies that offer a surreal, exaggerated look into American society are popular with European audiences. Neil Chue Hong, writing for the program of the Edinburgh University Film Society, described it as a "fairy tale for the nineties." He felt that Ashley simply oozed "innocent sexuality," and he savored the scene in which a family of circus performers in search of a large sequined shoe mysteriously appear with an elephant. He concluded his review with the observation that "people like this apparently do exist in America." Another reviewer, Damian Cannon, writing for the website Movie Reviews UK, described the film as a "masterpiece of visual exuberance."

*The Passion of Darkly Noon* never had a theatrical run in the United States, for obvious reasons, but it was released on video in 1996. Philip Ridley apparently gave up directing after making the movie and returned to his life as a novelist. For Ashley, the movie was yet another setback in her career, for the only thing worse than a bad review is no review at all—and the movie was totally ignored by the American media.

Ashley was hopeful of better things in 1995, although there was one carryover nightmare from 1994 that threatened to undermine her optimism: her mother's autobiography, *Love Can Build a Bridge*, had been sold to NBC television for a miniseries. Ashley was horrified, for to her way of thinking, that meant that her life was going to be held up to ridicule. She never liked the book because she did not feel it was truthful, at least concerning the events of her own life.

Directed by Bobby Roth, the miniseries starred Kathleen York as Naomi, Viveka Davis as the adult Wynonna, and Megan Ward as the adult Ashley (two child actresses played her at different ages). Ashley was asked to play her mother in the show, but the answer was, "Not just no, but hell no!" Then she was asked to narrate the show. Again, she said no.

"I wasn't interested in the miniseries," Ashley told Barbara Teasdall for Reel.com. "At the last minute, I did the voiceover as a favor to my mom because it was important to her. I'm reading some of this material going, 'This is dubious.' My name is not a combination of our hometown and something else. It's just not....So you just sort of throw up your hands and say, 'My reward is in Heaven.'"

Wynonna was equally opposed to the miniseries. Naomi tried to talk both daughters into going to the set with her to oversee production. Both daughters refused. "I felt so alone, so out of control," Naomi told the *Nashville Tennessean*. "When I would call home, they wouldn't even ask me what I was doing. They wanted nothing to do with it. That was so lonely for me because we are not that way. We are so supportive of each other."

"I was miffed with Mom," Wynonna told author Bruce Feiler. "[Naomi] spent more time building the media image of the Judds than I did, but still she let NBC turn our life into this sensational mother-daughter fighting thing."

Naomi did not see it that way. When she went to Los Angeles without her daughters to oversee production of the miniseries, she did what she had always done: she listened to her own drummer. Before leaving Nashville, she sought advice from Loretta Lynn, whose autobiography was made into the 1980 film *Coal Miner's Daughter*. Lynn told her, "Bird dog them, honey. Don't let them out of your sight."

Naomi followed that advice literally. She asked for and received a trailer that she could sit in so that she could watch the comings and goings of the crew. On the day they shot a scene in the old Ambassador Hotel, Susan King, a writer for the *Los Angeles Times*, visited the trailer, which was situated in the parking lot. Watching actress Kathleen York portray her was "beyond bizarre," Naomi said. "Last night, we sat here and watched dailies and it was the scene where I threw Larry out. We didn't see each other for a year-and-a-half. We were sitting and we were both crying. I said [to him], 'I am so glad you are here because this is really strange.'"

Timing is everything in the Judd family, and the timing of the miniseries could not have been worse for Ashley and Wynonna. It was bad for Ashley because she was struggling to get her career back on track, and a television show about her life as the abandoned Judd was not something that would have a positive effect. Wynonna was in much the same situation. After an impressive start, her solo career had waned. Record sales dropped and concert crowds fizzled. She fired her longtime manager, Ken Stilts, and replaced him with John Unger, a Princeton graduate who had no experience managing country music stars, but nothing seemed to help. In 1995, her career was headed for trouble and the implications of that were frightening.

Because Naomi was persistent—the timing of the series was *perfect* for her, because her music career was a thing of the past and she was searching for a new identity—Ashley agreed to do the voiceover and Wynonna agreed to record part of the soundtrack. When production on the miniseries wrapped, both daughters thought that particular nightmare was history (they could always leave the country when the program aired). But Naomi had other ideas. She volunteered both daughters to help promote the show.

Ashley and Wynonna joined Naomi for a *People* magazine cover photograph. Again, they thought they were done. But again, Naomi dragged them into another promotional project, this time for a cover photograph for *TV Guide*. Reluctantly they said yes, but the session turned sour when the photographer expressed an interest in putting Wynonna's son, Elijah, in the picture with them. Wynonna refused and the *TV Guide* representative threatened to pull the cover. Wynonna stood her ground and the magazine went ahead with the mother-daughter cover originally planned.

It went that way right up until the miniseries aired, although Naomi had one last surprise for her daughters. She had arranged for the entire family to appear on the *Oprah Winfrey Show* the very week the miniseries was scheduled to air. That was the ultimate nightmare for both daughters, but, ever dutiful, they agreed to do the show.

Oprah had done hundreds of shows about dysfunctional families, but none of them had ever joined her on stage to promote a television miniseries. Naomi kept smiling throughout the interview, but it was obvious to everyone watching that Ashley and Wynonna were there under duress. Both daughters appeared chilly toward Naomi throughout the program. At one point, Ashley almost jumped up out of her chair to proclaim that a particular scene from the miniseries was "fiction!"

By the time the show ended, the Judd family was exhausted, if only from the stress of sitting on a stage together pretending to be something they were not. When they returned to Tennessee, they fought for a solid week.

Reviews of the miniseries were generally good. Joyce Millman, a television critic for the *San Francisco Examiner*, found it "surprisingly perceptive and hugely entertaining." She wrote that Naomi "displays the same frankness here as in her book."

When Ashley and Wynonna viewed the miniseries they alternately wept and bristled. The show, even when it was off the mark, was every bit as schizophrenic as their lives. At one point, according to author Laurence Leamer, Ashley threw up her hands and left the room: "I can't watch this anymore. It's awful. I can't believe this."

Both sisters had worked so hard to be *somebody*. Unfortunately, adoring viewers of the miniseries did not see them for the richly complicated individuals they had finally become. Is there anything sadder than being loved for the wrong reasons?

Michael Mann began his career in the late 1970s by writing for high-action, low-budget television shows such as *Starsky and Hutch* and *Police Woman*, hardly the type of credits likely to attract the attention of Hollywood film companies. But by the mid-1980s he had become something of a cult figure with his production of the television series *Miami Vice*. The show's nonstop action and trendy dialogue made its costar, Don Johnson, a household name.

Although he had directed two feature films by that time—*Thief* and *The Keep*—neither did well at the box office. He was not considered an A-list director. All that changed with the success of

*Miami Vice*, for it provided him with a signature style of directing. In 1992 he was hired to direct *The Last of the Mohicans*, starring Daniel Day-Lewis and Madeleine Stowe. The movie was both a critical success and a box-office hit.

Mann followed that project up with a thriller that he wrote himself. Titled *Heat*, it was more than an action drama, although it was filled with gratuitous violence; it was also a psychological study that probed the minds of a master criminal and the dedicated cop who hunted him down.

For the role of the cop, Vincent Hanna, Mann chose Al Pacino. Probably best known for his role as Michael Corleone in the *Godfather* trilogy, he had, by the age of fifty-five, given a series of breathtaking performances in films such as *Serpico* (1973), *Sea of Love* (1989), *Scent of a Woman* (1992), and *Carlito's Way* (1993).

Mann considered Pacino perfect for the role. Born in New York City in 1940, he had street smarts, for he had grown up in the Bronx during a time in which it was possible to learn about organized crime and gang warfare without ever leaving the neighborhood. Pacino was tempted to consider a life of crime but found the possibilities offered by an acting career more to his liking.

Asked to play opposite Pacino, as the master criminal, was Robert De Niro, another New York-born actor. Three years Pacino's junior, De Niro also had an urban upbringing that taught him, at an early age, the dynamics of warfare in the streets. Before agreeing to do *Heat*, the Oscar-winning actor had done almost fifty films, including *Taxi Driver* (1976), *The Deer Hunter* (1978), and *Raging Bull* (1980).

The Pacino–De Niro pairing was a director's dream team. Previously, the two men had appeared together in *The Godfather II*. Although they were not in the same scenes together, their presence, even separately, provided chemistry to the film. Mann toyed with that chemistry in *Heat* by filming the two men separately, allowing the tension to build until the moment they stood face-to-face. As a device, it was ingenious.

The supporting cast was equally inventive. Diane Venora played Hanna's wife and newcomer Natalie Portman played his step-daughter. Amy Brenneman, who went on to star in the successful television series *Judging Amy*, played De Niro's love interest. Cast as members of De Niro's gang were Val Kilmer and Jon Voight.

Ashley Judd was offered the role of Charlene Shiherlis, Kilmer's screen wife. It was not a big part but it was an important one, and Ashley jumped at the chance to be in a movie with De Niro and Pacino.

The movie begins with De Niro and the members of his gang acquiring the tools of their trade. Kilmer purchases dynamite. De Niro steals an ambulance. Other gang members rendezvous at various locations in Los Angeles. Their target is an armored car containing over one billion dollars in bearer bonds. As the gang goes about its business, Pacino begins his day by making love to his wife.

The armored car heist, complete with synchronized explosions and high-tech action, was classic Mann, sort of a postgraduate replica of *Miami Vice*. After the heist takes place, the pace of the drama picks up considerably as Pacino is put in charge of solving the crime. With consummate skill, Mann juxtaposes Pacino's marital problems with the relationship issues that plague the various members of the gang.

Ashley's first scene is with Kilmer. They are having an argument over money. She argues that the eight thousand dollars he took for a previous job is not worth the risk. With her hair dyed blonde, Ashley looks dazzling, but not too dazzling to be a gangster's wife. She argues that, as a couple, they are making no forward progress. Kilmer orders her to shut up and get into the car.

"What am I doing in this rat bastard situation?" she snaps.

Ashley has an edgy look in her eyes throughout the movie. That may have been good acting, or it may have been the result of her continuing squabbles with her mother. More than once during the shooting of *Heat*, she had to break her concentration on the movie to attend photo sessions for Naomi's miniseries *Love Can Build a Bridge*.

Ashley's second scene calls for her to talk on the telephone to De Niro about her marriage. Kilmer has appeared unexpectedly on his doorstep and De Niro is justifiably concerned that the disharmony of his marriage might affect their criminal activities.

Later in the movie, a suspicious De Niro follows Ashley to a motel to determine if she is being unfaithful to Kilmer. She is cheating on him, of course, and when her lover leaves the motel room, De Niro goes to the door and demands to know the man's name. She is surprised to see her husband's boss but not particularly rattled at being caught. De Niro tells her to give Kilmer one last chance and Ashley agrees to play it his way.

Meanwhile, Pacino finds out about the affair, locates her lover, and pressures him to work with the police. Ashley's best scene occurs when her lover takes her to a police stakeout under false pretenses. There, police confront her and tell her that the only way out is to betray her husband: "You give up Chris [Kilmer], you get off clean."

Ashley pretends to go along with the police, but at a crucial moment she waves Kilmer away before the police can nab him. It is an extraordinary scene because she does it without ever saying a word. Amazingly, everything is done with her face.

One of the best non-Ashley scenes occurs when Pacino and De Niro meet in a coffee shop. It is the moment that Mann has made moviegoers anticipate. Each man talks about how hard his life has become. De Niro asks Pacino how he expects to have a happy marriage when he is out chasing criminals. Pacino wants to know how De Niro can have a good life when he is always running from the police. They part company with the certain knowledge that they are destined for a violent showdown.

When *Heat* was released in December 1995, critics were generally enthusiastic about the film. Mike Clark, writing in *USA Today*, praised it as having "rare psychological depth" and said it belonged in the "cop-movie Pantheon." *Austin Chronicle* writer Simon Cote noted that while Pacino and De Niro share little screen time together, their scenes are "poignant and gripping. Some might have expected the two to collide like forces of nature, but in a high noon scene that should go down in cinematic history, the two merely talk life and realize they are essentially the same."

What struck Roger Ebert of the *Chicago Sun-Times* was the way Mann played the tough-guy roles of the men off of the more accommodating roles of the women. "The wives and girlfriends in this movie are always, in a sense, standing at the kitchen door, calling to the boys to come in from their play." He suggests that Mann's writing and direction have "elevated" the story line of the film. "It's not just an action picture. Above all, the dialogue is complex enough to allow the characters to say what they're thinking: They are eloquent, insightful, fanciful, poetic when necessary."

Despite favorable reviews, the film grossed only sixty-seven million dollars, only seven million dollars above what it cost to make it. The film made money, but when investors sink sixty million dollars into a speculative project, they like to make more than a twelve-percent profit. Mann's stock as a director fell somewhat and he did not make another film for four years, not until 1999's *Insider*.

Ashley had hoped that appearing in the same movie with Pacino and De Niro would boost her career, but even though she got favorable reviews, it did nothing to focus attention on her potential as a leading lady. Not since *Ruby in Paradise* had she received the sort of praise that she needed to sustain a film career.

Instead, the media attention she received focused on a rumored romance with De Niro. She denied it and insisted that they were only friends, but whenever her name appeared in print in association with

De Niro, it was as a suspected lover and not as a fellow actor. That was not the sort of publicity she needed.

Whatever her actual relationship with De Niro, *Heat* marked the beginning of a long-lasting rumor mill that perpetuated stories that Ashley had a propensity for sleeping with her leading men. That was not a very flattering—or entirely accurate—assessment of her love life, but it did keep her in the news.

# Chapter
# Five

## *Back in the Spotlight (Clothing Optional)*

When HBO president Bob Cooper decided to proceed with a movie based on Marilyn Monroe's life, he knew the biggest problem would be in casting because the script called for two different people to portray the legendary actress. He would need one actress to play the part of Norma Jean, the ambitious would-be movie star, and another to play the part of Marilyn, the iconic sex goddess.

For Norma Jean, he chose Ashley Judd. He told *TV Guide* that it was because she had "a range and self-assurance that was very unusual for an actress her age." Ashley did not accept the role right away. Marilyn Monroe died in 1962, almost six years before Ashley was born. She had a historical appreciation of the actress, but she did not have an emotional attachment to her, as did many older Americans who had attended her movies.

Before giving Cooper her answer, she watched a number of Monroe's films. Only then did she feel confident that she could capture Norma Jean, the ambitious nobody who was hampered in life by the abuses of her upbringing as a child. "This shaped her—the way she loved, why she loved," Ashley told *Orbit* magazine. "It formed the foundation of insecurity that always haunted her. There was this desire to be a huge star that would somehow make up for the hurt in her childhood.

The role called for Ashley to be convincing as a damaged spirit that had the survival instincts of wounded buffalo. Yes, she could do that, she finally decided—in a heartbeat.

There was only one drawback. The script called for her to get buck-naked in a church filled with people. What would her family think? What would her inner self think? She gave that issue a lot of thought, then decided that getting naked in a church would be a piece of cake compared to the traumas she had been through the past year. After reading her mother's autobiography, she no longer felt the need to protect her from having a daughter that appeared nude on the silver screen.

There was more to it that that, of course. Only after watching Monroe's films did she realize how "mesmerizing" she was, she confessed to *TV Guide*: "I have a lot of admiration for her animal brilliance, her ability to survive, to know what she needed and how to go about getting it." Amen to that, her guardian angel must have thought.

Motivated by the exposure of the nude scenes, Ashley underwent a crash course in body shaping. Her favorite instrument of torture was the StairMaster, but she did more than her share of sit-ups to work off the extra poundage caused by her favorite Tennessee cuisine. Even so, she did not overdo it: Norma Jean had a smooth, rounded physique, unmarked by muscular definition, much like Ashley, and the only real problem area was her stomach, not a difficult set of muscles to shape at the age of twenty-eight.

In choosing an actress for the part of Marilyn, the HBO head could not possibly have found a better match for Ashley than Mira Sorvino. In some respects, one was the mirror image of the other. The daughter of respected actor Paul Sorvino, Mira grew up in a household in which the trappings of fame and celebrity colored her everyday decisions. Her first identity in life was as the daughter of a famous person.

Perhaps because of that, she developed a rich fantasy life at a very young age. She self-produced plays with her friends. "My friend Erin and I would play friends who'd run away to the woods, and we'd establish this whole play-life of how we had to forage for food and the traumas of being stranded there," she told *Interview* magazine. "I think I was hoping something magical would happen....Maybe my whole impulse to act is a case of wishful thinking, the need to live life in an extraordinary way instead of mundanely."

Despite her interest in acting, Sorvino was not certain she wanted it as a career. After graduation from Englewood High School in Englewood, New Jersey, she enrolled at Harvard University. In 1990 she was graduated magna cum laude with a bachelors degree in Asian studies. Just as Ashley went to France to become fluent in French, Mira went to Beijing, China, to become fluent in Mandarin Chinese. Just as Ashley's early decisions were influenced by a troublesome family situation, Mira's were influenced by her parents' divorce, an event she found very traumatic.

It was when she returned from China that she decided to become an actress. "I could not deny my heritage," she told Louis B. Hobson of the *Calgary Sun*. "I struggled for five years working as a waitress, showroom model, script reader and tutor for Chinese-Americans."

Mira's entry into acting occurred after she accepted a job as a script reader at Tribeca Productions in New York (the production company owned by Robert De Niro). Asked by Rob Weiss, the director of the 1993 film *Amongst Friends*, to help with casting, Mira brought in an actress that was so much like herself that Weiss gave the job to Mira.

Between 1993 and 1996, when Cooper approached her about playing Marilyn, she had appeared in several television movies and seven feature films, including Woody Allen's *Mighty Aphrodite*. Her performance as a porn queen in that movie earned her an Oscar in 1995. It was while she was promoting *Mighty Aphrodite* that she met writer and director Quentin Tarantino (the author of *Natural Born Killers*). They became lovers and maintained a relationship that lasted well into 1998.

The way Cooper saw it, a pairing of Ashley Judd and Mira Sorvino could not possibly go wrong. Not only were they both on the verge of major stardom, they were so much alike internally they would have made the perfect lesbian couple had they been so inclined. For someone looking for two actresses to play the same character at different stages in her life, Cooper's logic made perfect sense.

*Norma Jean and Marilyn* begins with the star's body being carted out to the ambulance, accompanied by newsreel-style narration on her death (she was only thirty-six). The focus then shifts to the early Norma Jean. Ashley is in a church, naked, but no one seems to notice. When the preacher asks the congregation to come down the aisle to be saved, Ashley joins the other church members as they proceed to the altar.

No one looks at Ashley's nakedness because no one can see it. It is symbolic of something else. It is, in fact, a recurring dream. Ashley is telling a man, a possible suitor, about the dream. "Like, it's the most natural thing in the world," she says. "Nobody looks at me funny....I mean, I have this dream all the time. There's never any sense of sin or shame in it." Then, to the man, she says, "Don't you just love being naked?"

During Ashley's solo segment of the movie, there are frequent flashbacks to Norm Jean's dysfunctional childhood. Her Marilyn is intelligent, manipulative, and promiscuous. She is sympathetic, not because of her vulnerability but because of her cynicism and manipulative will to succeed. She is ruthless, but only at her own expense.

Eddie Jordan is the boyfriend (played by Josh Charles). He is also an aspiring actor. When he tells Norma Jean that he just signed a contract with 20th Century Fox, making seventy-five dollars a week to begin with, Ashley is jealous of his success. They go dancing and he continues talking about it. Finally, she blows her stack. "Fuck your contact, Eddie!" she screams, breaking away from him on the dance floor. "Fuck your contract! Fuck your SAG card! Fuck Dana Andrews and fuck you!" In the car, an angry Ashley pledges to have sex with everyone it takes to become a star.

That path inevitably leads her to Johnny Hyde, an executive with the William Morris Agency. He does what he can to forward her career, but he runs into opposition. When he suffers a heart attack, Ashley visits him at his home. "I'd be lost without you, Johnny," she says, then attempts to make him feel better by exposing her breasts. She smiles sweetly, then leans over to allow him to caress her.

The script, which was based on Anthony Summers's book of the same name, stays true to the major events in Marilyn's life. For the famous calendar session, Ashley again gets naked and goes through the poses Marilyn made famous, though she never looks entirely comfortable doing it.

Ashley propels Norma Jean along though her failures and disappointments, right up to where she makes the transformation into Marilyn Monroe, at which point Mira Sorvino steps into the role. Interestingly, Ashley never goes away. She returns to confront Mira at crucial moments in her career.

For example, after an inept reading for studio executives, a tearful Mira goes to the restroom, where she encounters Ashley. The two women talk, with Ashley encouraging her to do better. When Mira says the people "out there" hate her, Ashley tells her not to worry about it. "They're all going to be kissing your ass when you're famous," she says. "And you're going to be famous, even if it kills me."

"But I did kill you," deadpans Mira. "How are you here?"

Like Ashley, Mira disrobes for a couple of scenes, although her topless and bare buttock scenes are never as revealing as Ashley's full frontal nudity. The scenes between the two women are interesting, but, despite the common interests and similar backgrounds, they seem lacking in some essential chemistry.

When the movie was aired on HBO in May 1996, it received mixed reviews from the critics. "A lot of fans will hate this movie," wrote Frederic M. Biddle for the *Boston Globe*. "But don't call it spitting on Marilyn's grave. For the most part, it's just a brutally observant take on a star we love. It's also a triumph for Ashley Judd and for HBO, the only network that seems able to pull off a biopic with panache anymore."

Ginia Bellafante, writing in *Time* magazine, said that Ashley's performance was "the high point of his absurd psychoanalytic adventure." The critic chastised Sorvino for not making Marilyn "sufficiently tortured" but praised Ashley for making Norma Jean "a feminist out of a Camille Paglia fever dream—a firecracker of a young woman fully aware of her ravaging sex appeal and ready to use it."

*New York Times* critic Caryn James barely noticed Ashley but thought Mira's portrayal of Marilyn was "dazzling." Despite that performance, the critic thought that the movie's script was "weak" and landed "on the silly side," further noting that "such a film is bound to be brilliant or loopy, and this one is even more outrageous than it sounds."

In an interview that followed the first airing of the movie, Ashley told Bernard Weinraub of the *New York Times* that she felt Marilyn Monroe's screen persona was dated. "We don't tolerate her kind of witty sexuality anymore," she explained. "It was so titillating and sweet. Now we have raw, gritty actresses who put it all out there with all kinds of nudity. It leaves less of a place to appreciate those famous shots of Marilyn, when she's walking down the street and swinging her hips."

Ashley barred her soul and her body in the movie because it was consistent with the script and because she knew it would attract attention. She did it for the same reason that Marilyn did when she posed for the calendar shots. Ashley told reporters that she felt Hollywood would look at her in a new light. She had always known she was destined for the big time. Now Hollywood knew it, too.

Naomi Judd was horrified enough by her daughter's performance—and by the fear that she had *become* Marilyn—that she asked her to accompany her to the UCLA Medical Center so that she could learn about the effects that such roles could have on the actress's immune system. "I worry about the roles she plays," Naomi told *Us* magazine. "Marilyn Monroe was one of the most pathetic, tortured human beings. Later, I said, 'Boy aren't they ever going to do a remake of *The Singing Nun?*'"

For Ashley and Wynonna, 1995 had been an "us against the world" year. Just as Ashley was determined to break out of her loser cycle in 1996 by making a new slate of movies, Wynonna was hell-bent on reestablishing her career with a new album.

In retrospect, there is something disturbingly self-destructive about the way she approached her reinvention. In January 1996, one month before the release of the album, she started doing interviews. She disclosed that she was pregnant again and would marry the father of her two children, Arch Kelley, before the March 15 kickoff of her tour. The new baby was due in July, which meant that during the tour her overweight frame would be ballooned out even more with her pregnancy.

The announcement concerning the baby and her upcoming marriage was obviously calculated to mitigate criticisms concerning her weight and her unmarried mother status, but it did just the opposite: it focused attention on her lifestyle and her weight problem at the precise moment she least needed it.

Like many recording artists who have hits when they look one way, then age into a different body type, she was perplexed as to why people would make an issue of the changes in her physical appearance. To her, it seemed cruel and unnecessary.

The truth of the matter is that country music and rock 'n' roll are both hormone-driven art forms. Elvis Presley would never have become a superstar if he had looked like Rodney Dangerfield. The success of the Judds had more to do with sex appeal than it did with the music they recorded. When Wynonna almost doubled her body size, she altered the formula needed for continued success as a recording artist.

In her own way, Wynonna attempted to compensate for those changes by shifting the focus of her music. Her new album, *Revelations*, had a rhythm-and-blues tinge to it. R&B was perhaps the only genre left in American music in which female singers could break the weight taboos.

"When I recorded *Revelations*, I was pregnant…wondering what was to be," she explained in a press release. "I remember saying, you know, each artist comes to this place where things aren't figured out, where you can no longer sit back and cruise. I was coming to the end of something. I remember saying, 'This album is about me. This has nothing to do with competing for a nomination or trying to get the sell-out crowd. This record has to do with my soul.'"

To express that soul on her new album, Wynonna turned to an eclectic blend of songs. "Dance! Shout!" was a high-energy gospel tune that Nashville gospel singer Gary Oliver had previously recorded. For the song, producer Tony Brown brought in a twenty-five-voice black choir, the Born Again Ministrels. "To Be Loved By You," the first single, was thought to be sensuous and romantic.

Lynyrd Skynyrd's "Free Bird," a 1970s rock 'n' roll anthem, was added to the mix for reasons known only to Wynonna.

The only thing really different about the album, besides the gospel and rock, was the phrasing she used. There had always been an edge to her vocals, but with this album she spotlighted a blues growl that she had long used in concert. It is not the sort of sound that transfers well to a CD, for it loses something in the translation. It made her sound angry and dissonant at a time when her competitors seemed joyous and in touch with the more hopeful aspirations of record buyers.

The press releases issued by Curb/MCA in support of the album were an odd blend of confession and bravado. They highlighted the "controversy" of her marital status and the "personal turmoil of almost Shakespearean proportions" that surrounded her life, while hyping her ability to ascend "to a new level of singing."

Even as that was going on, Wynonna seemed to say that she would be all right, even if the album was a failure. "There were times last year when I'd wake up at nine o'clock and have this overwhelming urge to put on my stage clothes and do a show, but I didn't have that," she said. "And I didn't have then—and don't have now, as is often supposed—some enormous business machine. I lived on my savings, I had this child inside me, and a lot of dreams....I learned that I could survive without singing. I certainly didn't want to, but I learned that I could."

Wynonna's media managers convinced her that the best way to deal with the issues that concerned her personal life was to confront them in a straightforward manner. In a January interview with Tom Roland of the *Nashville Tennessean*, Wynonna talked about her upcoming marriage to Kelley and admitted that she was sensitive to criticisms of being an unmarried mother. "I'm sure people in my family are worried, and the Baptists will have something to say," she said. "But I know God is a loving God and forgiving God. All I can do is get up off my butt and move forward."

In a prerelease interview with the *Boston Globe*, Wynonna tried to cast her problems in a different light. Her lifestyle was not the problem. Country music itself was the problem. "I'm looked at as a rebel in this town," she told Steve Morse. "People won't know what to do with me. But they know one thing is that I won't settle for less than what I believe. I don't care how many corporate million-dollar moments are part of Wynonna, Inc., I have to go home at night and know that I was honest about my art."

Wynonna could talk about her "art" all she wanted to, but such talk did nothing change the reality of the situation, which was that country music, for all its lovely sentiments, is basically a beer drinking and line dancing emotional laxative that addresses specific needs among those who listen to it. Ignore those needs and your career goes straight into the dumpster.

In 1996, those needs were defined by sex appeal as defined by Shania Twain, whose 1995 album *The Woman in Me* had then sold over twelve million units, making her the biggest-selling female country artist in history.

A great deal had happened since the Judds recorded their first album. For one thing, demographics had changed. In the mid-1980s, the country music fan base was mostly male and encompassed primarily a regional Southern and Western area that extended into Michigan and California. By the mid-1990s, the country music fan base was mostly female and had a global reach. In 1996, female country music fans were drawn to Shania Twain because of the way she looked—they, too, wanted to be trim and attractive—and because of the quasi-feminist tone of her song lyrics.

While Wynonna had holed up on her farm, a revolution had taken place in country music. She did not have a look that other women wanted to emulate, nor did the lyrics of her music seem to speak to the new generation of CD buyers. In her isolation at the farm, she had missed the signs of the changing times. At the still youthful age of thirty-one, she had become a music relic.

When *Revelations* was released, reviews were generally mixed. Michael McCall, writing in *Pulse!* magazine, said the album offered "tasteful material with delicate brushes of blue rhythm." He also said that she sang with "genuine soul." *Atlanta Constitution* writer Miriam Longino said the album was disappointing: "Wynonna is capable of much better than this." Writing about one of her concerts in mid-March, Robert Hilburn, pop music critic for the *Los Angeles Times*, wrote that she "may just be the most complete and gifted female singer of her generation—and we're not just talking country music."

Encouraging reviews notwithstanding, Wynonna was unable to isolate her tour from the repercussions of her personal life. There were signs of trouble even before the tour began. Interviewed on *Entertainment Tonight*, Wynonna hinted that Naomi was not entirely happy with her upcoming marriage. "Mom and I are so close," she said. "I don't know that Mom really can accept the fact that I'm moving on....But she's letting go. We talk about it a lot."

Within two weeks of the *ET* interview Wynonna and Kelley were married. If Wynonna thought that would mitigate the issue, she was wrong. As much as she wanted publicity about her new album and tour to focus on her music, it always seemed to gravitate to her personal life. Typical of the press she received during her tour was an article in the *National Enquirer* under the headline "Wynonna's Marriage Hits the Skids after 2 Months." The article quoted Wynonna as telling a band member: "Mama was right—I should have listened to her."

*Revelations* peaked at number two on the *Billboard* album chart and was certified platinum by May (representing sales of one million). Unfortunately, while sales proved that Wynonna still had a significant audience, it also proved that she was not in the same league with Shania Twain. Record executives predicted that the album would sell as many as two million units, but that was a long stretch away from Twain's twelve million. Wynonna did not want to be merely successful. She wanted to be the best, and that simply was not in the cards for her, not at this stage of her life.

At a party to celebrate the success of the album, Wynonna was petulant and uncommunicative with those who came to pay tribute to her. She expressed unhappiness at sales of just two million. She blamed the record company. She blamed the media. Then she blamed herself. "I'm trying to organize my life," she said, according to author Bruce Feiler. "I'm studying Stephen Covey. I'm working with Deepak. I'm looking for a personal trainer I can turn my life over to. I'm trying to decide what part of my life is for family, what part for fun, what part for interviews. Is that what the problem is? Is it me? Is it because I'm fat? Do I have to show my belly button and make sexy videos?"

The answer, of course, was yes, yes, yes. Music had changed, Wynonna had changed, indeed, life itself had changed since Wynonna's glory days with the Judds. The more Wynonna thought about fitting into that new world, the more frustrated she became. What she did not seem to understand—or remember—was that her entire life had been built around trying to fit a square peg into a round hole. Life had always been difficult for her. Why would it suddenly change now?

Wynonna is probably one of the most misunderstood singers in country music. There are individuals who love her because of her music. There are individuals who hate her because of the way she looks, whether it is because of her weight or because they think she looks like a lesbian (a long-standing criticism). The *real* Wynonna is a loyal sister and a forgiving daughter—and, by all accounts, a devoted mother to her children.

Why, she wondered throughout 1996, is that not enough?

Novelist John Grisham was inspired to write *A Time to Kill* after listening to the courtroom testimony of a young girl who had been raped and left for dead by an older man. He spent three years writing the story, often getting up at five in the morning to work on it before heading off to his job as a lawyer and member of the Mississippi legislature. After twelve publishers and sixteen agents rejected the manuscript, Grisham found a New York agent willing to represent him. The agent placed it with Wynwood Press, which printed five thousand copies and published it in 1989.

The novel did not sell out its first printing and quietly slipped into oblivion. Undeterred, Grisham wrote a second novel titled *The Firm*. When it became a bestseller, Wynwood issued *A Time to Kill* in trade paperback, selling an impressive quarter-million copies. The following year, Island/Dell published a mass-market edition that sold almost eight million copies. Grisham still considers it his best book.

"I watched a little girl testify one day who had been brutally raped," he explained in a press release. "I remember thinking, 'That poor child. If that was my little girl, I'd get a gun and this guy would be dead.' What I wanted to explore was what an all-white jury would do to a black father who did what every juror would want to do. And I wanted to explore race relations in a small town in the deep South, because it's where I'm from."

After the book became a bestseller, Grisham received offers right away from movie companies. However, since the story was autobiographical and special to him, he decided against selling those rights until he had a track record with a movie company he felt he could trust.

After Warner Brothers and New Regency translated his novel, *The Client*, into a movie of which he approved, he agreed to trust them with *A Time to Kill*, but only on condition that he retain approval over the script, the director, and casting for the lead roles. Movie companies seldom grant that type of approval to an author, but they readily agreed to do so, primarily because of the box-office success they had with *The Client*.

Joel Schumacher, who had directed *The Client*, eventually was chosen to be the director for *A Time to Kill*, but it was not a fast process. Over the course of three years, he had many conversations with Grisham about the film. At one point, he even traveled to Grisham's hometown of Oxford, Mississippi, to convince him of his vision for the film.

Together, Schumacher and Grisham decided on the actors for the leading roles. Samuel L. Jackson was asked to play the role of Carl Lee Hailey, the father of the young girl who was brutally beaten and raped by two white thugs. Devastated by the incident, he assassinates the two men charged with the crime. The story revolves around his efforts to find justice in a judicial system that has not yet proved itself free of racism.

Kevin Spacey was chosen to play the role of Rufus Buckley, a manipulative prosecutor with political ambitions. For the role of Jake Brigance, the lawyer who defends Carl Lee Hailey, they took a chance on newcomer Matthew McConaughey. Grisham had never heard of him, but Schumacher had seen his work in a 1993 comedy titled *Dazed and Confused*, and he felt he was perfect for the part.

McConaughey was asked to do a screen test and the results were shown to Grisham. He was impressed. "I watched the tape several times with my wife, Renee," he said in a press release, "and I called Joel [Schumacher] up and said, 'I love this guy.'"

Warner Brothers was reluctant to approve McConaughey for such a pivotal role but agreed to do so after Schumacker and Grisham insisted that he was perfect for the part. They rounded out the cast with Sandra Bullock, who was asked to play Ellen Roark, a left-wing, Boston-born law student at the University of Mississippi who finds herself attracted to both the case and Jake Brigance; Donald Sutherland, who plays the part of Lucien Wilbanks, a disbarred-but-noble attorney who serves as Brigance's mentor; and Ashley Judd, who was asked to play Brigance's wife, Carla.

Of all the parts, it was Ashley's that required the most subtlety. From the outset of the movie, Brigance is cast as the hero, the man who puts his life on the line so that Carl Lee Hailey can receive something approximating justice. Complicating things is the fact that Brigance is no liberal. He believes in the death penalty and he is not opposed to vigilante justice, especially when children are involved. He knows he would have done the same thing that Carl Lee Hailey did if the situation had been reversed and it was his daughter who had been beaten and raped.

It would have been easy for Schumacher to make the film a battleground over liberal-versus-conservative values. Instead, he shades the morality of the drama by allowing the conflict to put a right-wing lawyer in opposition to ultra-right-wing elements of the community. That shading is the reason Ashley's role was so important to film. Viewers never learn whether Ashley is a liberal. What they see is a wife who is opposed to her husband's involvement in a case that threatens the security of her family.

Ashley was asked to play the role with subtlety because it was mandatory that someone in the film elevate the story above liberal-conservative stereotypes. Confident of her ability to deliver such a performance, Schumacher felt she was capable of exploring depths of her psyche that had not yet been touched.

Ashley has eight scenes in the movie. In the first, she merely waves goodbye to her husband from the front porch of their house. It is not until the second scene that moviegoers see a blonde Ashley in all her cat-on-a-hot-tin-roof splendor. Splashed with baby oil to simulate sweat, she looks sensual but wifely. She tells her husband not to torment himself over the rape. He confesses that a conversation with the girl's father made him think that he might take the law into his own hands. She advises him to notify the sheriff. He promises that he will, but he does not.

After an effort to bomb their home is thwarted—and he refuses to withdraw from the case—Ashley decides to take their daughter to visit out-of-town relatives. He tells her he is sorry, but he cannot drop the case because his client is counting on him. To which Ashley responds, "I understand that, Jake. I just want you to remember that we're counting on you, too. What if something happens to you?"

He promises that nothing would happen.

"Watch you don't make your wife promises you can't keep," she says.

For most of the movie, Ashley appears to be an unsympathetic character, a wife who deserts her husband in his time of need. By the end of the movie, it is apparent that it is Ashley, not her husband, who occupies the moral high ground. She proves to her husband and to herself that there are some things in life that transcend black-and-white morality. That is why the role required subtlety to keep it from slipping into caricature.

At Grisham's request, *A Time to Kill* was filmed in Canton, Mississippi, a small town on the outskirts of Jackson, the state capital. The production attracted a lot of attention, not just from the locals, who were delighted to get hired as extras, but also from the national media. Among those who showed up to conduct interviews was CBS News anchor Dan Rather, who brought a camera crew to tape a segment for the network's weekly newsmagazine *48 Hours*. "You know, I worked in Mississippi a long time ago [covering the civil rights movement], spent quite a bit of time in this state," Rather told the *Atlanta Constitution*. "It was a particularly tough time in this country, a tough time for Mississippi. But it was a real good education for me....I'm a believer in experience, and this is an ongoing story: can we hold together as a nation?"

It was a surreal scene for everyone involved. Grisham wrote the novel to interpret an injustice. Schumacher did the movie to interpret the novel. Rather did a news segment to interpret the movie. And the *Atlanta Constitution* published a story to interpret Rather's interpretation of Schumacher's interpretation of Grisham's novel. Add to that carnival dozens of extras roaming the streets in Ku Klux Klan outfits and you have a spectacle of irony, Southern style, that will long be remembered by local residents.

During filming, the irony continued when the film crew rented apartments on the Ross Barnett Reservoir, a thirty-thousand-acre lake named after the most controversial governor in Mississippi history (it was Governor Barnett who presided over the race riot that occurred at the University of Mississippi in 1963). When they weren't working, crew members played on the lake on jet skis and soaked up the view from an outdoor hot tub.

Local residents treated the actors and crew like royalty. "It was a really fantastic movie-making experience," Ashley told *Interview* magazine. "There was a lot of decency and kindness and consideration going around. On top of it, there was the most fabulous homemade food. Sisters from a local church baked for the movie. Every morning there were cinnamon rolls and these little cream-cheese rolls, and in the afternoon there was everything from homemade black-walnut fudge with marshmallows to the most delicious vanilla cupcakes, homemade blueberry pies with a crust on top spelling out the initials T T K [*A Time to Kill*]."

Not staying at the scenic apartments on the lake were the lead actors. Instead, they lived in rented houses in a nearby residential neighborhood. Ashley and Matthew McConaughey were so taken with each other that they shared a house, giving rise to a romance that kept gossips busy during the entire shooting.

The relationship ended on the day the movie wrapped. "Matthew and I loved each other, but he went through an incredible change during the filming of [the movie]," Ashley told the *Calgary Sun*. "By the end of the film, he was not the same man. He was entering a new world and a whole new phase of his life. He needed time and space to explore it and I knew I had to give him that time and space."

Interviewed by NBC, McConaughey admitted that they had had "a really nice relationship" during the filming. "If you've ever spent time with Ashley you've seen the presence that she has," he explained. "She comes into a room, all eyes go to A. J. very quickly."

When the movie was released in the summer of 1996, the reaction of critics was predictable, with most of the focus on Grisham instead of the movie. Mike Clark, writing for *USA Today*, described the film as "a handsome but riotously cluttered melodrama with maybe 145 subplots, it's the latest and least in a soulless string of preordained multiplex hits from the John Grisham warehouse."

*Rolling Stone* film critic Peter Travers acknowledged that Ashley was "gifted" and that Sandra Bullock was "adorable," but felt the movie was too busy: "Audiences expecting more Bullock or more weighty import from *A Time to Kill* will have to adjust expectations and settle for the kick of a good yarn."

*Time* magazine's Richard Schickel predicted that the movie would induce a sense of déjà vu among viewers: "Yes, we have intruded in this dust, killed this mockingbird before. But that was back in the days before lawyer jokes."

Ashley left Jackson, Mississippi, in a deep depression. It was not just the failed relationship with McConaughey that disturbed her—her heart did not really seem to be in it anyway—it was everything that had happened over the past two years. Naomi's autobiography and the resulting miniseries had done major damage to her self-esteem and to her concept of family. On top of her own feelings, she had to deal with her father's reactions. Two months after the miniseries aired, Michael Ciminella gave an interview to the Ashland *Daily Independent* in which he admitted that he was not Wynonna's father. He challenged Naomi's interpretation of the circumstances of their marriage by saying that she had tricked him into marrying her because of his family's wealth.

"She has spent her career saying what a horrible person I was when she, in fact, is the one who didn't stand up and do what is right," he told the newspaper. "She let me take the rap for something I did not do."

Ashley's world was a war zone. Not only were the various members of her family at odds with each other—and with themselves over issues of self-loathing regarding their careers and personal lives—Ashley was in conflict with herself over her failed romances and seemingly stalled movie career.

Naomi's intentions were good, but her way of dealing with Ashley's unhappiness was to criticize, in a polite way, her daughter's relationships with men and her career ambitions. And why not? Those were the same issues that had plagued Naomi since the day she found out she was pregnant with Wynonna.

Wynonna had much the same fears for Ashley. "I don't worry

about Ashley professionally, but is she going to fall in love with every guy that she's in a movie with?" she told *Us* magazine. "I'm actually concerned about her becoming so global."

Just exactly how many of Ashley's leading men she has had romances with is a closely guarded secret in the Judd family, but Ashley has admitted to dating only two of her leading men (McConaughey and one actor whose name she refuses to provide).

On top of all the emotional baggage she brought home from Jackson, she suffered from a lingering cold that she simply could not shake. "I was real raw and tender," she told Bernard Weinraub of *Interview* magazine. "I felt pretty ravaged...and all of a sudden I thought, 'Oh my God, I think I'm depressed.' This is what people do when they're depressed. The sickness was brought on by emotions and I realized that my body was not going to get better until I looked at my emotions."

It was at that point in her life that Ashley entered therapy with her mother. Through hypnosis and intense therapy sessions, some of which involved tearful confrontations with her mother, Ashley was able to unearth a wide-range of suppressed feelings about her childhood, especially about being abandoned. To her surprise, she discovered that she was not simply hanging out alone all those years, as she thought—she was lonely.

Ashley had fooled no one more cleverly than she had fooled herself. She had been laughing on the outside and crying on the inside for most of her life. No offense intended to Matthew McConaughey, but the fact that she would travel to Mississippi and set up housekeeping with an actor she knew little about—and then break up with him when the movie wrapped—was a cry for help that Ashley recognized when she returned to the commonsense reality of her Tennessee farmhouse.

In addition to therapy, Wynonna offered a more homespun remedy. Backstage, at the Country Music Association Awards, she introduced her sister to a nice boy named Michael Bolton, a singer who had recently broken up with actress Nicolette Sheridan. A fling sounded like a good idea to Ashley, who did not want to entirely drop her long-standing habit of self-medicating her emotional problems with male companionship. By September, Ashley and Michael were an item in the tabloids, especially after they were spotted at a New York fashion show, smooching as if no one else was in the room.

In December 1996, when Ashley was asked to be the guest of the grand marshal of the Ashland, Kentucky, Christmas parade, she took Michael with her. They rode together on a float as the parade wound its way through downtown Ashland.

Standing in the crowd was Dixie Johnson, Ashley's high school math teacher. When Ashley spotted her, she elbowed Michael and pointed in the woman's direction; then she shouted, her voice rising above the din of the marching bands: "That's my math teacher! Hey, Mrs. Johnson!"

Dixie Johnson waved back, confident that Ashley was going to do just fine in life.

Director John McNaughton had a reputation as a maverick long before the former carnie and constructor worker ever decided to make a movie titled *Normal Life*. His first film, *Henry: Portrait of a Serial Killer,* was held up for three years while studio executives debated the wisdom of its nonjudgmental examination of real-life killer Henry Lee Lucas. Finally released in 1989, it eventually became a cult favorite and established McNaughton as a provocative and irreverent filmmaker.

He followed that film with *Borrower,* a science-fiction thriller about an alien with an exploding head, *Sex, Drugs, Rock 'n' Roll,* a look at performance artist Eric Bogosian's one-man off-Broadway show, and *Mad Dog and Glory*, a dark comedy starring Robert De Niro, Bill Murray, and Uma Thurman. Although *Mad Dog and Glory* was a mainstream Hollywood film and starred actors with proven box-office appeal, it never caught on with the public and received mixed reviews from the critics.

*Normal Life* was McNaughton's follow up. Written by Peg Haller and Bob Schneider, it was based on a true story about a cop who falls in love with an emotionally unstable woman he meets in a bar. A straight-arrow who plays by the rules, he soon finds himself confounded by the difficulties inherent in a relationship with a woman who drinks too much, uses drugs, and likes to spend money like there is no tomorrow. In order to make her happy, he must sell his soul and go against everything he believes in.

To play the role of the cop, McNaughton turned to *Beverly Hills 90210* heartthrob Luke Perry. At the age of thirty, he seemed ready for a role with an edge to it (he left the television series in 1995). Previous movies included *Buffy the Vampire Slayer* (1992), *Terminal Bliss* (1992), and *Scorchers* (1991).

To play the role of the woman, McNaughton needed an actress who could be convincing as a psychotic dream-buster. It was essential for the actress to be both charismatic and believable as a normal woman in order for her transformation into psychosis to be convincing. He turned to Ashley Judd. He had no idea that she had issues of her own and was undergoing therapy; he had been impressed by the intensity of her acting in previous movies and her willingness to shed her clothing in the name of art.

Ashley did not disappoint. It was her first co-starring role since *Passion of Darkly Noon* and *Norma Jean and Marilyn*, which had aired earlier that year on HBO. She was desperate to prove herself again, not just to moviegoers but to herself and her family. As a result, her acting in the film was provocative and disturbing, almost spellbinding in its intensity. It some ways it was her most brilliant performance since *Ruby in Paradise*.

Ashley's best scene occurs when she leaves Perry and moves in with a lesbian coworker. Perry tries to win her back by explaining his love for her. As they walk along the sidewalk of a closed strip mall, Ashley tells him she can't take it any longer. "I'm not a normal person," she says.

Perry says that does not matter: "Just don't leave me," he pleads.

They embrace and then commit a crime together that unravels everything in their lives that they have fought to salvage. As a couple, they were doomed from the first day they met, but it is a credit to the acting of Ashley and Perry that viewers were allowed to hold out hope for them until the very end.

Ashley did things in this movie that she never dreamed she would do before a camera. In one scene she mutilates herself with a knife, cutting her breasts and stomach with an expensive knife that they have argued over. In another, she suggests masturbation with a pistol that she rubs against her body.

In all, she has six nude scenes. Almost always the nudity is paired with emotions far removed from sex. In one scene, Perry comes into the bedroom and finds Ashley holding a pistol to her head. She is topless and oblivious to her nudity. It is gratuitous and has nothing to do with the emotions sizzling inside her head. He puts a gun to his head and suggests that they kill themselves at the same time. Faced with the reality of his actions, she backs down and says she is sorry.

Sex is in fact an important issue in their relationship. Early on, she informs him that she has never had an orgasm. Not until she learns that he is a bank robber is she able to have an orgasm with him. Incredibly, when Ashley has simulated sex with Perry in the beginning of their relationship, at a time when she is not supposed to be able to have orgasms, her nipples are visibly flaccid. Later, when she is supposed to be having orgasms, her nipples are erect. How Ashley was able to accomplish anatomical feat remains a mystery.

McNaughton was able to make *Normal Life* for $2.75 million, a small amount by 1996 standards. When he turned the edited film in to Fine Line Features and Spelling Films International, he was shocked to learn that they had decided against a theatrical run and were going to release it directly to video after a showing on HBO television.

That is the worst thing that can happen to a movie because it sends a message to the director and actors that the film is not up to theatrical standards. McNaughton was incensed. "I think it really came down to the fact that it really wasn't their sort of picture, and they could dump it, still make a tidy profit, and not have to work," he told writer Nathan Rabin. "Which, as I've often said, is something they're very good at."

There was so much controversy over the film that Fine Line Features finally agreed to put the film in a handful of theaters around the country, including Nashville, San Francisco, and Chicago. Reaction to the film was not what McNaughton expected and critics were divided among those who passionately liked the film and those who passionately hated it.

"Judd, so good in *Ruby in Paradise,* is frighteningly real here as a woman who lives for pleasure, but, finding it fleeting, would just as soon blow her head off with one of her husband's guns," wrote Barbara Shulgasser in the *San Francisco Examiner.* "Judd's performance is reminiscent of Jessica Lange's in *Blue Sky* and *Frances,* no surprise as she shares Lange's aching vulnerability and powerful sexuality."

Roger Ebert, writing in the *Chicago Sun-Times,* described it as the type of movie "you watch with the same fascination as a developing traffic accident. Part of its success is due to the casting. Ashley Judd, so warm and likable in *Ruby in Paradise,* here plays the kind of woman you would cross the room, or the state, to avoid." Said *Rolling Stone*: "Ashley Judd flares like lightning. Her hot, sexy and violently unsettling performance...is a high-wire act that would win her a stack of awards if this indie film had any chance of a run before being shipped off to video."

In the unimpressed camp was Edward Guthmann of the *San Francisco Chronicle:* "Ashley Judd hasn't demonstrated much subtlety in her recent films, but in *Normal Life*...she eats everything but the camera. Playing a suicidal, emotionally explosive psycho, Judd rants, stomps, shakes her wig, points a gun to her head and leaves her poor co-star, Luke Perry, looking catatonic in the shadow of so much overacting."

Also unhappy with the film was Chuck Dowling, who wrote in the online Jacksonville Film Journal that Ashley's character was "one of the most evil, despicable, frustratingly ridiculous and unsympathetic female characters in movie history."

After its brief theatrical run, *Normal Life* retreated to the obscurity of video stores. Five years later, the film was difficult to locate anywhere.

Ashley was stunned by the failure of the film and embarrassed that it had gone so quickly to video, as if it were just another skin flick by an ambitious porn queen. Despite what some critics said, she knew she had delivered a passionate performance. Not only had she bared her breasts, she had bared her soul. What did people want from her, anyway? How much bad luck could one actress stand? If Ashley were not already in therapy, the failure of *Normal Life* would certainly have sent her there.

# Chapter
# Six

## *Kiss the Girls and Make Them Cry*

Ashley was still depressed when 1997 began, but she had several projects lined up that gave her encouragement, plus her relationship with Michael Bolton was on track, and if nothing else, that took her mind off of her other problems. She was not sure where that relationship was going—she sometimes wondered why, at the age of twenty-eight, she had not experienced a series of sustained relationships like other women her age—but she was not overly concerned about that. It would happen, she told herself, when it happened.

"I'm hurt by what I see in Hollywood—the broken marriages, the inability of people to have a life plus a career," she told the *Arizona Republic*. "I'm going to live my life the way I want, and if they don't like it that's their business, not mine. I firmly believe there can be a balance. I don't believe God said, 'Little Judd girl, you can have this, but you can't have that.' I plan to have it all."

At that point in her life, her career and her farmhouse were the two things in her life that gave her the most comfort. She had reached a stage in the remodeling of her home that she had become extremely fastidious. Guests were asked to leave their shoes at the door and they were expected to volunteer for a household chore that would pay tribute to the house, whether it was washing the dishes or sweeping out a room.

She explained the shoe mandate by saying it was to protect the floor from the ever-present dust on the farm, but if she had looked deeper into her own psyche she would have understood that her real goal was to keep guests from tracking up her life, cluttering it with unwelcome emotional demands and distracting social complications.

What she desired most in life was the inner strength to focus on her film career. In that realm, Bolton was most supportive. "Ashley is a genius," he told NBC television. "I think she's Oscar bound."

Going into 1997, the project that fascinated her most was *Kiss the Girls*, a thriller based on James Patterson's novel. She ended up with the script in a roundabout way. While she was filming *Heat,* producer David Brown sent her a script for an upcoming project of his, titled *The Saint.* He sent the script for a second project, titled *Kiss the Girls,* to actress Elizabeth Shue. Somehow—Brown says he does not recall exactly how—Ashley and Elizabeth switched scripts in a complicated move that would have baffled Sherlock Holmes. The way it played out, Elizabeth was given the female lead in *The Saint,* playing opposite Val Kilmer (Ashley's screen husband in *Heat*) and Ashley wound up with the female lead in *Kiss the Girls.*

Ashley was impressed by David Brown's résumé. Not only was he the husband of *Cosmopolitan* magazine editor Helen Gurley Brown— the go-girl-go guru of women who choose career over family—he had amassed an impressive string of producer credits, including *Jaws, The Verdict, Cocoon,* and *Driving Miss Daisy.* They were the types of successful movies with which Ashley wanted to be associated.

To direct the film, Brown chose Gary Fleder, a television director ("Homicide," "L.A. Doctors," and "Tales from the Crypt"). Before taking on *Kiss the Girls,* he had directed only one movie, *Things to Do in Denver When You're Dead.* It was a curious choice, but Brown saw something in the style and the pace of his television work that interested him.

For the male leading role, Brown approached Samuel L. Jackson, who turned it down because he felt it was "too misogynistic." Brown then turned to Morgan Freeman, with whom he had worked on the award-winning *Driving Miss Daisy.* He had not had a strong role since 1994's *The Shawshank Redemption,* and he readily agreed to do the project. In the film he plays Dr. Alex Cross, a Washington, DC–based forensic psychologist who is called in to help investigate a series of North Carolina abductions.

Ashley plays the role of Kate McTiernan, a young physician who relaxes by going to a gymnasium to kick-box male opponents. Before production began, Ashley did what she could to research the character. She approached the supervisor of the resident program at Vanderbilt Medical Center in Nashville, who put her in contact with a second-year resident named Amy Johnson. The women had two things in common: both were born in the South, and both dutifully had followed a liberal arts education until they discovered their true vocation.

Johnson gladly allowed Ashley to tag along with her on her rounds. "I was witness to one dramatic situation: she was preparing a woman to go home, essentially to die, when she suddenly realized the primary physician had not made his patient aware of the true situation," he told the *Nashville Tennessean*. "She was totally honest, direct, did not mince words, but at the same time she was marvelously tender and beautiful."

Ashley used that experience to shape a similar scene in the movie.

For the first fifteen minutes of *Kiss the Girls*, the focus is on Freeman as he meets with local detectives and probes for clues about the psychological profile of the man responsible for the abductions. Ashley enters the picture when she becomes one of the victims. As she sleeps, an intruder enters her house and awakens her.

"What do you want from me?" she asks.

"Everything," he answers.

The intruder sprays Ashley with a knock-out drug and takes her to a secret place. When she awakens, she is in a dingy room with little furniture, and her wrists are tied to the bed. She sees a man in the shadows and asks why she has been brought there, to which the man responds, "To fall in love." The man warns her not to try to escape or to use her kick-boxing skills against him.

After he leaves the room, Ashley calls out and learns there are other women being held captive there. They respond to her questions from their individual cells. When the man returns to Ashley's room to give her an injection, she kicks him and escapes from the building. He pursues her and as he closes in on her, she jumps from a cliff into a mountain stream. Later, she is found alive and taken to a hospital.

Freeman is in her hospital room when she awakens. Together, they decide to pursue the abductor and rescue the other women. Ashley's first riveting scene occurs when she speaks at a press conference. With her face bruised and scratched, she thanks the doctors who helped her recover and the young boys who fished her out of the stream. She tells the families of the missing women not to give up hope, that their loved ones are still alive. Then, looking into the television cameras, she speaks directly to the abductor.

"I broke your rules, just me," she says. "None of the other women helped. So if you're looking for someone to blame, blame me."

It was Ashley doing what she does best, delivering an emotional monologue. The scene following the press conference continued that intensity in an exchange with Freeman. He wants her to remember every detail, every nuance about her capture. She does the entire scene with her eyes closed so that she can play it out as if it were a monologue. As she speaks, important clues emerge. The scene ends with her breaking down in tears, expressing regret about leaving the other women behind. It was a brilliant scene, made even more impressive by her decision (or the director's decision) to deliver the lines as if she were delivering a monologue.

Ashley also has a good action scene at the end of the movie, when she slugs it out with the abductor. She doesn't have a body type that lends itself to high-end physical scenes, but she makes the most out of what she has and she can be very effective in scenes that require her to be athletic. Directors do not like actresses who are not naturally athletic to get too physical during shooting because invariably they injure themselves and shut down production. Ashley was no exception: she sprained her ankle during one of the action scenes.

Typically, Ashley works out before filming begins so that she will be in shape for whatever the director throws her way. For *Kiss the Girls,* she continued her training during shooting. "She ran every day to stay in shape and didn't shy away from the physical stuff," Freeman told *Biography* magazine. "She is incredibly disciplined and extremely willing to do whatever the role calls for."

Judd was equally flattering of Freeman. She repeatedly told reporters that he "took her breath away" as an actor. There were times during the filming when she was so overcome by the strength of his acting that she stopped delivering her lines and gazed at her costar with awe, bringing production to a standstill.

When the movie was released and she started doing interviews to promote it, she sometimes found herself defending the violence depicted in the film, both implied and actual. She defended it by pointing out that the movie had been toned down considerably from the book, which was quite explicit in the violence and sexual abuses that took place in the story. "I love that word, prurient," she told Bob Strauss of the *Boston Globe.* "But the screenplay wasn't prurient—the books is so much more nasty. And Morgan Freeman is the ultimate bastion of dignity, so I never worried for a second."

Critics were almost unanimous in their praise of Freeman, but Ashley's performance seemed to slip beneath their radar. No one praised her work and no one accused her of delivering a substandard performance. "Freeman and Judd are well-cast, but this adequately assembled thriller is more clinical than emotional, limiting even its better actors to establishing their competence and little more," wrote Mike Clark for *USA Today.* "Someone find a spare room in the woods for those responsible."

Peter Stack of the *San Francisco Chronicle* found Freeman's performance compelling and credited him with saving the movie from itself. About Ashley, he wrote, "This young actress is getting awfully good at turning potentially gelatinous characters into substantive people who spark viewer interest."

When Ashley attended a private showing of the movie at Paramount's Hollywood studio, she invited Naomi and Wynonna, along with Robert Carnegie, her acting teacher at Playhouse West. "I told her afterward that I thought she was the Tiger Woods of actresses," says Carnegie. "They put her in movies that require an extraordinary amount of emotion and reality because if you don't have that in movies like that, it will just collapse. But if you have an actress doing the part with enormous conviction and deep feeling, then you buy into it and you go along with it and that is what Ashley is capable of in the emotion that she displays. She is just a world-class actress. Whenever anyone asks me what I consider the ideal representation of the work we do at Playhouse West, [I say] it is Ashley Judd. She's just perfect insofar as what we try to achieve. I don't think she has nearly reached her capabilities yet. She is still young and growing. She is going to get better and better."

After the showing at Paramount, an insecure Ashley talked to Carnegie about returning to Playhouse West for additional training. "I told her I didn't think that was necessary," he says. "Her technique is so solid and she puts so much emotion into her films that the better thing to do would be to live life, experience life, and recuperate between her ventures. I told her, 'Let's leave well enough alone'—and she went along with that."

When Ashley read the script for *The Locusts*, she thought it was "beautiful." Written by John Patrick Kelley while he was a student at New York University, it had been optioned by a Hollywood producer. "The script circulated around Hollywood for years, developing a certain cachet," Ashley told the *Nashville Tennessean*. "Several actors I know told me they thought it was the best screenplay they had ever seen. But somehow it never got produced."

Disappointed by negative reactions of this work, Kelley, who had moved to New Orleans after leaving the university, bought the script back and searched for financial backers so that he could do something with it himself. Eventually, he found two backers, Bruce Franklin and Marc Ezralow, who agreed to produce the film.

With financing in place, the next task was to find a director. Kelley was chosen, even though he had never directed a film. He had never even had one of his scripts made into a movie. For him, it would be on-the-job training.

When the task turned to casting, things got even more interesting. For the female lead, they signed Kate Capshaw, wife of legendary producer and director Steven Spielberg. A former Ford model, she had made her acting debut in the early 1980s, appearing in two films, *A Little Sex* and *Windy City,* both of which got good reviews. She followed up those successes with a role in *Indiana Jones and the Temple of Doom,* directed by her future husband Steven Spielberg. Her acting in that movie was so spotty that it took years for her career to recover.

In 1991, Capshaw married Spielberg, converted to Judaism, and began raising a family (she has had five children with Spielberg). Even so, she did not abandon her film career. From 1991 to 1997 she had roles in five feature films, including *Love Affair* and *How to Make an American Quilt,* none of which made her a household name.

Capshaw brought more to the film than her talent: she brought her daughter from a previous marriage, Jessica Capshaw, who was given the role of Patsy; and she brought Vince Vaughn, who was given the male lead. Earlier that year Vaughn had been cast in Spielberg's *The Lost World: Jurassic Park.* Although he had appeared in only two movies at that point in his career, he was considered an up-and-coming actor. The fact that three major parts were given to actors with close ties to Spielberg eventually gave rise to speculation that the Spielbergs had more than an artistic interest in the film, that perhaps Steven and Kate were closet investors in the film.

Rounding out the cast were Jeremy Davies, who was given the part of Joseph "Flyboy" Potts, and Ashley Judd, who was asked to play the passion-hungry Kitty, Vaughn's love interest. The film was shot on location in Texas at four sites, including Sealy (population 5,248), a sleepy town located three hundred miles from the Mexican border. The town is fifty-eight miles from the nearest commercial airport and projects an image of stoic isolation, which was exactly what the filmmakers wanted to convey.

*The Locusts* begins with the proverbial stranger with a secret (Vaughn) coming to town. When he asks where he can find work, he is directed to a cattle ranch run by the forty-four-year-old Capshaw, an aging, alcoholic widow, who obviously has an attic full of demons in her twisted psyche. Living with her on the ranch is her twenty-one-year-old son Flyboy (Jeremy Davies), who has remained mute ever since his return from a mental hospital, where he received shock treatments on a regular basis.

Capshaw not only hires Vaughn on the spot, she allows him to live in the carriage house, presumably so that he will be available to satisfy her lusty sexual appetite. As Capshaw pursues Vaughn, he understandably pursues the eager-to-trot Ashley. To the surprise of some, Ashley never gets nude in this movie, although she does

Ashley Judd

*From the collection of Alan L. Mayor*

*The Judd family. Photo by Alan L. Mayor.*

*Delta Burke shows up for Wynonna's first number-one hit as a solo artist. Photo by Alan L. Mayor.*

*The Judds backstage after the County Music Awards show. Photo by Alan L. Mayor*

*The Judd girls with Tammy Wynette and Loretta Lynn. Photo by Alan L. Mayor.*

Prince of Egypt *premiere in Nashville. Left to right: Beth Neilsen Chapman, Ashley Judd, Mindy McCready, Wynonna Judd, James Stroud, Faith Hill, Randy Travis, Linda Davis, Jeffrey Katzenberg, Clint Black, Vince Gill, and Reba McEntire. Photo by Alan L. Mayor*

Prince of Egypt *premiere in Nashville brings out the stars. Left to right: Charlie Daniels, James Stroud, Wynonna Judd, Jeffrey Katzenberg, Ashley Judd, and Gary Chapman. Photo by Alan L. Mayor*

*Ashley Judd and Michael Bolton at* Ebony *magazine's "Celebrate the Dream: 50 Years of Ebony Magazine." Photo by Ron Wolfson.*

*Actress Ashley Judd at the 56th edition of the Venice Film Festival, September 5, 1999. Photo by Piovanotto/LePresse.*

*Actress Ashley Judd and actor Morgan Freeman chat at the party following the premiere of Judd and Freeman's film* Kiss the Girls. *Photo by Fred Prouser, Reuters/Hulton Archive.*

*Ashley Judd arrives at the 72nd annual Academy Awards, March 26, 2000, in Los Angeles. Photo by Bob Riha Jr.*

*Ashley Judd attends the TNT All-Star Tribute to Joni Mitchell at the Hammerstein Ballroom in New York City, April 6, 2000. Photo by Laura Walters.*

*Ashley Judd, winner of "Favorite Actress" for the suspense category, at the sixth annual Blockbuster Entertainment Awards, May 9, 2000. Photo by Chris Weeks/Liaison Agency.*

*Ashley Judd portrays Jane Goodale, a New Yorker who is determined to succeed both professionally and in her romantic life, in the film* Someone Like You. *Photo courtesy of 20th Century Fox.*

*Los Angeles premiere screening of* Double Jeopardy. *Photo by Brenda Chase/Online USA, Inc..*

*Driver Dario Franchitti of Great Britain and Ashley Judd during the Medic Drug Grand Prix in Cleveland, Ohio, June 28, 1999. Photo by Robert Laberge/Allspor.*

*Ashley Judd and fiancé, racing driver Dario Franchitti, arrive for the 73rd Academy Awards, March 25, 2001 in Los Angeles. Photo by Reuters/Win McNamee/Hulton Archive.*

participate in a steamy sex scene with Vaughn that suggests oral intercourse.

The rehearsal for the scene was a real nightmare for Vaughn, but he did not explain why until some time later. Because he was ill when shooting began, a doctor gave him an injection in his buttocks and covered it with a Band-Aid. He was wearing jeans but had on no underwear at the time. He went immediately from the doctor's office to the rehearsal. "So Ashley and I had to rehearse a hugging scene, and her hand went in the back of my pants and I started to freak out," he told *Cosmopolitan* magazine. "I'm thinking, 'She's gonna think. 'This guy's got no underwear on and he's got a huge Band-Aid on his ass.'" Being a Southern lady of worldly sophistication, Ashley thought no such thing; she simulated sexual gratification, as so many Southern ladies before her had done, then went on about her business.

As the plot progresses, the sexual tension increases. Both Capshaw and Ashley want Vaughn, but he is strangely drawn to Davies, ostensibly to help him escape the emotional nightmare he is living. That is a high-minded motivation, to be certain, but beneath it lurks the sexual tension that exists between the two men.

Vaughn decides that his mission in life, before he drifts to another ranch, is to free Flyboy of his mother's domineering control. It becomes an obsession for him, even to the point of distracting him from taking advantage of the generous, no-strings-attached sex offered by Ashley and Capshaw.

By the time the plot unravels, moviegoers are subjected to thinly disguised themes of infidelity, incest, homosexuality, promiscuity, and betrayal. In the event those themes are too subtle for some audience members to appreciate, a bull castration is thrown in as sort of an all-purpose thematic wrap.

When *The Locusts* was released in 1997, critics savaged it with something akin to the gore of the castration scene in the movie. Under a headline that read "Crawling 'Locusts' Leaves Lust in the Dust," *USA Today*'s Andy Seiler had pleasant things to say about Ashley—she is "spunky and likable"—but little good to say about the movie: "It's hot, it's sultry and everybody's smokin'....Too bad the movie never catches fire."

"The talented Judd has one of the most thankless roles of her fresh career," wrote Jack Mathews for the *Los Angeles Times*. "As Kitty, she isn't asked to do much more than appear sexy and flash Kodak smiles. She does both with ease, but there's too much going on behind the actress' eyes to waste in throwaway roles." He went on to

129

compare the script to a "terrible Tennessee Williams competition."

*Chicago Sun-Times* critic Roger Ebert seemed genuinely baffled. He praised John Patrick Kelley's talent "for rhythm, for mood, for gothic weirdness"—and he even had kind words for the performances, especially Ashley's confident delivery of her lines—but the movie itself seemed dated to him. "The movie is not bad so much as it's absurd," he observed. "Its material is so overwrought and incredible, so curiously dated, that it undermines the whole enterprise."

Allen Johnson, writing in the *San Francisco Examiner,* ignored Ashley's performance in his review, which was just as well for her because he found little in the film to like. Wrote Johnson: "*The Locusts* is one of those weird Southern dramas where the skeleton in the family closet still has decaying flesh and everyone and everything is hot and sweaty, including the iced tea."

*The Locusts* went quickly to video and to the United Kingdom, where it was marketed under the title *A Secret Sin.* John Patrick Kelley has done no movies since then, and that is a shame since he did a good job as a director. It was the script that was the real clunker in this project. It is surprising that an experienced actress like Capshaw would want to get involved with a script driven by such an abundance of over-the-top dialogue, but perhaps not so surprising that Ashley would do so.

To Ashley, a well-written script is one that deals with serious themes and allows the actors to use as many monosyllabic words as possible. About that she is only half right. The history of good prose has been the writer's ability to convey serious thoughts and emotions with as few words and syllables as possible. Art, more often than not, is determined by what is left off the page, not what has been underlined.

When Ashley read the script for *The Locusts,* she was impressed by the seriousness of themes dealing with sexual and emotional dysfunction, and by the dialogue, which seemed reminiscent of something Tennessee Williams might have written. But the reality was that the dialogue was terribly overwritten and often so wordy it seemed an unintentional caricature of the genre it sought to emulate.

The script might have worked as a dark comedy in the erotic thriller genre, especially since no one in *The Locusts* ever has their sexual needs satisfied—and that is amusing if you think about it, since someone takes a drag on a cigarette in nearly every scene (a sure sign they are *not* having sex)—but the script was interpreted by the director/writer as a serious drama instead of a quirky satire and it never stood a chance at the box office, where audiences quickly picked up on the artistic gaff.

*The Locusts* was the third substandard motion picture Ashley had made in four years. As far as her career was concerned, she was her own worst enemy. Even when critics hated those movies, they almost always complimented Ashley on her acting. The problem was not with her acting skills, which were considerable, but with her judgment—and lapses in that area are understandable in view of the depression she had experienced for the previous two years. Depression is a disease that relies on bad judgment for nourishment; unfortunately, Ashley sometimes acquiesced in a feeding frenzy, to the detriment of her career.

Wynonna released two albums in 1997, *Collection* and *The Other Side*, but neither went platinum. With svelte beauties like Shania Twain and Faith Hill dominating the charts and creating a new image for country music, Wynonna seemed out of the loop. She tried to compensate by shifting her music away from country toward a more blues-oriented style. For example, *The Other Side* included a song written by blues-rock guitarist Kenny Wayne Shepherd (he even played guitar on the recording).

More important than her song selection for those two albums was her delivery. For some reason, she decided to highlight a distinctive growl reminiscent of the blues mamas of the 1940s and 1950s. It was probably fun for her to do, but it did nothing to enhance her music and it usually came across as a very grating distraction. Wynonna has one of the best voices in country music, but it is not the sort of vocal instrument that can be successfully molded into something else: she is what she is.

At the age of thirty-four, Wynonna suddenly found herself a senior citizen on country radio, joining the likes of Johnny Cash, Willie Nelson, and other stars who saw their careers all but end on radio after a long run of hit records. They compensated by performing in concert, where they always could count on enthusiastic crowds of older fans who remembered their music. Wynonna saw that handwriting on the wall.

In 1998, after disappointing sales for both albums, Wynonna put together another tour. Only this time, unsure of her audience, she looked for a touring partner who could expand her fan base. She approached Ashley's beau, Michael Bolton, who was happy to team up with Wynonna for a tour. He was in much the same situation with his career. He, too, had released two albums in 1997 (one of them a collection of operatic music), neither of which were competitive on the charts. Perhaps he thought a pairing with Wynonna would expand his fan base into her country territory.

They called it the Voices Tour, a bit pretentious perhaps, but the title at least tried to address the differences in the two singers' styles. Besides, what were their choices? It Takes Two? Double Your Trouble? Or, perhaps, Double Indemnity?

Reviews of the tour were generally good, but critics seemed to prefer Wynonna over Bolton. "Sassy Wynonna Steals Show from Bolton," read the headline in the *Deseret News*. "Although Bolton was actually the headliner, it was the one with the big hair that had the bigger show," wrote Scott Iwasaki. "Yes, Wynonna, as she prefers to be called, stole the show with her sass, spunk and attitude."

Kevin Johnson of the *St. Louis Post-Dispatch* felt Wynonna's performance was "warm and natural" and Bolton's was too emotional. "The gutsy Judd was a little bit country and a little bit rock 'n' roll, not diving too deeply into either but finding a comfortable midpoint," he wrote. "While some might say she's betraying her country roots, broadening her horizons this way—and this well—exposes her to a larger audience."

One of the interesting things about the tour was the insight it showed into the state of Juddland. Whereas audiences once were treated to Wynonna's interactions, in person or long distance, with Naomi, they now received doses of Ashleymania. Each night Wynonna dedicated "Come Some Rainy Day" to her sister and she never missed an opportunity to mention her name. The sisters were closer now than they ever had been.

On occasion, Ashley joined the tour. Indeed, one of the brightest moments of the tour occurred when Ashley and Naomi both showed up one evening. Together, they decided to play a trick on Bolton. Each night, their routine was for Wynonna to join Bolton on stage to sing "It Takes Two." This time, instead of Wynonna walking out on stage, Ashley stepped out into the spotlight, microphone in hand.

As far as anyone in the audience knew, Ashley was singing the duet with him. Unknown to the startled Bolton—and the audience— it was Wynonna who was doing the actual vocal from a backstage microphone. As if that bit of trickery was not enough to torment Bolton, Naomi appeared on stage doing Chuck Berry's patented duck walk.

"Michael completely flipped out," Naomi later told the *Tennessean*. "I have never seen this sophisticated, together man lose it. But he did."

Of course, what seemed like good ole down-home fun to the Judds did not necessarily translate that way to Bolton, who took his career quite seriously. Photos taken during that time of him and Ashley usually showed her with sparkling eyes and a radiant smile—it was probably the most intense love affair of her life; she used words like being "blown away" and "powerful" when describing the relationship to others—but Bolton never seemed to have joy in his eyes and, more often than not, appeared bored and disinterested.

Whether it was because of Ashley's stage trick or Naomi's duck walk during one of his favorite songs—or something else entirely—Bolton bailed on Ashley before the year ended. Apparently, not everyone has what it takes to become a Judd.

Ashley has a habit of working on films with first-time directors. Whether that is by accident, simply attributable to the luck of the draw, or because first-time directors tend to be her own age, thus eliminating the likelihood of troublesome generational differences of opinion, may be known only to Ashley and her therapist.

At any rate, for her next movie, *Simon Birch*, she went to work for first-time director Mark Steven Johnson, whose previous movie experience had been as a screenwriter (*Grumpy Old Men*, *Grumpier Old Men* and *Big Bully*). Actually, for *Simon Birch* he had signed on as both the director and the screenwriter, which meant that his main job was to adapt John Irving's novel *A Prayer for Owen Meany* into a screenplay and then to direct the movie using his vision of the story and not Irving's.

*Simon Birch* is about an eleven-year-old dwarf whose physical condition has left him with little hope of meaningful longevity. Perhaps as a way to cope with what he knows is an uncertain future, he imagines that he has been put on earth to serve a special purpose. He is not certain what that purpose is, but he believes in it with all his heart.

Simon's best friend is Joe Wenteworth, the son of an unmarried mother, Rebecca Wenteworth, who has steadfastly refused to disclose the identity of his father. Much of the story centers on the relationship between Simon and Joe, and their efforts to make sense of the universe.

Unlike Joe, who tries to follow the rules, Simon is a rebel and an outcast. He relishes getting into trouble and he uses his physical condition as a weapon when sparring with adults who think he is on the wrong side of God's plan. At times it seems to the townspeople as if Simon is a child of Satan, especially when he accidentally kills

Rebecca Wenteworth at a Little League baseball game. Simon is devastated by the accident, for Rebecca had been like a mother to him.

Of course, it is the entire town that is wrong. Simon really is on a mission from God—well, two divine missions actually: one that will solve the mystery of Joe's mysterious birth and the other that will earn Simon a reputation as a town hero. Getting to those two intersections of truth is what the film is all about.

To play the role of Simon Birch, producers chose newcomer Ian Michael Smith, a three-foot-one-inch dwarf who suffers from Morquio Syndrome, a disease that affects the skeletal structure. The part of Joe Wenteworth went to Joseph Mazzello, a veteran of eleven feature films, including *Radio Flyer*, *Jurassic Park*, and *The Wild River*. In what was the most mysterious casting decision of the movie, Jim Carrey was asked to play the role of the adult Joe Wenteworth. Carrey is only on screen for a short time, but his voice can be heard throughout as the narrator.

Ashley was asked to play Rebecca Wenteworth. It is a small part, but she radiates goodness and caring. She has no memorable lines, but her presence in the film is extraordinarily strong. As usual, Ashley fought hard to get the part. Two big-name actresses were approached about the part, but it turned out that one had a scheduling conflict and the other could not come to financial terms with producers Laurence Mark and Roger Birnbaum. Ashley had her agent keep tabs on the negotiations and when the studio reached an impasse with the other two actresses, Ashley waltzed into the part.

The story was filmed in Ontario and Nova Scotia, but Ashley's screen time in the movie was so limited that it only took three weeks to complete her scenes, so she barely had time to soak up the Canadian culture and scenery. The best part of making the film, for her at least, was her interaction with the children, especially Ian Michael Smith.

"We would goose him, and he would cringe," she told the *Lexington Herald-Leader*. "We all had the willy-nilly laughs. I would ruin takes I would be laughing so hard." The laughter was so prevalent that the director simply threw up his hands at one point and allowed the giggles to stay in the film.

Paradoxically, Ashley was still battling depression while making the film—mood swings compounded by doubts about her movie career. She telephoned Wynonna and Naomi often, the sad tone of her voice betraying her mental condition. One day she called Wynonna, who was not at home, and left a message on her answering machine. When the call was returned, it was by Wynonna's son, two-and-a-half-year-old Elijah, who left a message on Ashley's machine that assured her in soothing tones that everything was going to be all right. Touched, she kept the message as a souvenir.

When *Simon Birch* was released, critics praised Ashley's performance but pounced on the movie for being too sappy. Jack Mathews, writing for the *Los Angeles Times*, opened his review with the observation that the sap was going to flow early that year. "*Simon Birch* is a dreadfully sticky affair," he wrote. "Johnson, on is maiden voyage as director, treats every scene as if it were a bonbon, almost too precious to consume, and Marc Shaiman's score is a running series of mood cues."

Equally overdosed on the saccharine content of the movie was *New York Times* critic Stephen Holden, who wrote: "*Simon Birch*, Mark Steven Johnson's insufferably precious 'reduction' of John Irving's popular 1989 novel...might be described as the movie equivalent of a piece of stale angel food cake. Bite into it, and what you'll find is a nearly flavorless mixture of air and sugar and more sugar and a texture so parched that a mouthful is almost impossible to swallow without risk of choking." He went on to say that Simon's deathbed scene had to rank "among the ten most bogus" in Hollywood history.

Incredibly, one of Ashley's hometown newspapers, the *Nashville Scene*, published a review that mentioned her only in passing, although it did concede that she was "luminous" in the role. "Some read Irving's novel and find a powerful story about the intersection of politics, friendship, and faith," wrote Noel Murray. "Mark Steven Johnson read it and used the opportunity to film a two-hour Hallmark card. *Simon Birch*'s intentions are noble, but its sentiments are paper-thin."

For Ashley, the movie's release was just more of the same. She could see a definite pattern. Critics either ignored her or slammed the movie and praised her wasted performance. She had few detractors among the critics, but what good was faint praise when the movies that she starred in were trashed? She sometimes wondered if the critics saw the same movie that she had worked on with such a passion. She always gave her best—and sometimes her best bordered on being magnificent. So why, then, could no one bring themself to give her anything back in return? It was the questions—not the answers—that kept her under gray clouds. Ashley did what any dedicated artist would do under the same circumstances: she moved on to the next project.

When Ashley read Marc Behm's 1980 novella *Eye of the Beholder*, she thought the role of Joanna Eris would be perfect for her, and she pressured director Stephan Elliott for the part with all the zeal and determination of a tobacco lobbyist. She was attracted to Elliott's enthusiasm about the film (he put up his own money) and his passion for movies in general, plus at thirty-six years of age he was only five years her senior.

An Australian filmmaker who had only three movies to his credit—*Frauds, The Adventures of Priscilla (Queen of the Desert)*, and *Welcome to Woop Woop*—Elliott had written the script for *Eye of the Beholder* himself, a clue to Ashley that he would, as director, adhere closely to the screenplay she had read (not always the case when directors do not write the script). Sometimes actors find unpleasant surprises waiting for them when filming begins. "Cut to sunrise" can become "cut to nude jog."

When Elliott finally got around to offering the role to Ashley—he wanted to give the role to an older woman, so as not to have a femme fatale—she almost turned it down, not because she had something else in place but because her viewpoint about the character had changed since first reading the script.

Joanna Eris was a cold and calculating woman who had been abandoned twice as a child. Ashley's first reaction had been compassion for her. Only later did the relevance of the character's childhood to her own childhood sink in and give her pause. But for the grace of God she might have become that wretched creature herself!

Ashley said yes to Elliott, but with serious misgivings.

Also signed to the movie was Ewan McGregor, a twenty-eight-year-old Scottish actor who had studied acting since the age of sixteen, when he joined the Perth Repertory Theatre. Before taking on the role of Eye in *Eye of the Beholder*, he had appeared in fifteen feature films, including *Trainspotting* (1996), *Nightwatch* (1998), and *Star Wars: Episode I—The Phantom Menace* (1999), in which he played the coveted role of Obi-Wan Kenobi.

McGregor was not Elliott's first choice for the male lead. The director already had gone through his top-ten list without success, when he ran into McGregor in a neighborhood bar (this was before the release of *Star Wars*). They started talking and bonded almost immediately. Elliott told him about the film, and McGregor's enthusiastic responses convinced him that the actor understood the role better than anyone else.

Rounding out the cast were Jason Priestley as a violent, spaced-out drifter ("Nobody would ever ask Jason to do anything like that," Elliott told the *North Shore News*. "When he got there he just went wild...he looked at me with this little glint in his eye and said, 'I've been waiting for this.'"); k. d. lang as Hilary, Eye's contact person at the agency (Lang's involvement was the icing on the cake for Ashley, who, at the age of eighteen, made the singer a clover chain out of admiration for her work); and French-Canadian actress Genevieve Bujold (probably best known for her riveting performance in *Anne of the Thousand Days*), as Dr. Jeanne Brault, an over-the-top dominatrix therapist.

The plot of *Eye of the Beholder* revolves around Eye's surveillance of targets assigned to him by the British embassy in Washington. No ordinary spy, he has a troubled past and an obsessive need to get involved in his subjects' lives.

Joanna crosses his path early in the movie when he encounters her while investigating the blackmail of his boss's son. He follows the suspect to his apartment and watches through his high-tech equipment while Joanna stabs him to death. In the first of several nude scenes in the movie, Joanna undresses and drags the man's body, wrapped in plastic, to a dock, where she dumps it without visible distress.

Abandoning his assignment, Eye follows Joanna across the country on a train, where she meets a man who shows her a stash of jewels he is transporting. She kills him and takes the jewels, which she sells at the next stop.

Eye stays in the shadows, watching her every move. When she reaches her apartment, he takes one next to hers. Ashley's second nude scene occurs when Joanna takes a bubble bath. By that point the voyeuristic Eye is clearly obsessed with her. He rigs cameras so that he can peer into her apartment.

In one scene, Joanna is pursued on the street by a thug. When a car hits him, she walks away from the scene of the accident. Seeing her is a sleazy cop who follows her to her apartment and tries to shake her down for a few dollars. Thinking he has scored both money and sex, he leans over to kiss her. She pulls out his gun and shoots him.

On the run again, Joanna takes up with a wealthy, blind winemaker. She taunts him into marrying him. When he picks her up in his limo to take her to the church, someone shoots into the car, causing an accident that kills the winemaker. Joanna flees the city, but has car trouble. She is picked up by a drifter who takes her to the next crossroads. When she refuses to do drugs with him, he beats her up and injects her with the drug of his choice while she is unconscious.

From there, Joanna goes to Utah, where she is apprehended by several carloads of police on the street. Eye opens fire on the police, allowing her to escape. She catches a flight to Alaska, where she gets a job in a diner as a waitress. Eye follows her and finally works up the nerve to ask her out on a date. She says she is too busy. Undeterred, Eye returns to the diner at closing. This time, realizing that she may have been identified by diners, she is friendly toward him and agrees to leave with him.

In Ashley's best scene in the movie, Eye offers to help her get a house. "Getting a house isn't a problem," she says. "That's easy enough. What do you do in a house? When you wake up in it? What do you do on Christmas in a house? I mean I'm supposed to be so young and I've nothing to show for myself except a big sense of loss."

Surprised by her comments, Eye asks her what she has lost.

"I've lost my childhood. My youth. My father. My husband...my daughter. She wasn't any bigger than a minute. Barely had a name... and spookiest of all I lost my angel. I had a guardian that looked after me."

Making the movie turned out to be one of the oddest experiences of Ashley's career. She rented a house while she was in Montreal, but she was unable to sleep in the master bedroom. Instead, she climbed into the attic and slept there each night because it reminded her of her grandparents' house.

"I played a character who is so aloof that my whole lifestyle became very aloof," she told her friend Salma Hayek for *Interview* magazine. "If someone knocked on my door, there was a part of me that went into a rage, because I wanted to be isolated and alone. I mutated into something that was a little to my detriment—not to mention unpleasant for other people—because I was a raging meanie!"

Ashley did not much like herself during shooting. She especially did not like the way she looked. Her character was not glamorous. She was psychopathic and her face was meant to reflect the void in her spirit. How could she possibly make people like such a despicable person?

Ashley's eyes often looked tired because of the hard hours she spent commuting to the Wildcats' basketball games, but instead of covering that up, the makeup artist amplified it even more by putting dark lines under her eyes. On top of that, since her character used wigs as a necessary tool of her trade, Ashley had to wear several in the film, including one—the short Prince Valiant cut—that she especially disliked.

No movie Ashley had ever made took such a toll on her spirit. Joanna was not a sympathetic character. She represented the worst of humanity. Far from the security of her farm and family—and entombed in a cold, dreary environment void of blue sky and white clouds—Ashley felt the painful futility of Joanna's existence.

Considering Ashley's love of the French language, it is odd that she did not take advantage of the Montreal location to explore the local culture. Instead she cowered like a trapped animal and seldom left her house unless it was to report to a shoot.

Ashley repeatedly tried to breathe life into the character, but Joanna's emotional development was overly restricted by a psychobabble script that tried to be more than it was capable of and, in doing so, limited options for the actress. In the end, Ashley simply surrendered her own will and allowed Joanna to step into the abyss.

"[Stephan Elliott] is so original," Ashley told Heather Svokos of the *Lexington Herald-Leader.* "The movie is going to look fantastic. The shots blew my mind. I'm going to be glad I'm in it, and I'm going to be proud of the performance, I can already tell, but it was just a weird film-making experience. That is not a movie I would make again."

When production on the film wrapped at sunrise on May 26, Ashley went to her rented house, crawled into the attic for six hours sleep, then caught a flight back to Nashville, where the daffodils and jonquils were in bloom.

Ashley did not have many visitors while she was working in Canada, but one greatly appreciated visit was made by actress Salma Hayek, also in Canada to make a movie. Salma and Ashley had bonded as friends some time before in a Hollywood restaurant, where they had met for lunch. During the course of the meal, Salma spilled wine on her white shirt. Seeing Salma's discomfort, Ashley took a napkin, dabbed it with wine, and stained her own shirt in a show of solidarity. How odd the two of them must have looked to passersby— two striking women with matching wine stains. And what exactly were they laughing so hysterically about?

One of the traveling tricks Ashley has learned while making movies is to take things from home with her. She ships her own sheets, pillows, and quilts to the location and she decorates her hotel room or rental house with things from her farm. "I have an oversize acrylic envelope that I travel with," she told *Us* magazine. "Into it I fit these stuffed animals that my godmother's mother made from fabric scraps, an angel mobile that I hang from the ceiling and packs of flower seeds from the hardware store. I punch holes through their tops and hang them up to make instant flower bouquets."

Sometimes she gets a little too carried away with that entire home-away-from-home concept. Once, while staying in the state suite at the Imperial Hotel in Vienna, she and boyfriend Michael Bolton moved the antique furniture around to give the suite a homier feel, only to be told that they would be switched to other rooms because the Palestinian leader, Yasir Arafat, had arrived at the hotel and needed the suite.

Before going to Montreal, Canada, to film *Eye of the Beholder*, Ashley had an "escape" clause written into her contract that stipulated that she would be able to leave the production site to attend University of Kentucky basketball games if the team made the finals. The University of Kentucky Wildcats did indeed make the 1998 finals. As a result, Ashley shuttled back and forth to the games from Canada, much to the approval of UK fans, for the actress had proved herself to be a very vocal supporter at the games.

"I started being intrigued [with UK basketball] in about the first grade," Ashley explained to *Kentucky Monthly*. "There is a kinship you automatically feel with Kentuckians. I have so deeply bonded in hotel lobbies with total strangers after a Kentucky win. We have something so special in common. Basketball love is a very real thing."

As it happened, the 1998 finals overlapped not only with the production schedule for *Simon Birch* but with that year's Academy Awards ceremony, at which Ashley had agreed to be a presenter. Five days before the awards show, Ashley, wearing no makeup and making no pretense to be glamorous, met with Jeannine Stein, a reporter for the *Los Angeles Times,* at the Peninsula Hotel in Beverly Hills to discuss that year's fashions.

"Couture is a given," Ashley said, responding to questions about the dress she will wear. "I think it's really important to maintain a sense of individuality. It's not to say that when something is popular you avoid it like the plague, but make it your own."

Stein, who had no idea just how strongly Ashley would exert her sense of individuality at the awards show, had no problem understanding why various designers had vied for the opportunity to clothe the actress: "Nary a blemish on that sweet-as-apple-pie face, a figure most women would kill for—what's not to like?"

The night before the awards-show telecast, Ashley went to the tournament game that pitted the University of Kentucky Wildcats against UCLA (the Wildcats won 94 to 68). The next scheduled game for the Wildcats was against Duke University, a longstanding powerhouse in college basketball.

Ashley was a nervous wreck when she showed up at the Shrine Auditorium in Los Angeles. She had skipped the rehearsal the night before so that she could attend the game, and she really was not focusing on the task at hand. When she gets excited about things, she tends to zone out her surroundings. That night as she slipped into a slinky, slit-to-the-crotch Richard Tyler gown, all she could think about was the upcoming basketball game.

When it was her turn to announce an award, she strode out onto the stage, smiling broadly, seemingly unaware of the lower level camera that had drawn a bead on her. Several steps from the podium, her dress billowed briefly, giving the audience a glimpse of a certain shadowy place between her legs. Since it was live television, it could not be edited out for viewers watching the ceremony at home.

Immediately after the ceremonies, Ashley left for the next basketball game, leaving damage control to her publicist, who promptly insisted that Ashley had not been "naked underneath." Asked to explain the use of that phrase—did it refer to body glitter or perfume?—the publicist did not elaborate.

Ashley attended the game, which saw the Wildcats defeat Duke in a close contest (86 to 84), and then move on to oppose Stanford University (Wildcats 86, Stanford 85), before facing off against Utah in the final game of the tournament. To Ashley's delight, the Wildcats defeated Utah 78 to 69, thus taking home the school's seventh NCAA championship.

Later, once the championship dust had settled, Ashley, still pumped over the victory, talked about the dress incident with Heather Svokos of the *Lexington Herald-Leader*. Asked if she was wearing underwear, Ashley said, "Yeah—I'm a pretty simple person, so I shrug and I say, 'Of course I was.' And then I drop out of the conversation. If I wanted to make a big brouhaha, I could point out a myriad of things ranging from, 'That's how Richard Tyler made the dress' to 'That's how he's been showing them for two seasons.'... Everyone can have a fashion victim moment, you know?"

Ashley explained that she had been surrounded by people in the dressing room who cared about her, people whose advice she cherished, and no one had thought the dress might be too revealing. Then she added: "If I had it to do over again, of course we'd stitch the thing down a couple inches. But I don't, and I can't."

That summer Ashley did something she had done only once before. Invited to a charity auction in Nashville with her mother and sister, she took the stage and nervously sang, after four false starts, the gospel standard "Goodnight, The Lord's Comin'."

"It's no longer just the Judds," said Wynonna. "It's the Judds Women."

Among the items sold that day were a crossword puzzle filled out and signed by Barry Manilow ($50), a visit to Naomi's farm ($7,100), and one of Ashley's yellow satin shirts ($140). The event was the unofficial kickoff of Nashville's Fan Fair celebration, which brings about twenty thousand country music fans to town each year to meet and listen to the performances of their favorite stars.

Singing with Naomi and Wynonna was a difficult thing for Ashley to do, for it was about more than singing; it also was about dealing with her feelings of alienation and abandonment, something she had been mastering in recent months.

"At some point everything comes up in your life and you can either layer upon layer your evasion or you can be brought to your knees and deal with it," Ashley told *Interview* magazine several months earlier. "It turns out I had never really grieved for a lot of stuff. It was not ideal growing up, but that's not to say we didn't have love. It's just that having love and having trauma are not mutually exclusive. I saw and felt a lot of things that broke me. And I had never let myself be broken."

The mini-concert was symbolic, of course, but confronting symbols was essential to her recovery from depression. It took courage for her to stand before an audience with her mother and her sister, but it was an outward sign that life was beginning to have meaning to her again.

Ashley also showed courage in another area of her life that summer. She agreed to go to Suriname, in South America, on assignment for *Marie Claire* magazine. The idea was for the actress to live out her college ambition of becoming a Peace Corps volunteer by spending a week in a remote jungle village.

Ashley pursued the assignment with typical zeal.

Asked to rough it without the comforts and convenience of running water and electricity, she never once complained, although she once wanted to when a native girl who was braiding her hair told her that she was a Mariah Carey fan.

"That, I must say, is the only time wished for something I did not have," Ashley later wrote, "namely a cell phone, so I could call Mariah and ask her to sing 'Always Be My Baby' to my new friend."

Ashley adjusted to the challenges that environment presented when it came to maintaining minimum standards of personal hygiene (the only bathing location was in a river infested with piranhas) by recalling childhood visits to Kentucky relatives who preferred their bathroom facilities outside the house.

Constantly on the lookout for hostile wildlife, she never once had to do battle with a python or rabid jungle monkey. "I'm not intimidated by nature and I found nothing fearsome, despite the jungle's reputation," she wrote. "The only encounter I had was being chased back to the hut by a mosquito which seemed to be the size of my hand."

When "The Life I Might Have Lived," the article she wrote for *Marie Claire,* was eventually published in May 1999, Ashley was disappointed by the way it had been edited. She felt the editors had not understood what she was trying to do in the piece and had deleted the best of her writing. Even so, she had nothing bad to say about the editors. On the contrary, she said she understood why they did what they did.

To compensate for that disappointment, she asked University of Kentucky officials if she could deliver her paper, as originally written, in a speech before a scholarly audience. The university thought that would be a fine idea.

When Ashley arrived at the lecture hall, she was flanked by an entourage of reporters, television cameramen, deans, and professors. Wearing a white T-shirt, a yellow-and-red skirt, and Nike Airs, Ashley stood before the audience, her hair pulled back into a ponytail, looking more like a student than a lecturer.

Ashley gave the students a brief history of Suriname and described its geography. She described the people as being "very rhythmical" and she said the women possessed "an incredible knowledge of the jungle's healing plants."

If someone asks you how you slept the previous night, it is a faux pas of the highest order to be flip about it, she explained, for the natives take it very seriously. Another thing to avoid: do not show your thighs because it is considered the most erogenous zone of all. She would have committed those mistakes—and more, she admitted—if Peace Corps volunteers had not briefed her on the customs.

At the end of the lecture, she agreed to take questions.

"Wow, what a sense of power!" she laughed, according to the university's *Arts & Sciences* magazine. "As a kid I used to play teacher with my friends, but I never thought I'd have deans and professors raising their hands to me."

After the lecture she ate pizza with a group of honor students and then participated in a class discussion with a drama class. Were there times in Ashley's life when she wondered what life would have been like if she had pursued an advanced degree in anthropology instead of acting? Certainly. That is why excursions like this were beneficial for her. They helped keep her grounded. She put as much thought and passion into her lecture as she did into a movie role, yet when the presentation was over, there was only applause in the auditorium. No one rose to their feet to review the lecture or toss barbs at her for perceived lapses of judgment or good taste. The lesson was obvious: Movie critics could learn a thing or two from these students.

When *Eye of the Beholder* was released to theaters in January 2000, the reaction of the critics was swift. Everyone liked Ashley and Ewan McGregor, but they hated the film. "Judd is a hot-blooded actress, but the movie is cold and bloodless (aside from all the blood)," wrote Mick LaSalle in the *San Francisco Chronicle*. "*Eye of the Beholder* attempts to convey emotional dislocation and passion at the same time. All we get is distance."

*Entertainment Weekly* critic Ty Burr said he would gladly pay cash money to watch Ashley read hog reports but was at a loss when it came to *Eye of the Beholder*. He concluded the disastrous movie was not the actors' fault. "It's writer-director Stephan Elliott who gets the laurel and hearty handshake for this puppy," he wrote. "Clearly he set out to make a perverse, damned romance about a watcher who loses all perspective. Just as clearly, he fell into the same trap."

Like the other critics, Peter Travers of *Rolling Stone* seemed to almost feel sorry for Ashley. "Joanna's case history is spelled out: She's an orphan who grew up to be victimized by men and even doctors.... Elliott sees this sociopath as an abandoned innocent in need of a cuddle," he wrote. "Judd, often trapped in pop trash...while her fine work in indie films (*Ruby in Paradise, Normal Life*) goes unseen, works hard to reconcile the contradictions in Joanna, but it's an uphill battle."

# Chapter
# Seven

## *Intruder among the Llamas*

*ouble Jeopardy* got off to a ragged start. Veteran Hollywood producer Leonard Goldberg offered the female lead to Ashley Judd and she accepted, but before anything could be put into writing, studio executives objected on the grounds that she did not have the name recognition to ensure the film's box-office success. Some of her movies had done very well with the critics, but others had bombed with both critics and theatergoers.

Goldberg then offered the role to Jodie Foster, who accepted. Ashley took the rejection with good grace but stayed in telephone contact with Goldberg, asking him every two weeks if Foster was still on board. What did she have to lose? She loved the script and just knew it would be a major box-office draw.

Six months into preproduction—and just three months away from filming—Foster informed the studio that she would be unable to do the film. When asked why by executives, she told them that she needed to take some time off (what she did not tell them was that she was pregnant). Goldberg again mentioned Ashley for the role, but studio executives instead offered it to Meg Ryan, who declined. The script then went to Michelle Pfeiffer, who also passed.

Pressed for time, studio executives gave Goldberg a green light for Ashley, but only on the condition that they find a name actor to attach to the film. "We managed to talk Tommy Lee Jones into playing the detective who is chasing her," Goldberg told the *Calgary Sun*. "He was the box-office name the studio needed."

A veteran of more than thirty feature films, including *Men in Black, Batman Forever,* and *The Fugitive*—and not to mention a costarring role in *Lonesome Dove*, one of the most successful miniseries in television history—Tommy Lee Jones was exactly the type of actor needed to star opposite Ashley.

After he played Woodrow F. Call in 1989's *Lonesome Dove*, audiences associated him with that character so much that no matter what roles he subsequently played, the first reaction of the audience was always to think of him as a man who was flawed but determined to do the right thing as he saw it. That was exactly what Goldberg and the studio executives wanted him to be in *Double Jeopardy*.

Jones was also a good match for Ashley. Born in Texas and only eight months younger than Naomi, Jones possessed that same peculiar, Southern-laced irreverence for authority and single-minded dedication to tradition that colored Ashley's viewpoints. At Harvard, where he roomed with future vice president Al Gore, he played offensive guard on the Harvard football team and graduated cum laude with a degree in English literature.

But for a few ironic twists of fate, Jones might have been the perfect father or lover for Ashley; he was psychologically and emotionally more like her than any actor she had ever worked with. Typically, whenever she went out of her way to be nice to him—such as baking him a birthday cake—his response was "thank you ma'am."

Rounding out the cast were Bruce Greenwood, the Canadian actor who played Ashley's real-life stepfather in *Naomi & Wynonna: Love Can Build a Bridge* (this time, he did not play Ashley's stepfather, he played her husband); Annabeth Gish, who played Angie, the devious friend; and Benjamin Weir, who played Matty, her young son.

Bringing that divergent group of people together—and making sense of a flawed script—was director Bruce Beresford, a former film advisor to the Arts Council of Great Britain who is probably best known for his period films and opera productions, though he had several Hollywood successes with movies such as *Driving Miss Daisy, Crimes of the Heart,* and *Tender Mercies.*

Beresford had several surprises working on *Double Jeopardy*, but none compared to the experience of interacting with Ashley. Said Beresford to *Elle* magazine: "Ashley's intensely interesting to watch… she's both well-read and devout, and it's not an affectation." He was further impressed that she gave dinners for the cast and crew and said grace before each meal.

As usual Ashley put up a good front for Beresford and the cast and crew. All of the confusion about whether she would play the female lead in the movie had occurred while she was making *Eye of the Beholder.* When she finished that movie in Montreal, she had only six weeks to spend at her home before flying to Vancouver, British Columbia, to start work on *Double Jeopardy.*

Prior to leaving for Canada again, she rented a five-bedroom house in Vancouver and shipped an assortment of comfort trophies such as quilts and linens from her farmhouse. Still slightly bruised emotionally from filming in Montreal, she asked both Wynonna and Naomi to visit her, though when asked about her mother's presence in the city she laughingly said she was there to massage her feet.

Actually, the trip that Naomi and Wynonna made to Vancouver to visit Ashley was not a sign that Ashley was losing her battle to overcome depression. On the contrary, the fact that she would ask her mother and sister for support during that time is an indication she was overcoming that battle. Emotionally, Ashley was in good shape, despite the career and personal disappointments of the past twelve months. She was even beginning to see her career in a realistic perspective. In an interview with the *Lexington Herald-Leader*, she admitted that her work pace to date had been a bit much. "I don't know how many more movies I'm gonna make," she said. "I don't want to make as many as I have. Like, one a year, maybe. One every two years. Just super-special material I feel compelled to be involved with. Because there's some life to live."

Ashley could afford to slow down somewhat. She was now earning one million dollars per film. The only thing that could entice her to rev up her schedule would be more money—and never in her wildest dreams did she think that would happen.

*Double Jeopardy* begins with Ashley talking to her four-year-old son (Benjamin Weir) about sailing. It is the great passion of her life. By the time the day ends she is presented with a sailboat by her husband (Bruce Greenwood). That night, they leave their son with a sitter and take the boat out into the sound. They make love that night (Ashley's customary nude scene), but when she awakens, there is blood on the bed and her husband is gone. She finds more blood on the deck and picks up a bloody knife just as a Coast Guard ship pulls up alongside.

Ashley is charged with murdering her husband. At the trial, the prosecutor plays a tape of Greenwood's call for help. He said he had been stabbed. It was compelling evidence and Ashley was convicted and taken off to prison. Before leaving, she asks her best friend (Annabeth Gish) to keep her son.

At the prison, Ashley becomes a subject of debate among the other inmates. They look at her and wonder how long she will make it before cracking. Someone bets five cartoons of cigarettes that she will kill herself inside of six months.

At first, Gish brings Weir by to visit on a regular basis. Then the visits stop and she no longer hears from her or her son. Finally, Ashley tracks her to San Francisco (she has moved there from

Washington). She puts Weir on the phone. While Ashley is talking to him, the door opens and he screams out "Daddy!" The telephone disconnects.

It is a turning point for Ashley. She returns to the prison dorm with the certain knowledge that she has been set up for murder. A disbarred prison lawyer tells her about double jeopardy. She tells her that she can hunt him down when she gets out and legally kill him: "You can walk right up to him in Times Square and pull the fuckin' trigger and there's nothing anybody can do about it."

(That is not exactly true. The law says you cannot be tried twice for the same crime in the same jurisdiction; if you go to another jurisdiction to kill someone you were convicted of killing elsewhere, you could be tried a second time).

Faced with the truth, Ashley works out in the gym and runs every day, preparing herself physically for the day she is released from prison. After six years she is granted parole and sent to a halfway house managed by Tommy Lee Jones. He is a hard-nose, no-nonsense parole officer and it is clear from the moment they meet that they are destined to clash.

Desperate to find her son, Ashley breaks into the school where Gish last worked to see if she left a forwarding address. She finds none, but she does obtain her social security number, a piece of information that she knows can be used to locate her. Before she can make her escape from the school, she is captured by police. Jones picks her up to take her back to the halfway house. He is incredulous that she would risk returning to prison.

"You cannot know what it is like to sit in prison for six years and think of nothing else in the world but your son," Ashley says. "Did I make the right choice? You asked the wrong question....I didn't have a choice." It is Ashley's best speech in the film, but it has an odd sound quality to it, as if it were dubbed.

While they are on a ferry, Ashley drives the car off into the water and swims to shore. Free at last, she begins her search for her son. When she arrives at Gish's last address, she learns that she has died in a suspicious accident. A neighbor tells her that Greenwood took the boy and moved away. She tracks Greenwood to New Orleans and confronts him at a bachelor's auction. It is Ashley's best scene in the movie.

They agree to meet in a cemetery so that Ashley can get her son back. Instead, she is knocked unconscious and dumped into an occupied coffin inside a tomb. When she awakens, she sees a corpse lying next to her. The remainder of the movie deals with her escape from the tomb and her final confrontation with Greenwood—and, of course, her reconciliation with her parole officer and her son.

*Double Jeopardy* proved to be a very physical film. Ashley insisted on doing most of her own stunts, including the one in which she is trapped inside a submerged car. Part of it was filmed in a water tank, but other parts were shot in the ocean. Beresford was generally cooperative with her, but when it came time to shoot a scene in which Ashley's character jumps from the roof of a building, he shot it with a stunt double while Ashley was at lunch. The stunt she enjoyed the most about, she later joked, was one in which she got to punch Jones.

The only scene in the movie that really got to Ashley was the one where she was placed inside the coffin. "I cried all day when I did that," she told the *Toronto Sun.*" It really upset me. I think it was because it was coming to the end of the movie, and we'd already said goodbye to everybody. And there was something about lying still for twelve hours that promoted having thoughts about my own mortality."

During filming, Ashley was interviewed for *Playboy* magazine by Robert Crane, who described her as "fearless" and "drop-dead gorgeous." She invited Crane to the movie set for the interview and talked to him between scenes.

At one point, Ashley was asked to change pants for the next scene. Instead of going to a dressing room, she dropped her pants right there on the set in front of Crane and the crew and slipped on another pair. Not surprisingly, Crane asked her what she had against wearing underwear. She told him that she thought underwear was uncomfortable, to which he asked, "Aren't you putting underwear workers out of a job?"

"It's also affecting the need for laundry detergent," she answered good-naturedly. "My mother instigated all of this....She happened to remark in public that I don't wear underwear, and it's followed me ever since. I'd like for it to go away."

Was Ashley wearing panties when she changed trousers? Crane didn't say.

After wrapping up the film, Ashley returned to her Tennessee farmhouse to rest and recharge her emotional batteries. By September 1999, her mood was bright and sunny. September was always nice in Leiper's Fork. It was still hot, but not the stifling kind that took your breath away. Fall was on the way, and that was the best season of all in that part of Tennessee.

When *Double Jeopardy* was released on September 21, it grossed over twenty-three million dollars the first week, making it the number-one movie in the nation. By February it would net over 115 million dollars. Ashley became an "overnight" box-office sensation. Although the big movie she had dreamed about since the days of *Ruby in Paradise* had become a reality for her, she continued to tell reporters that her other movies were "gems" to her if no one else. Actually, the more people talked about the success of *Double Jeopardy*, the less she was able to enjoy it, because it seemed to suggest that her prior body of work was not important, and she did not feel that way.

Not surprisingly, movie critics pounced on *Double Jeopardy*. Writing in the *Chicago Sun-Times*, Roger Ebert, normally a fan of Ashley's work, was critical of the film. "[It is] not a successful thriller," he said. "This movie was made primarily in the hopes that it would gross millions and millions of dollars, which probably explains most of the things that are wrong with it."

Walter Addiego of the *San Francisco Examiner* thought it was a "good-but-not-great melodrama" that had its share of "snappy" action scenes. About Ashley, he wrote: "[She] does a nice take on the avenging angel (yes, she says she's just after her son, but you can smell payback in the air): She's crafty and hardy and intent on redressing the wrong done her, but maintains her dignity and sense of humor."

Writing for *Entertainment Weekly*, Ty Burr good-naturedly chastised other critics for dumping on the movie because it "it didn't stop to make sense on the way to the bank." If the film had been shot in 1949 with Ida Lupino, he observed, the same "biscotti-munching" critics would be praising it as an "unsung feminist film noir."

Ashley was so interested in the reaction of moviegoers that she crept into the back of a theater that offered audiences an early screening. "It played like a rock concert," she told the *Lexington Herald-Leader*. "It was almost an audience participation, like I remember *Jaws* being when I saw it in the third grade. I've enjoyed the critical success with some of my movies, but to have a really entertaining audience-pleaser was a different kind of pleasure."

September 27, 1999, was an especially nice day for Ashley, for she had a houseguest. Earlier in the year, at a friend's wedding reception, she had met a handsome Scottish race-car driver named Dario Franchitti. He was not terribly well known, but his star was on the rise (the previous year, he had placed second on the Championship Auto Racing Teams' Indy circuit). They hit it off right away and started going out (secretly, of course). By September they were inseparable.

That afternoon, Ashley and Dario were in the kitchen washing and drying dishes, the very picture of domesticity. Across the road was a herd of llamas. In the field next to the farmhouse was a pasture, specked with wildflowers, that seemed to stretch for miles. On the other side of the house was a stand of timber inhabited by songbirds and wild squirrels.

Ashley felt safer at her farmhouse than at any other place on earth. A paved road ran past her house, but there was seldom any traffic on it. Just about the only people who traveled it were families that lived on the other side of the Judd farm.

She had come to think of the farm as a compound. "I do think of it that way sometimes," she told the *Toronto Sun*. "And I think that oftentimes the way I appreciate it is rooted in fear. No, not fear of losing it all. Fear of recognition, fear of fans, fear of intrusiveness. The reason that it's become so sacred to me now is because it protects me and buffers me against what you-all call celebrity."

None of that went through her mind while she and Dario washed dishes. She only thought about her safety when she was away from the farm, out in the world of big cities and suspicious strangers. That is why, when she heard a knock at the front door, she yelled instructions for the caller to let himself into the house. She assumed it was one of the workmen who had been making repairs around the house.

After she dried her hands, wearing shorts and a T-shirt, she went into the front room. To her surprise, she was confronted by Guy Paul Dukes, a thirty-two-year-old Kentucky man who previously had been spotted watching her house. She had filed a police complaint against him and obtained a restraining order to keep him away from her property. Apparently he did not think Ashley would recognize him, for he showed her a police badge and told her he had just "stopped by."

Ashley insisted that he leave her house. By that time, Dario entered the room and escorted the man out the door. Then he wrote down the man's license plate number and gave it to Ashley. When Dukes drove away, Dario, a driver IMG Motorsports has called "one of the best drivers in the world," chased after him in one of Ashley's cars, staying in touch with her on a cell phone. Meanwhile, Ashley called the police.

Working together, Ashley and Dario were able to give police enough information to apprehend Dukes in nearby Franklin. He was arrested and taken to the criminal justice center, where he was booked on charges of criminal trespass and criminal impersonation of a police officer.

Ten minutes after the chase began, Williamson County deputy sheriff Grant Benedict arrived at Ashley's farmhouse. "She was upset and angry," he later recalled. "Angry that he would show up the way he did, because he knew he was not supposed to be there. She was agitated, but she wasn't terrorized."

*Double Jeopardy* had just been released and Benedict had seen the movie in a local theater. In a community filled with country music superstars, Ashley had a different kid of celebrity: she was a motion picture star, and that carried more weight. As Benedict took down information about the incident, he noticed that Ashley had a telephone in each hand and managed to talk to him while carrying on two other conversations.

"She was very pleasant and actually had a good attitude," he says. "She was adamant that she had a private life and he was to stay away from it."

After the interview, Ashley went to the criminal justice center and filled out the paperwork for a warrant against Dukes. Three days later, at a bail bond hearing, his bail was set at fifty thousand dollars. Dukes told court officials that he was a resident of Louisville, Kentucky, where he worked for a security service earning $6.75 an hour. Asked if he owned any property, he answered no, except for a car valued at $6,800.

Based on that information, Dukes was assigned a court-appointed attorney, who worked out a plea-bargain deal with the prosecutor. Dukes waived his rights to a trial by jury and pleaded guilty to the charges of criminal impersonation and stalking. He was sentenced to six months in the workhouse on the criminal impersonation charge and eleven months, twenty-nine days on the stalking charge. Both sentences were suspended by the judge, who placed him on probation for eleven months and twenty-nine days and ordered him to go no closer than one hundred feet to Ashley and her residence. Said the judge: "Once this order is entered, you are to have no contact, you are not to follow, stalk or harass Miss Judd again." To which, Dukes responded: "It won't happen again."

In the weeks following the release of *Double Jeopardy*, Ashley found herself in the odd position of defending violence in films. She did defend the film, although she did have problems with the poster, which proclaimed, "Murder isn't always a crime."

Of course, it is always a crime, she said, explaining to reporters, somewhat defensively, that she felt the poster was trying to make a legal point about an important provision of the Constitution. When questioned about Hollywood's right to make violent movies, she was unwavering. "To me, it's about personal accountability," she told *EW Daily*. "I don't think you can legislate content. The point where that ends and other kinds of censorship begins is way too porous."

At age thirty-one, Ashley's concept of the Constitution was still evolving, but it stood in stark contrast to the views of her mother. Shortly after the Judds became a successful recording act, a reporter at a Nashville newspaper began a biography about the duo. In her autobiography, Naomi proudly wrote that she asked friends and relatives not to talk to the reporter. It was an odd admission.

While everyone has the right not to do an interview—just as radio program directors have the right not to play records and movie critics have the right not to review movies—the act of asking someone not to do an interview is tantamount to pressuring a program director not to play a song or influencing a movie critic not to review a movie. It can be construed as racketeering if favors are offered in exchange for inaction or silence.

To Ashley's credit, I found no evidence that she asked friends or associates not to talk to me in the preparation of this book, but that does not mean that she is entirely at ease with the First Amendment. On the contrary, questions about her family life often send her into either depression or her own peculiar brand of quiet rage. Because of her upbringing, she has tried to stake out a portion of her private life that she can feel proud of, but that is difficult when reporters are constantly asking her questions about it.

When Ashley gets sore at the press, it has more to do with the answers than the questions. She does not like to talk about her romantic relationships because so many of them have failed and it pains her to be reminded of that. She does not like questions about her family life for much the same reasons. How can she repair the damage of her childhood if strangers are always asking her questions about it?

The media present quite a quandary to the Judds. They know they can have no success without it, yet they resent the price they must pay to have the sort of media coverage that will ensure them success. Their philosophy can best be expressed by a reworking of a popular phrase—The press: you can't live with it, and you can't live without it.

That point was made evident after the release of *Double Jeopardy*, when Naomi spoke to *USA Today* about her support of an organization called Appeal to Hollywood, a right-wing pressure group whose goal is to pressure Hollywood filmmakers into limiting the use of sex and violence in the media. While explaining her support of the group, Naomi told the reporter that she had asked Ashley not to star in *Norma Jean and Marilyn* because "Pop and I wouldn't watch it."

Naomi went on to tell the reporter positive things about Ashley's career, but editors included only those comments that addressed the issue at hand—and that was the issue of censorship. When the article was published, Naomi was horrified that Ashley would think she said only negative things about her career. She called Ashley and told her she intended to complain to the editor about the way her comments were edited.

Surprisingly, Ashley did not overreact. That may have been because she had other things on her mind. In a September interview with Luaine Lee of the Scripps Howard News Service, done several days before the stalker incident, she broke her own rule and talked about her personal life, explaining that a relationship she had the previous year had taught her a valuable lesson: "It's amazing how not being with someone is actually the act that completes you." In spite of that failed relationship, she admitted, "the ideal of marriage" was "highly desirable."

During an October interview with Douglas J. Rowe of the Associated Press, Ashley sometimes had tears in her eyes. It had only been two weeks since the stalker incident at her farmhouse and she was still emotional about it. Plus, she was exhausted by the media blitz. She complained to Rowe about the personal questions she was always being asked by interviewers. "I don't mean just the messes," she said. "I even said to Mom...'You know, let's not sing our special songs. Because that's our stuff. And if you don't protect yourself you're not going to have anything left....I would much prefer to have a very private and very separate life from my work."

A few weeks after that interview, Ashley went to Queensland, Australia, to watch Dario race. When a photographer attempted to get a photograph of her in the pits, she got into a scuffle with him, according to the *Scottish Daily Record*, which reported that she hurt her ankle while pushing away the photographer and had to be carried out of the pit by one of Dario's crew members.

Who could blame her? In recent weeks, her privacy had been invaded by a stalker, her mother had unintentionally trashed her movie career in the press, and reviewers of *Double Jeopardy* had either belittled her previous movies while praising the thriller or they had cut the thriller to shreds while praising her earlier movies. The photographer just picked the wrong day to pursue Ashley.

Getting physical with a photographer is not the recommended way to express a grievance, but Ashley's therapist must have been thrilled because it indicated that she was now expressing her anger and not internalizing it as depression.

The relationship between Ashley and Wynonna is like a see-saw. When one is up, the other is down—and vice versa. That is not necessarily a bad thing. Just as both sisters had to learn how to deal with their mother, so did they have to learn how to deal with each other. By 1999, they had the routine down pat. It was the duty of the sister on the "top" to give comfort to the sister on the "bottom." Usually, those positions would be held for days or weeks at a time, but sometimes the two sisters could reverse positions several times in a single day. No big deal: it was all part of being a Judd.

Bad things had happened to Ashley in 1999, to be sure, but for the most part she was on the upswing. She was in love. *Double Jeopardy* was a box-office hit. When people heard the word Judd, they thought of Ashley, not Naomi or Wynonna. Ashley was in the driver's seat of the Juddmobile—and she relished that role.

Life for Wynonna was just the opposite. Her marriage to Arch Kelley fell apart in 1999 and ended in divorce. Terms of the divorce were kept secret, but word leaked out to the *Nashville Tennessean* and the *Star* that Wynonna paid Kelley $250,000 and retained "primary custody" of their two children. Angered by the publicity, Wynonna dragged Kelley back into court, charging that he had violated their agreement by selling his story to the *Star*.

The presiding judge agreed with Wynonna and sent Kelley to jail for fifty days after finding him guilty of criminal contempt. In sentencing him, the judge cited the publication of his comments in the *Nashville Tennessean* and the *Star*. Kelley posted bond and was released after several hours in jail; then he appealed to the State Court of Appeals and won a temporary stay in the sentence.

When the case finally made its way back to the judge's courtroom, both Kelley and the judge were ready to cut a deal. Kelley pleaded no contest to the contempt charge and agreed to drop his appeal. In return, the judge agreed to suspend the fifty day sentence with the understanding that it would be reinstated if Kelley did not return the money paid to him by the *Star*. In addition, Kelley was ordered not to discuss any of the couple's legal disagreements with the children until they both reached age eighteen.

It was a nasty public fight, exactly the sort of thing Wynonna hoped to avoid by having a secrecy clause in the divorce agreement, but like most things that send Judd adrenaline pumping, it, too, subsided in time.

Throughout it all, Wynonna was working on a new album. Titled *New Day Dawning*, it was mostly a collection of cover material, such as the Fabulous Thunderbirds' "Tuff Enuff," Joni Mitchell's "Help Me," and Macy Gray's "I Can't Wait to Meetchu." Four songs on the album were recorded with Naomi, an unfortunate resurrection of the Judds. Reviewing the album for *Entertainment Weekly*, Alanna Nash wrote: "Wynonna says she's not as interested in paving a new road as she is in forging a connection. That's fine for sales. But it also makes [it] merely a good album from an artist capable of greatness."

Wynonna had sold about nine million albums as a solo artist, but most of those had been for her first two albums. Sales had tapered off in recent years to the point where Curb and MCA Records were unable to reach an agreement to continue the contract. Wynonna moved over to Mercury Records, the home of Shania Twain, in the hope of finding an older, more-mature market for her records.

Over the past twenty years, Mercury Records has carved a niche for itself with older record buyers by signing successful artists who have been unable to hold onto the youth market that initially made them famous. Johnny Cash is an example. He was dropped by CBS Records when sales plummeted. He moved over to Mercury and recorded several successful albums before giving up on Nashville entirely and moving on to a West Coast record company.

At thirty-six—and still overweight—Wynonna had no hope of ever again capturing the youth market. She had mixed feelings about working with her mother again, but the economic reality was that Naomi had an older fan base and that was where Wynonna was headed with her material. The songs Wynonna recorded with Naomi were placed on the album for a reason. They planned a Judds reunion tour in the year 2000. The album was viewed as a promotional tool for the concert tour and vice versa.

Ever practical, Wynonna and Naomi gave a New Year's Eve reunion concert in Phoenix, Arizona, before proceeding with plans for an all-out Judds tour in the spring. More than twelve thousand tickets were sold for the concert, making it almost a sellout.

Because it had been eight years since the Judds performed together, the *Nashville Tennessean* sent music writer Tom Roland to Phoenix to cover the concert for local readers. "In many ways, it represented a new Judds," he wrote, explaining that the new harmonies were "even smoother than in the past."

As an added attraction, Ashley was offered up to the audience as the emcee. In typical fashion, she injected as much drama into the event as possible, saying it represented a new chapter in the Judds's story of "struggle, loss, triumph, and redemption."

When the Judds walked out on stage and sang the first song, "Love Can Build a Bridge," the audience gave them two standing ovations. That level of enthusiasm continued throughout the show, and when it was over individual audience members told reporters that they hoped the reunion would be permanent.

When the tour began in February, it was billed as the Power to Change tour. More than twenty cities were booked for the Kmart-sponsored tour, including Chicago, Detroit, Atlanta, and Minneapolis. "We partnered with Kmart because it fits what we stand for," Naomi said in a press release. "They understand women and their life challenges, and are all about 'changing for the better'…and we're the poster children for change." To which Wynonna added: Fame has given us a voice, but we're ordinary people that extraordinary things have happened to. We've had lots of hard times but look what's happened to the three Judd women: That is the power to change."

"The three Judd women"—that phrase was the difference this time around for the Judds. There were three Judd women when the duo first went out on the road fifteen years ago, but Ashley was never acknowledged. This time, it was the actress daughter who was the brightest star. During the tour, reporters asked all the expected questions about the Judds—"how does it feel to be back together again?"—but the most pertinent questions always seemed to center around Ashley.

When *Tulsa World* reporter John Wolley interviewed Naomi prior to the Judds' concert in that city, he asked about Ashley. Would she be included as she was at the performance in Phoenix? "That was a special thing," Naomi said. "She's not going to be with us all the time. In fact, she's getting ready to do two more movies right now. But I do have a bunk saved for her on my bus, and it's possible that she could be with us in Tulsa. She'll be here whenever her schedule allows."

As the tour entered the month of March, Naomi began a countdown to the final show. Eleven shows left—ten, nine, eight…. She dreaded the end of the tour, for it had given her new life, but she saw things in Wynonna's face that let her know that it would have to end.

"The only time we came close to talking about [the future] was the second night of the tour," Naomi told Robert Hilburn of the *Los*

*Angeles Times."* We were in our hotel bathrooms and I said, 'OK, kiddo, tell Mama what's on your mind.' I could see that something was troubling her, but she couldn't bring herself to say it because of her loyalty, so I had to say what I knew she was thinking. I said, 'You are afraid you are going to get lost in this, aren't you?' And the tears started rolling down her cheeks."

Actually, there had been a bit of role reversal for the tour. This time it was Wynonna who was the mother figure; she constantly reminded Naomi to rest and take care of herself. One thing that surprised Wynonna was the pride she felt watching her mother on stage. Naomi did things with the audience that Wynonna would never be able to do. Wynonna attributed it to Naomi's "prissy butt" attitude. Seeing Naomi strut about the stage grated against Wynonna's nerves and soothed her at the same time. That did not make sense to her, that she could possess negative and positive feelings at the same instant, but it was the nature of her relationship with her mother.

When the tour finally ended, mother and daughter returned to their farms near Nashville and took stock of their lives. Maybe they would tour again as the Judds. Then again, maybe they would never tour again as the Judds. Naomi threw herself into a weekly radio program that she broadcast from her farm.

That summer, Wynonna decided to sell her home and move into another home nearby. She took stock of her life and went through her closets and storage bins looking for items to sell at a yard sale. "Wynonna Judd's Moving Sale," read the advertisement. "Antiques, silver, crystal, furniture, clothing, kitchen items, memorabilia, Christmas items, toys and much more!"

The three-day sale began on August 25, 2000, and was held at Wynonna's house. After all those years of protesting her lack of privacy, she held a public sale at her house and invited the entire world. It was a bizarre event, even by Judd standards.

Among the items offered for sale were a $35,000 1949 Ford pickup, an $18,000 Harley-Davidson motorcycle, "tons" of shoes, unopened *Buns of Steel* videos, boxes of false eyelashes, Judd photos and posters, a black leather jacket priced at $850, and a pink, faux-fur coat priced at $100. More than one thousand people showed up for the sale and, while the big-ticket items did not sell, the tables were raked bare by fans hoping for a piece of the Wy.

Wynonna was there, but she never left the house. Instead, she perched in a window and watched, keeping in touch with the sale workers via two-way radio (shades of the window imagery in the movie *Psycho*).

"I should have had a lemonade stand, as well," she told the *Nashville Tennessean*. "When you have one thousand people come to your yard sale, that's not normal, but I've never been anyway, so I feel we're all even. I've got a lot of stuff and a lot of friends. I'm grateful today." Wynonna said she planned to spend the money on her new house.

Psychologically, the yard sale raised interesting questions. Was Wynonna selling off those artifacts that she associated with the Judds? Was she ready to make a clean break from her mother? Creatively, did she feel weighted down by the past?

Not present at the yard sale was Ashley. It was unusual for her to miss a sisterly function, but this one was so far off the Judd radar that she pretended it never happened. That is a shame, for the sight of Ashley hawking shoes and photographs, no doubt with the grace and poise of a *Price Is Right* model, would have been something to witness.

Leaving the yard sale, one music fan gushed that she had purchased Wynonna's pajamas and fully intended to sleep in them.

In late December 1999, Ashley and Dario decided to get married. But they kept their engagement a secret until after Naomi and Wynonna completed their tour. Ashley was as surprised as anyone that she had fallen in love with Dario. She had always thought that race-car drivers were macho exhibitionists like professional jocks. That was not the case with Dario. He was quiet and reflective, and attentive to her needs—just the opposite of the arty crowd to which she always had been drawn to find a mate.

Whenever she went to races with him—and that was often in late 1999 and early 2000—she was amazed at the way racing fans cheered for him. Instead of hearing "Ashley, give me a big smile" she heard cries of "Dario! Dario! Dario!" She found the spectacle riveting, especially with the roar of engines in the background.

Ashley was so taken with the racing atmosphere that she asked Dario to give her some pointers so that she could race in celebrity competitions. It was at one of the celebrity races in which she was driving that Dario's jeweler showed up with a ring he had found for the couple. It had taken him four months to find the right ring: It was made of 150 mico-pavé diamonds. There was no question that Dario could afford it. His earnings that year, according to *Talk* magazine, totaled a cool $3.6 million.

Ashley was so excited about the ring that she could barely contain herself. Soon she and Dario were rolling around on the grass like a couple of pups. Later, when she went to a script reading for a new movie, she was still beaming with joy. "She was on cloud nine," actor Hugh Jackman told *McCall's* magazine. "She was telling everyone, 'Oh, my God! Look at it!'"

Being in love was not a new experience for Ashley, but it was the first time she felt she would not be disappointed. In the past, her work served as a substitute for romance. Now it was the crowning glory. As a result, she attacked her work with a new vigor and optimism.

Ashley's next project was a public television production of Arthur Miller's *The Ryan Interview*. She played the part of Fredricka Rose, a big-city newspaper reporter sent to write a puff piece about a centenarian named Bob Ryan (played by veteran actor Eddie Bracken). She is unhappy about the assignment since she thinks her time could be better spent elsewhere, but she does her best to charm the old man into telling her what she thinks she needs for the article. The more Ryan speaks, the more interested she becomes in his stories. By the time the interview ends, the old man has expanded her humanity and transformed her life.

The half-hour-long drama was shot in high-definition video by Kentucky Educational Television and supplemented with a documentary featuring Arthur Miller speaking about America's treatment of the elderly. The audience was reminded to pay closer attention to older citizens.

Ashley accepted the role because the program was produced in Lexington, Kentucky, and she felt a loyalty to her home state, but the larger issue of the plight of senior citizens was one that was important to her. Although her emotions and opinions changed frequently, the one thing that seemed never to change was her social consciousness. Regardless of the heights and deep valleys of her life and career, Ashley could always be counted on to have a heart. It is her most endearing—and enduring—quality.

In June 2000, Ashley flew to Austin, Texas, and checked into the Four Seasons Hotel to start work on her next feature film project, *Where the Heart Is*. It is not well known outside the film industry, but in recent years Austin and the surrounding area have become a choice location for filmmakers. That year alone, according to the Austin Film Office, Hollywood did $120 million worth of business with the city. Austin-made films included *Spy Kids*, *Miss Congeniality*, *The Great Waldo Pepper*, and *The Getaway*.

*Where the Heart Is* was adapted from the Oprah Winfrey–sanctioned novel of the same name by Billie Letts. It is about a seventeen-year-old pregnant girl from Tennessee, Novalee Nation, who sets out for the bright lights of California and somehow gets diverted to Oklahoma, where she discovers her talents and her true destiny after giving birth to her child in the local Wal-Mart.

Ashley plays the part of Lexie Coop, a nurse with four children who befriends Novalee Nation after she has her baby. It was a supporting role (at thirty-two, she was too old for the starring role), but Ashley took it because she liked the script. Chosen for the part of Novalee was Natalie Portman, a young actress with whom she shared film credits in *Heat* (they had no scenes together).

At nineteen, Portman was considered the hottest up-and-coming actress on the scene, following scene-stealing roles in *The Professional, Beautiful Girls, Anywhere But Here,* and *Star Wars: Episode I—The Phantom Menace,* in which she played Queen Amidala. Despite the buzz going around about her celebrity, there were real questions about her involvement in *Where the Heart Is.*

The role called for a Southern accent. Would the Israeli-born and New York-raised actress be able to bring it off? There were questions about her ability to carry a movie as the star. As a supporting actress, she had a reputation as a scene-stealer. Would she be able to hold her own with a veteran cast of supporting actors? Then there was the matter of her personality. The actor she would be required to relate to the most was Ashley Judd. On the surface, at least, they appeared to be totally different types. Would there be sparks or chemistry between the two women?

Complicating all of the above was the fact that the director, Matt Williams II, had never before directed a motion picture. His career had consisted entirely of television work. As a producer and writer for shows such as *Roseanne, Home Improvement,* and *Thunder Alley,* he had built up a glowing reputation for work on the small screen. Would those skills as a producer and a writer transfer to the big screen? Just as important, would he be able to control a cast of veteran actors that included, in addition to Ashley and Portman, Stockard Channing, Joan Cusack, and Sally Field? These were five very strong-willed women, each of whom had opinions about how a movie should be made.

As important as those questions were, they all took a back seat to the first obstacle that greeted the cast and crew when they arrived in Austin—the intense heat. June and July can be brutal in Texas, especially for people not accustomed to ninety-degree-plus heat. The hotel was air-conditioned, of course, as were the vans that transported them to the various locations, but the comfort usually ended there.

Most of the scenes were shot in Round Rock, which is about twenty miles north of Austin, and in Lockhart, which is about thirty miles south of Austin. In the old days, the two towns were known mostly for their contribution to the Chisholm Trail, a route used by cattle ranchers to movie their herds north into Kansas. Today, Lockhart, with a population of twelve thousand, and Round Rock, with a population of sixty thousand, are best known for the ways in which they have adapted to modern life.

Lockhart promotes itself as the Barbecue Capital of Texas, thanks to the Texas legislature, which once passed a resolution so-naming the city. It is also known as a filmmaking center, primarily because of the many movies made there, including *Texas Justice* and *Honeysuckle Rose*.

One of Lockhart's attractions is its old-fashioned courthouse and town square. "One of the reasons the film industry likes to come here is because they can film with relative ease," said Lockhart mayor Ray Sanders. "We make it easy for them to do so. The townspeople who do go out and watch the film [being made] are not intrusive."

Director Matt Williams used the Wal-Mart stores in both Lockhart and Round Rock in the film, and he used the Lockhart town square for several scenes. "I went down and watched a couple of shootings," says Mayor Sanders. "I was amazed to see how they converted, in July, part of the square into a Christmas tree lot, and how they made the snow on the ground with cotton, and [how they] wet down the streets to get the reflection while they were shooting. It was just amazing."

Lockhart resident Beverly Annas, an extra in several scenes, enjoyed watching Ashley and Natalie interact, although she was unfamiliar with Natalie's work. While the crew set up the scenes, Annas noticed that Ashley and Natalie usually stood together and talked, keeping their distance from the extras and crew. At one point, Natalie left to make a telephone call and Ashley picked up a magazine and thumbed through it.

"The only time I was close to [Natalie] was in the grocery store, because we were standing at one of the checkout lines," said Annas. "I didn't talk to her. They tell us not to talk to the stars. I thought she was cute."

One of the high points for Mayor Sanders occurred when Ashley walked past him on the set. He didn't speak to her or otherwise bring attention to himself because that would have broken an unwritten rule. "Most of the folks like to glance at them, but they don't interfere in any way," he said. "I would certainly like to meet the stars, and if that should happen it would be great....The film companies have been excellent. They have no qualms letting our folks go down and view the scenes as they shoot them."

One of the scenes that interested Annas was the one in which Natalie gives birth to her baby inside the local Wal-Mart. Moviegoers saw sheets of rain pounding against the store's windows, but she saw a water truck spraying water against the windows. Said Annas, a second grade teacher when she is not working as an extra: "One of the reasons I enjoy being an extra is because I find all the behind-the-scenes stuff very interesting. I could just sit for hours and watch them set up scenes."

As *Where the Heart Is* begins, Natalie, who is obviously pregnant, and her boyfriend, played by Dylan Bruno, are saying goodbye to family and friends at their mobile home in Tennessee. They are on their way to the promised land of Bakersfield, California. Because Natalie has "never lived anyplace that didn't have wheels under it," she hopes to find a house that has a view of the Pacific Ocean.

As they drive through Sequoyah, Oklahoma, Natalie asks Dylan to stop at the local Wal-Mart so that she can go to the bathroom. After taking care of business in the Wal-Mart, she returns to the parking lot, only to discover that Dylan has abandoned her. On the spot where the car was parked, she finds her only worldly possession, a camera.

Hopeful that he will return for her, she waits for him outside the store. It is at this point that she meets Sister Husband, the character played by Stockard Channing. Since she is employed at the town's official greeter, she presents Natalie with an assortment of gifts and coupons, and a small buckeye tree potted in a paint can.

By the end of the day, when it is apparent that Dylan is not going to return, Natalie sets up house in the Wal-Mart, surreptitiously living in the store while she figures out what to do next. One day, while living in the Wal-Mart, Natalie goes to the local library to find a book that will give her tips on how to care for her buckeye tree. There she meets the librarian, played by James Fain. He falls in love with her on the spot.

When Natalie finally goes in labor, it is Fain who leaps through the front window of the Wal-Mart to deliver the baby. The following morning, when Natalie awakens, she is in the hospital being cared for by Ashley's character, Lexie Coop. Ashley comforts her, tries to answer her questions, and brings her baby to her.

"Am I in trouble?" asks Natalie.

"What for?" responds Ashley.

"For living in the Wal-Mart."

Soon Ashley and Natalie are best friends. Since the biggest task facing both women is determining exactly how they fit into the overall scheme of things in the universe, it is a friendship based on mutual support and understanding

Ashley's best scene occurs when she goes to Natalie for help after being beaten by her boyfriend, whom she caught in the act of molesting her children. She moves in with Natalie until she is able to get back on her feet.

One night, as they sit out on the front steps, Ashley opens up to her. Natalie asks her if she is all right. Ashley says no and they hold hands. During a three-minute monologue, Ashley recounts the events of the night she was beaten.

"How do men like that find my kids?" Ashley asked. "How did he know he could do such a thing to us? He had to be looking. He was looking for women like me who are alone with children, women who are stupid and they [the children] saw through him. They could tell he was evil. All I saw was a Buick."

It was a powerful scene in which Ashley paced her emotions with dazzling skill. It was Ashley at her best, in the driver's seat of her favorite vehicle—a monologue. She was so convincing, in fact, that Natalie was momentarily mesmerized by Ashley's delivery. "She's the best actress I've ever seen up close," Natalie told the *Nashville Tennessean.* During that scene, she found herself "just watching her work. I had to keep reminding myself that I was supposed to be in the scene as well."

The day after that scene was filmed, Ashley and Natalie went to a movie theater to see Portman's new film, *Anywhere But Here.* It is about a mother, played by Susan Sarandon, who uproots her teenage daughter and takes her on the road with her to chase after a dream. Ashley sobbed all through the movie.

When Ashley and Natalie first arrived on the set, director Matt Williams saw a problem right away. The two women looked too much alike to play the roles of friends. They looked more like sisters. Williams solved that problem by asking Ashley to dye her hair blond. There were other problems. Ashley has a more voluptuous figure than Natalie and she is much taller. Natalie knew she would have to wear a prosthetic device beneath her clothing to make her look pregnant, but she was surprised that Williams asked her to wear padding in her bra to make her breasts look larger.

Natalie thought that was hilarious. Once, while being interviewed by *Mademoiselle*, she reached into her bra and yanked out the fake breasts to show to her interviewer. "I'm not waif-thin, but I'm small, so they make me wear fake boobs," she told the interviewer. "Otherwise they say I look boyish."

With the Texas heat sizzling, Ashley felt sorry for Natalie wearing all that padding, so she showed her how to put an icepack between the prosthetic device and her stomach. It was their little secret. The heat remained a problem throughout the shooting, especially when they were required to wear winter coats for a Christmas scene, but Ashley and Natalie, packing ice the way gangsters pack heat, remained cool and calm at all times, only adding to their images as unflappable babes.

Another problem Natalie encountered involved the infant used in the movie. An only child, there were no younger siblings in her family, so she never learned how to hold infants. To remedy that, Williams hired a nurse to stay on the set at all times, so that she would be there to give tips to Natalie about the infant.

Natalie very much got into the role on a pregnant teen. In her off-hours, she slipped into her padding and went to Wal-Mart and walked among the store's regular customers, none of whom recognized her (the store made that possible by taking down *Star Wars* posters that bore Natalie's likeness). She wanted to find out how the customers would react to a pregnant teen. Everyone noticed her, it seemed, although some people stared at her with obvious contempt, as if she were a "ho" on the prowl.

Fears that Ashley and Natalie would not get along were totally unfounded. Despite their differing backgrounds—Natalie is a Jew and Ashley is a charismatic Missionary Baptist (in the Deep South, it is a black denomination; in Kentucky, it is a hillbilly denomination)—they found they had a great deal in common. Both women like to read and often carry books with them on location. Both have a passion for education (Natalie was attending Harvard at the time). Both have parents who mean well but who are demanding and often cause problems in their lives.

When a writer for *Entertainment Weekly* showed up on the set to conduct interviews, he asked Ashley what it was like working with Natalie. "It's hot here," Ashley quipped. "Or is that just her career?"

Between scenes, Ashley and Natalie played card and board games, and tested each other with brainteasers. Natalie thought that Ashley was the smartest person she had ever met. Sometimes she went to Ashley's trailer to visit and play with her white cockapoo and her cat. The dog is named Buttermilk and the cat is named Buttercup. When they had nothing else to do, they had a competition to see who could come up with the most "butter" names for future pets.

The two women developed a relationship that continued after the film wrapped. When Natalie returned to Harvard, they became e-mail buddies and Ashley often sent her things in the mail that she thought would be helpful to her at school. "A lot of people you work with will tell you they'll keep in touch," Portman told *Premiere* magazine. "Ashley really does it....She says, 'I'll send you this.' And it arrives the next week."

Ashley knew the routine. When *Where the Heart Is* was released in April 2000 and the reviews started coming in, critics were divided on the movie's merits. The headline for Wesley Morris's review in the *San Francisco Examiner* was "All Heart, No Brain." "There is a force powerful enough to keep America's boys and men away from a Hollywood movie that puts Ashley Judd in the comforting arms of Natalie Portman," he wrote. "It's call love. And when there's no basketball, baseball, golf, hockey or mud wrestling attached to it, you've just got love, which is what [this movie] has to give."

*Chicago Sun-Times* critic Roger Ebert had problems with the "contrivance, coincidence" and "improbability" of the plot, but he had good things to say about the cast. "Portman is quite an actress," he wrote. "Here she's the calm eye of the storm, mightily aided by Judd, who brings a plausibility to Lexie that the character surely needs...every time I looked at Portman or Judd, I was aware that whatever else Sequoia [*sic*], Oklahoma, may lack, it obviously has makeup and hair facilities to rival those in Beverly Hills."

Wrote Todd Camp in the *Fort Worth Star-Telegram*: "The film's inevitable 'chick flick' label is well-deserved—this is a movie about women...but that doesn't make it any less enjoyable for male audiences. Its bigger hurdle is class-related. Anyone who's never had to hold their car's hatchback open with a broom will have a hard time relating to what it's like to walk in Novalee's flowered house slippers."

All those questions about Matt Williams's ability to leap from television to motion pictures were answered by the critics, who invariably chastised him for the way he directed the film. Observed the *San Francisco Chronicle*, Williams "delivers a piece that is sweetly middle of the road, but the sights along the way are not much to write home about."

Usually front and center when her movies are released, Ashley stayed in the background this time, and did few interviews to promote the movie. That did not mean, of course, that magazines stopped writing about her. *Movieline*, not a publication that has devoted a lot of ink to Ashley's career, selected her number one in its third annual Hollywood 100 Most list. She was also chosen "Most fantasized about by castaways."

Truthfully, that was the core element of Ashley's sex appeal. While men might lust after the likes of Claudia Schiffer or Pamela Anderson, they fantasize about women like Marilyn Monroe and Ashley Judd, less-than-perfect physical specimens that project vulnerability and indomitability as the same instant. As beautiful as she is, Ashley still seems accessible, and that is the secret to her success.

Ashley appeared fully clothed in the May 1999 issue of *Playboy*, but the feature was easily the sexiest in the magazine. That was because of the way she toyed with readers' fantasies. Asked whether English words should be allowed into French usage, she said no. "OK, blow job in French is *la pipe*," she explained. "Who wants to say *la blow job* when they can say *la pipe*?"

# Chapter
# Eight

## *Love Carries Ashley into Ya-Ya Land*

It was a big day for Emily Westermeier, a Franklin High School senior who turned eighteen on January 24, 2001, five months before graduation. To celebrate the occasion, her parents, Dr. and Mrs. Thomas Westermeier, took her to Amerigo's restaurant in Cool Springs Mall, an upscale shopping center in Franklin that is frequented by country music stars, musicians, record executives, and producers.

Trouble was the last thing on Dr. Westermeier's mind that evening. A pathologist, he had put in a full day at an area hospital. He just wanted to relax and honor his daughter on her birthday. In the weeks leading up to the birthday dinner, they discussed what they could do to make the evening special. Emily pointed out that she was turning eighteen, the magical age of consent, and she preferred to be treated as an adult.

Well, in that case, someone joked—how about a stripper? Everyone laughed, but the more they talked about it, the more perfect it seemed. A male stripper would be a real hoot, especially right there in the restaurant among the other diners.

Dr. Westermeier called Pro Entertainment, a Nashville firm that specializes in male and female exotic dancers, and booked a male dancer for the twenty-fourth. It is not generally known outside the city, but Nashville has one of the largest adult entertainment communities in the South. One of the best-known lap-dancing establishments in the country is located just a block off famed Music Row, where most of the record labels are located, and there are a half-dozen topless nightclubs within a five-minute drive of the music district. In addition to the nightclubs and home-delivery adult entertainment services, there are listings for nearly two hundred escort services in the telephone directory. Many a country music hopeful has gotten her start as an after-hours escort. Ironically, the official voice of the music industry, the Country Music Association, had a porn link on its website as late as December 2001, although when questioned about it, embarrassed officials said it was an accident and they promptly removed it from the site. Undoubtedly, the site did get there by mistake, but the incident is indicative of the city's overall fascination with pornography.

Sex is a bigtime industry in Nashville, contrary to its down-home, flag-waving image, and people in the city and surrounding area are not hesitant to turn to the industry for entertainment, whether the intent is serious or humorous in nature. For Dr. Westermeier, ordering a male stripper for his daughter was nothing more than a family joke, a memorable way to mark her passage into adulthood.

Through the luck of the draw, thirty-year-old Chris Pearce was the dancer assigned to Emily. He had only been stripping for three months, so performing in a packed restaurant in a shopping mall was not an everyday experience for him. When he arrived at the restaurant he was shown to the Westermeier table, where he launched into his routine without formality. He placed his boom box on the table and hit the play button, unleashing the sounds of "Freak Me" by Silk.

A number-one hit in 1993 on the urban contemporary charts, "Freak Me" quickly became an anthem for female audiences, especially among soul sisters. Pearce had found it to be a very effective number with the women he entertained, so he incorporated it as his theme song. Emily Westermeier was delighted.

Rocking his hips to the music of Silk, he pulled away his shirt and then his trousers, stripping down to his shorts. It was at that point, while he was shaking his booty for the pretty Emily, that Naomi Judd appeared, seemingly from nowhere, and confronted the dancer. "She got me by surprise," he later recalled. "She grabbed me on the neck and shoulder area and pulled me down. I fell and the girl fell and the back of her head banged on the table."

Amid the chaos, Naomi admonished Pearce that his dance was not appropriate behavior in a restaurant. "She was not yelling," Pearce said. "She was just angry about the situation. She looked pretty angry."

After she had her say, Naomi stormed out of the restaurant with her husband, Larry Strickland, an odd thing in itself since she recently had filed for divorce. Emily and a couple of her friends followed Naomi out into the parking lot, where a heated argument ensued. Emily told Naomi that she had ruined her birthday party. When Emily returned to the restaurant, Pearce was packed up and ready to go. He was not interested in finishing the dance. Said Pearce: "I was done after that."

Naomi denied ever touching the dancer. "The unexpected

spectacle of a semi-nude man openly simulating intercourse on a young girl was shoved in my face," she told the *Nashville Tennessean*. "I was having a quiet meal at the dinner hour in a family restaurant not dreaming I'd come face to face with a lewd act you'd only see in a strip joint."

The following day Pearce filed assault charges against Naomi, but subsequently dropped the charges. A short time after that, he gave up dancing entirely.

Two weeks later, Naomi appeared on Bill Maher's *Politically Incorrect* television show and shocked the other guests by demonstrating the hip-swiveling dance she had witnessed in the restaurant. When Maher sidestepped her pelvic thrusts, she danced for the other guests, who recoiled in mock horror. Said one of the guests, U.S. senator Barbara Boxer, "She's scaring me."

Also frightened by Naomi's bizarre behavior were Ashley and Wynonna. Was Naomi having health problems again? Had the pressures of faded stardom finally gotten to her? Neighbors told newspaper reporters that Ashley and Wynonna were concerned about their mother's behavior and watched her very closely in the days after the incident. Ashley was concerned enough to postpone her marriage to Dario.

A dark cloud hung over the seventy-third annual Academy Awards ceremony held on March 25, 2001, at the Shrine Auditorium in Los Angeles. There was talk of an actors' strike and recent setbacks on Wall Street had put everyone in a dour mood. Everything seemed smaller that year: the parties, the media hype, the movies—everything!

Ashley arrived at the auditorium wearing a low-cut blue gown with a layered skirt. With it she wore layers of jewelry around her neck, wrist, and head that contained more than two hundred carats of diamonds valued at over $750,000. It was her third year in a row to be a presenter.

Dario accompanied Ashley to the event, his face showing none of the disappointment the couple felt over postponing their marriage plans. Actually, he was happy to just be alive. The previous month he had crashed his car during a test drive at the Homestead-Miami Speedway in Florida. He awoke in a hospital with brain contusions, fractures of the pelvis and left hip, and no memory of the crash. Ashley took him home to her farm and nurtured him back to health.

Outside the auditorium, Ashley told a television interviewer that she and Dario were there to people-watch. Asked about her gown, she said it was designed by Giorgio Armani. "We had it organized weeks ago, so of course I sat at home smug, knowing I was all taken care of, when half the girls in town were running around in a panic," she explained. "I actually sort of designed the dress around these necklaces which Dario and I saw [last summer]."

Ashley looked stunning in the gown, but not everyone agreed that it was the right dress for the occasion. After praising Julia Roberts, Marcia Gay Harden, and Renee Zellweger for their gowns, *Entertainment Weekly* selected Ashley as one of the five worst-dressed women at the affair.

Ashley fared slightly better than Bjork, who wore a white, fluffy outfit that resembled a giant bird. Actually, the magazine's complaint about Ashley had less to do with the dress than it did her jewelry: "The three-time Oscar presenter should heed the adage attributed to Diana Vreeland: Take off one accessory before leaving the house."

It is a wonder that it was Naomi and not Ashley who made news by attacking a stripper. Every time Ashley left the house or made a movie, there was always someone snipping at her—or so it seemed. One wonders how successful lawyers or doctors would hold up under the pressure if every time they tried a case or performed surgery, their work was critiqued in newspapers and magazines. Ashley had been publicly insulted more times than she could count, but she was learning, finally, to ignore it.

As far as Oscar nights go, the evening was unusual both for the restrained and sophisticated comedy of host Steve Martin and for the way in which music received more attention than the movies. The star of the show was perhaps the least photogenic person in the auditorium, Bob Dylan. Except he was not really there; his appearance arrived via satellite from Australia.

Nominated in the Best Song Performance category for "Things Have Changed," part of the soundtrack for *Wonder Boys*, Dylan sang an abbreviated version of the song live, bringing the audience to its feet. Said actor Jeff Bridges: "Every time I see Bob Dylan I get the feeling of being so happy that I'm alive at the same time he is."

To no one's surprise, Dylan took home the Oscar.

Ashley carried out her duties as a presenter with her customary charm, although there were complaints later that she dipped too far into the well of down-home wit. Large crowds make Ashley anxious, as does public speaking. She does as little of that as she can get away with and still remain a motion picture star. It is the reason why fans never see her on talk shows chatting with the likes of Jay Leno or David Letterman. She is one of the most articulate actresses on the scene, but she feels ill at ease going one-on-one with talk show hosts, especially if the shows are taped before a live audience. She once did a sit-down interview on *Live with Regis and Kathy Lee*, but she seemed stiff and overly precise in her responses, as if she were conscious of being graded.

Aside from sharing the bright-lights-big-city experience with Dario, the highlight of Ashley's evening seemed to be a private conversation with actress Winona Ryder at a post-Oscar gala. Both women seemed animated as they talked and Ashley looked truly relaxed for the first time that evening. Perhaps she was simply grateful that her mother was not there to reenact the encounter with the stripper. For Ashley, life's small victories were *everything*.

When Ashley first read Laura Zigman's best-selling novel *Animal Husbandry* in 1999, she identified with the main character who, after being dumped one time too many, decided that men were animals without any control over their libido. But it was not until she found out that producer Lynda Obst had acquired the film rights to the book that she began thinking of herself as the right person to play the lead in the movie. As she always did when there was a part in which she was interested, she instructed her agent to investigate the possibilities.

As a producer, Lynda Obst had demonstrated a real knack for romantic comedies. She had begun her career as an editor at the *New York Times Magazine* and at *Rolling Stone*, where she was the author and editor of *The Rolling Stone History of the Sixties*. She emerged from those experiences as a confirmed pop-culture junkie.

When Peter Guber, chairman of Casablanca/Polygram, offered Obst a position as his protégée in 1979, she jumped at the chance. Her first assignment was to develop the movie *Flashdance*. By 1989, she had formed her own production company with Columbia Pictures, producing films such as *This Is My Life* and *The Fisher King*, starring Robin Williams and Jeff Bridges. Over the next few years, she made a name for herself working in the romantic comedy genre. Her *Sleepless in Seattle*, starring Meg Ryan and Tom Hanks, was a major box-office hit in 1993.

When Obst directed her efforts toward casting, Ashley Judd was not the first person she thought of for the female lead. The script, penned by Elizabeth Chandler, had Meg Ryan or Julia Roberts written all over it, but if she used Ryan in another romantic comedy critics would invariably compare it to *Sleepless in Seattle* and accuse her of doing a remake. She offered the part to Julia Roberts, who accepted—and then later withdrew from the project.

It was while Ashley was filming *Where the Heart Is* that she learned about Roberts backing out of the project. As it happened, Bill Mechanic, then the head of Fox, visited the set of *Where the Heart Is* (another Fox project). While he was there, Ashley cornered him and let him know that she was interested in doing *Animal Husbandry*.

By the time Ashley's agent inquired about the script, Obst had decided she needed to find an actress with name recognition who had not oversaturated the romantic comedy market. In comedy, it is sometimes a disadvantage to be too well known.

When Ashley read the script, she wept. "It was a great romantic comedy with a lot of meat on its bones," she told the *Lexington Herald-Leader.* "I had read many samples of the genre that were so forgettable, or maybe slightly entertaining for the duration of the read, but nothing I could possibly stay motivated for and interested in for three months!"

Besides the intellectual appeal, the story had an emotional connection for Ashley. At age thirty-two, she was somewhat mystified by the mechanics of male-female relationships, not an uncommon occurrence among women who have grown up in a household without a full-time father. Women learn about men though their interactions with their fathers. As a result of her upbringing, Ashley did not have a clue about what a healthy male-female relationship looked like.

When Ashley told Obst that she wanted to play the part of Jane Goodale, the producer was not interested. She thought Ashley might be too Southern for the part. Not until Ashley insisted on a meeting with Obst did the producer change her mind.

"Ashley has that elusive quality that makes a great movie star," Obst explained to *Entertainment Tonight*. "She is your girlfriend, she could be you, you root for her and genuinely like her." Obst liked her enough to boost her salary from her previous high of one million dollars to four million dollars.

*Someone Like You* offered Ashley more than a movie part, it offered her a cause. Once she signed to do the part, she researched it the way an anthropologist would research human behavior in a lost Amazon tribe. The bottom-line rationale of the movie is that men are animals that follow the behavior of other animals, particularly cattle. After they mate, bulls move on to the next cow. That explained everything to Ashley, who often wondered why she had been dumped by so many men for no apparent reason.

"Even if it's crackpot science, this script had some anthropology in it," Ashley said in an interview for the Internet Movie Database.

"And I'm someone who once or twice in college tried to have an original thought. I related to [the lead character] because she tried to take an intellectual tactic to sort out her emotions and you don't usually get that in a romantic comedy."

With Ashley aboard, Obst turned her attention to finding two male leads and two supporting actresses. For the role of Ray Brown, Ashley's live-in boyfriend, Obst turned to Greg Kinnear, a former talk-show host who found a niche in romantic comedies, with roles in almost a dozen feature films, including *You've Got Mail*, in which he played opposite Meg Ryan, and *As Good As It Gets*, for which he received an Oscar nomination for Best Supporting Actor. What made him seem perfect for the role in *Someone Like You* was a comment he made to *Maxim* magazine in the fall of 2000: "There are two things a man can follow: his heart or his...*that*."

With Kinnear as the red-herring man-boy, Obst had to find a real love interest. Hugh Jackman, a thirty-two-year-old Australian-born actor, had only made four feature films, but his most recent, *X-Men*, had been a box-office success. At six-two, he had the sort of rugged good looks that Obst knew would appeal to female audiences. He was given the role of Eddie Alden.

If there was one thing that Obst had learned making romantic comedies it was that the supporting cast was as important as the lead actors in making the film a success. For the two female supporting roles, she turned to veteran actresses. Ashley's boss in the movie, a talk-show host named Diane Roberts, needed to be a woman in her late forties who still possessed considerable sex appeal. Ellen Barkin, who had made a career of portraying sexy, offbeat leading ladies, seemed perfect. Marisa Tomei, who won an Oscar for her performance as Joe Pesci's girlfriend in *My Cousin Vinny*, was tapped for the role of Liz, Ashley's girlfriend who talks her into writing a relationship column for a men's magazine. Rounding out the production menagerie were Naomi Judd, who was given a small part as a makeup artist, and Wynonna, who cowrote and sang the song "You Are" for the closing credits.

Ashley began this project with a good feeling about the outcome. She had never done a comedy, but she felt she could be convincing as a comedic actress because, growing up, she had always been the butt of family jokes. Whenever Naomi and Wynonna needed to release a little pent-up frustration, they directed their aggression at Ashley in the form of humor, using her as their emotional pincushion. Ashley learned at an early age to deflect that aggression by turning everything they said into a joke. A well-spun quip can go a long way in smothering the fires of misplaced aggression. Ashley just figured that she would do on the set of *Someone Like You* what she had done in real life.

The best scene in the movie occurs while Ashley and Kinnear are at dinner. She has given up her apartment to move in with him, but after a six-week burst of passion, he begins to grow distant and unresponsive. The showdown comes over dinner. Kinnear tells her that he cannot "do this" anymore.

"Do what?" Ashley asks.

"Us," he says.

"I thought we felt the same way. Incredibly lucky to have found the thing."

Kinnear ends up walking away from the table.

Although the anguish and perplexed consternation displayed by Ashley in the scene shows her at her best, it is not the most memorable moment in the film. That distinction goes to a scene that has nothing to do with either good acting or well-timed humor. It occurs when she tells her roommate that she is a former cheerleader.

To prove it, she does a cheer in her underwear, complete with paper towels for pompoms. It is the one scene in the movie that lingers in your mind long after you leave the theater. Ashley knew it would be a good scene, so she left nothing to chance. Even though she had childhood experience as a cheerleader, she did not depend on that to get her through the scene. Instead, she returned to the University of Kentucky and asked the cheerleaders there to help her be convincing in the scene. They gave her more than advice; they gave her the cheer itself, which they worked up especially for her.

"Maybe we're all entitled to one victorious moment as adults when we vindicate a childhood dream and I loved cheerleading so much when I was a kid," Ashley told CNN's *Showbiz Today*. "I just thought it was the height of achievement....To get to cheer in a movie, I acquitted myself of the cheerleading virus."

One of the really odd things about the movie was the way director Tony Goldwyn had all the female actors munching on food in nearly every scene. The obvious reason was to play off the symbolism of "cows" grazing while the "bulls" took care of business, but the munching was so prevalent that it became an annoying distraction to the dialogue. Watching the women eat was too much like watching motorists eat while driving their cars. It made you want to shout, "Keep your eyes on the frigging road (script)!"

After work on the movie was completed, Obst discovered that studio executives had misgivings about the title. They felt *Animal*

*Husbandry* worked for the book, but they wondered if it might sound too much like a science project to work as a motion picture. Their doubts about the title were seemingly answered when Ashley went on the Conan O'Brien show before the release of the movie to promote it (an indication of her dedication to making the movie a success). At one point, O'Brien jokingly asked if the sequel to *Animal Husbandry* would be "*Crop Rotation.*" That comment was enough to stampede the studio executives. The title was changed to *Someone Like You.*

When production on the movie wrapped, Ashley was in love with both Dario and her career. Just as she felt that her relationship with Dario had elevated her optimism about life in general, she felt that *Someone Like You* had escalated her to another career level. Unfortunately, that bipolar lovefest was short in duration. When the movie was released in April 2001, the critics were not all in a loving mood.

"Movies described as 'escapist' usually promise the audience a glimpse of lives more glamorous and eventful than their own, but *Someone Like You* and its ilk deliver a kind of reverse escapism," wrote A. O. Scott for the *New York Times.* "You escape from them, back into a life you know couldn't be as shallow, as predictable or as empty as what you have just witnessed."

Owen Gleiberman, writing in *Entertainment Weekly*, saw nothing funny about the movie. At best, he found it an innocuous take on *Sex and the City.* "It was originally called *Animal Husbandry*," he sniffed. "And while the producers were throwing away that title, they might have done well to chuck the movie along with it."

*Chicago Sun-Times* critic Roger Ebert found fault with both the premise (the old-cow–new-cow theory) and its representation of a behind-the-scenes look at a television show, especially the moment when Ashley burst on the set, stepping between the camera and the star of the show, to deliver a monologue about what she has learned about men. "The chances of a production assistant standing in front of the star of a TV show and talking for several minutes are approximately zero, especially since, let's face it, she's babbling," he wrote. "Her speech reminded me of something in a barnyard. It's not a cow, although it's often found close to one."

*Rolling Stone*'s Peter Travers was one of the few critics that liked the movie. He was especially impressed by Hugh Jackman's performance. "[He]...is funny and touching in a role he rescues from macho caricature," Travers wrote. "His scenes with the dazzling Judd have a poignancy that soars above the chick-flick herd into the realm of sweet magic."

Ashley seemed to take the hits from the critics with more resignation than in past years. Perhaps it was because she was in love and nothing else really mattered. Or perhaps it was because it finally dawned on her that what critics thought and what audiences thought were two separate measurements of a film's success. Did she want to make films for the critics or did she want to make films for the people who purchased the tickets? For the first time, the business of movie making began to make sense to her.

At the New York premiere of *Someone Like You*, Ashley was joined by Naomi and Wynonna. Photographs taken during the event showed Ashley front and center, with mother and sister in the background. The gesture was more than a courtesy; it was symbolic of the changing fortunes of the Judds. By 2001, Ashley had achieved a level of fame that exceeded anything the Judds had been able to experience as recording artists.

The photographs taken that day reveal a subdued Wynonna standing behind Ashley, her arms wrapped lovingly around her waist. There is genuine pride in her face, a reflection not only of her support of Ashley's movie career but a testament to her newly forged emotional bond with her sister. It had taken more than thirty years, but Wynonna and Ashley were finally sisters in every sense of the word.

Naomi was a different story. Photographs of her at the event show a woman with too much rouge on her cheeks, an ominous sign of possible depression. The china doll of country music looked fragile and isolated, like something you would find atop a wedding cake—smart, stylish, yet oddly detached. Small wonder: in the weeks following the embarrassing incident with the male dancer, she broke her right ankle after stepping into a hole on her farm. The accident made her feel helpless and, to Naomi, that was the worst feeling in the world.

Naomi had been publicly supportive of Ashley's engagement to Dario, but it came at a time when she had filed for divorce from Larry, so her perception of the institution of marriage was probably not what it should have been. As they say in country music, she had not had good luck with the men in her life. She was only fifty-five, but her singing career was effectively over and her main partners in life, Ashley and Wynonna, were showing growing signs of independence.

What was a woman of fifty-five who had lost her career—and who was in the process of losing her daughters—supposed to do with the rest of her life? Wynonna and Ashley understood, finally, that they were not the answer.

One of the odd things about the relationship between Wynonna and her mother was the way they talked to each other through the media. They would have a fight, but instead of settling it between them, they explained the problem to the news media in an effort to gain leverage in the argument.

Wynonna resorted to that old device in the summer of 2001 while talking to a reporter from the *Macomb Daily* of Mount Clemens, Michigan. Since Wynonna was booked for a concert at Freedom Hill Amphitheater in suburban Detroit, the reporter had called Wynonna at her farm to get a pre-concert interview.

Instead of talking about the concert, Wynonna told the reporter about the "nightmare" she had experienced touring with her mother the previous year. She advised anyone thinking about going back to live with his or her parents not to do it. The problem she had with Naomi on the road, she explained, was that her mother still treated her like a child. "I'd be rockin' on stage and getting into it, and she'd come over and want to pinch my cheeks and hold my hand," Wynonna said. "I'd look at her and think, 'This can't be happening.'"

Naomi questioned her about similar issues while they were out on the road, but Wynonna kept quiet, allowing the tears running down her cheeks to speak for her. Not saying what should have been said to her mother had bothered her for a year. Finally, she spoke to Naomi through the reporter, knowing full well that the article eventually would be sent to her mother by the clipping service. It was learned behavior. Naomi's favorite method of disciplining Wynonna as a young woman was to tell embarrassing stories about her to the media. Perhaps Wynonna thought that the news would be easier for Naomi to take if it came from a stranger. Naomi has always benefited from the kindness of strangers.

Wynonna followed up that bit of news later in the summer with an announcement that she intended to marry D. R. Roach, her road manager. The co-owner of a concert security company based in Nashville, Roach was a longtime friend and business associate of Wynonna and Naomi. Said Wynonna: "I know that we can make it through anything because we have been coworkers and friends for the last ten years. We laugh constantly and learn something from each other every day."

The six months leading up to Ashley's marriage to Dario were not uneventful. In June 2001, Ashley went to Detroit to participate in an auto race called the Celebrity Team Challenge. With only three laps to go, Ashley was in the lead when her car crashed into the tire barrier on turn number three. She was not hurt, but her car engine went dead.

Thinking she was out of the race because of the crash, she climbed from the car only to be told by a racing official that she must restart the car and rejoin the race. She did with only three laps to go, but it was a nerve-wracking experience because the latch on the left-rear passenger door broke, causing the door to swing open and shut as she went in and out of turns. As a result of the crash, she dropped from first to twenty-first. After the race, she told reporters that they could start calling her "Crashly Judd."

It was not the only disaster she averted that day. Ashley also settled a lawsuit with a Kentucky-based entertainment journalist who wrote a story for *USA Today* that she did not like. She did an interview with *Entertainment Tonight* in which she made disparaging comments about the writer. He perceived them to be libelous and filed a lawsuit against both Ashley and the television show. Terms of the settlement were not disclosed.

When Ashley became engaged to Dario, everyone assumed she would have the wedding at her farm, where her mother could properly supervise it. The farmhouse was where she fell in love with Dario and where they learned they could live together as a couple. It was a magical place for Ashley, where she learned what she had inside herself as both a woman and as an actress. The fact that she and Dario decided to get married in Scotland was as much a statement about her evolving relationship with her mother as it was a declaration of love for her husband-to-be. In many ways, it was Ashley's declaration of independence.

The wedding date was originally set for January 31, 2002, in the Scottish town of Bonar Bridge, but it was subsequently changed to December 12 when the couple learned that Skibo Castle in Dornoch would be available for the earlier date. Built in the 1800s by American steel magnate Andrew Carnegie, it was later converted into an exclusive country club and hotel. It was the site where American pop singer Madonna had married movie director Guy Ritchie the previous year.

Ashley had two reasons for moving the site of the wedding. The first was atmosphere: Skibo Castle was more impressive than the site they had chosen in Bonar. The second was because officials at Skibo Castle had a reputation for maintaining a high degree of security for events scheduled there. Security was a major issue with Ashley. After the experience with the stalker at her farmhouse—and the legal tangle with the entertainment writer—Ashley wanted to make certain that unwanted guests, including the media, could be held at bay.

The night before the wedding vows were exchanged, Ashley and Dario slept in separate bedrooms, as is the tradition there, and ate breakfast in separate dining rooms. After kissing Ashley goodnight, the next time Dario saw her was when she walked down the aisle before three hundred invited guests in a white silk-and-satin gown designed by her favorite designer, Giorgio Armani. Dario wore the traditional Scottish kilt.

Wynonna served as maid of honor, while Sandra Bullock handled the bridesmaid duties. Best man was Dario's brother, Marino. Naomi attended the ceremony, but she was not involved in the proceedings. Instead, she sat in the audience with guests that included Gwyneth Paltrow, Edward Norton, Hugh Grant, Michael Douglas and his wife Catherine Zeta-Jones, and Robert De Niro.

Within minutes after the Catholic priest began the ceremony, alarms sounded at the castle as fire engines rushed onto the grounds to extinguish a fire that started in one of the hotel's golf carts. By the time the firemen arrived, the hotel staff had knocked down the flames. Inside the castle, the ceremony continued without interruption. Naomi and Wynonna sang "Love Can Build a Bridge" and Wynonna's backup singer, Kim Fleming, sang "Ave Maria."

Once Ashley and Dario were proclaimed man and wife, they escorted their guests to a banquet hall where a Nashville band entertained everyone with the down-home melodies and heel-kicking rhythms of Tennessee and Kentucky country music. The wedding took place without a glitch, and Ashley got her wish: no stalkers were apprehended and the American news media barely even noticed the event.

Ashley began 2002 with a new life and three new movies, starting with *High Crimes*, a thrilled based on Joseph Finder's best-selling novel. Costarring with her was her crime-solving partner from *Kiss the Girls*, Morgan Freeman.

*High Crimes* is about a Harvard law school professor, played by Ashley, who defends her husband in a military court after the Army declares him a deserter and charges him with participating in a mass killing in El Salvador. Assisting her at the trial is an ex-judge-advocate attorney played by Freeman.

*High Crimes* was filmed mostly in San Francisco, where Ashley lived at the Pacific Heights home of a family friend from Kentucky, and at the now closed Alameda Naval Base, which was used for the military scenes. The filmmakers created consternation among locals when casting calls went out for extras with really short haircuts. Fortunately, Ashley was not asked to shave her locks.

Ashley enjoyed working with Freeman on *Kiss the Girls* and by the time they wrapped *High Crimes* they had built a friendship. Later in the year, when Freeman opened a blues nightclub in Clarksdale, Mississippi, named Ground Zero, he flew Ashley and Wynonna to the Delta on a Lear jet to participate in the festivities.

Freeman, who has a home in nearby Charleston, Mississippi, grew up in Greenwood, the home of blues legend Robert Johnson. Because he came of age at a time when the music of the Mississippi Delta literally surrounded him every place he went, opening a blues club seemed like a natural thing for him to do at this point in his life.

When he invited Ashley and Wynonna to the club's opening, they jumped at the chance to sample firsthand the exotic music of the Delta. It is hard to know what they expected, but surely the freestanding building constructed in the early 1900s, with paint peeling off the well-worn doors, was not it.

The club looked like a juke joint, which was intentional, a reminder of years past when white Southerners slipped in the back doors of black juke joints to revel in the blues. Only on this night the situation was reversed, with whites outnumbering blacks, another sign of the times—the blues had lost its influence with African-Americans.

Black customers were welcome at the club, but its success depended on white blues lovers nostalgic for the past. Ironically, while it was once possible to travel the famed Highway 61 and hear blues emanating from the shanties that lined the highway, that scenario had been replaced by the early 2000s by the neatly manicured homes of white, middle-class Southerners who spent their evenings sipping wine and revving up their CD players with the music of Muddy Waters, Jimmy Reed, and B. B. King.

By the time the Judd sisters arrived at the club, Freeman had shucked his jacket and joined his wife, Myrna, on the dance floor. Always an unpredictable dresser, Ashley wore a low-cut black dress and a 1920s-style flapper hat pulled down almost to her eyebrows. Wynonna was dressed in black, her long red hair flowing onto her shoulders from beneath a massive black hat.

Before the night was over, both sisters were enticed up on the stage, where they posed with Freeman for photographers after being introduced to the cheering audience. "We got all generations here, all walks of life, black, white, and it's all about the blues," Wynonna told a correspondent for *Premiere* magazine. "It's also very Morgan—he's so inclusive. We adore him."

When Ashley and Wynonna left that evening to fly back to

Nashville, the last thing they saw in the club was a message written on the front door: "Mothers lock up your daughters, we're going to party until the last blues fan faints." It was late when they arrived back home, but not to worry: Naomi probably left the porch lights on for them.

Ashley's second film of 2002 was *Divine Secrets of the Ya-Ya Sisterhood*, which was released in June. Ashley was a late addition to the film. She was filming *High Crimes* when she began receiving emails from *Ya-Ya* director and screenwriter Callie Khouri, urging her to accept a role in the film.

Ashley played hard to get, which only made Khouri more determined. Khouri had never directed a film and she knew she would never direct another if she did not nail this one perfectly. She and Ashley had a lot in common. Raised in Kentucky, Khouri went to Purdue University to study landscape architecture, but she ended up switching majors to get a degree in drama. After graduation, she moved to Nashville, where she lived with her family for a short time until she left for Los Angeles in 1982 to study acting. When it became apparent that she would not be successful as an actress, she took a job as an assistant with a music video production company. It was while working at that job that she began writing a script that ultimately was titled *Thelma & Louise*.

Although *Thelma & Louise* was a big box-office and critical success in 1991, assisted no doubt by the amazing on-screen chemistry between the lead actresses, Susan Sarandon and Geena Davis, it surprised everyone by winning an Oscar in only one category—Best Original Screenplay.

To win an Oscar for a first script is a major accomplishment; Khouri overnight went from being a complete unknown to becoming the toast of Hollywood. That was fine as far as it went, but Khouri's real ambition was to become a director. For the next four years, she attended an endless stream of meetings with studio executives, during which she tried to sell herself as a director. Not until 1995 did she land another movie deal, this time for a script titled *Something to Talk About*. It was made into a successful movie starring Julia Roberts, but she was passed over for the director's job. The rejection broke her heart and she "cried a river" over the incident.

The following year, producer Bonnie Bruckheimer, who had bought the movie rights to the book *Divine Secrets of the Ya-Ya Sisterhood*, asked Khouri if she would adapt the screenplay. Khouri turned down the offer because she feared being branded a chick-flick writer. The job went to a male writer, Mark Andrus. Two years later, when the project still had not gelled, Bruckheimer went back to Khouri to ask for her help. The offer was simple: doctor the script and you can be the director.

Khouri would not believe her good fortune. For nearly a decade she had been begging, plotting, and scheming, all without success, to land a director's job. Now Hollywood was coming to her. Despite reservations about being involved in another chick flick, she said yes, fearing she would never have another opportunity to direct. Besides, this was her main area of expertise: women bonding with other women.

*Divine Secrets of the Ya-Ya Sisterhood* is about a prominent young playwright, Sidda Lee Walker, who lives in New York, a long way from her Louisiana roots but not far enough from her eccentric and domineering mother, Vivi.

When *Time* magazines does a profile on Sidda, all hell breaks loose in Louisiana when Vivi thinks she has been slighted in the article. War breaks out between Sidda and her mother, prompting Vivi's three childhood friends, known to each other as the Ya-Ya Sisterhood, to intervene in an effort to bring peace. They do that by telling Sidda things about her mother she never knew. The story that emerges is one of how Vivi and the other members of the Ya-Ya Sisterhood have maintained their unusual friendship for more than forty years, documenting their adventures in a scrapbook packed with old photos, letters, and dried corsages.

The challenge faced by Bruckheimer and Khouri was in assembling a cast that depicted the Ya-Ya Sisterhood in three tiers: in the present day as matronly women, as young women enjoying a zest for life, and as adventuresome children.

For the playwright/daughter they chose Sandra Bullock, a Virginia-born actress whose box-office appeal had exploded since her 1994 hit, *Speed*. A veteran of nearly thirty feature films, including *A Time to Kill* (1996) and *Demolition Man* (1993), she had just the edgy quality the script called for. Bullock had known Khouri for a long time, but when she first learned about the movie project she was hesitant to tell Khouri of her interest for fear of jeopardizing their friendship. There was no need to—Khouri already had her in mind. Bullock was delighted. Explained Bullock to the *Hollywood Reporter*: "It's a chick flick, it's a book I loved, and I loved what [Khouri] did script-wise."

For the role of Vivi, they went to Ellen Burstyn. The Oscar-winning actress who has been dazzling audiences for nearly forty years with her roles in *Last Picture Show* (1971), *The Exorcist* (1973), and *Alice Doesn't Live Here Anymore* (1974), had the experience and the emotional savvy to deliver an emotionally distraught mother who, while treading close to the edge of parental anarchy, somehow manages to keep her balance.

They balanced out the cast with Maggie Smith, Shirley Knight, and Fionnula Flanagan as the older women, with four newcomers as the children and with Jacqueline McKenzie, Kiersten Warren, and Katy Selverstone as the young adults. The only major male role went to James Garner, who plays Shep Walker.

By early 2001, Bruckheimer and Khouri had everything in place, except for casting the role of Vivi as a young adult. They needed someone who could depict the young Vivi as a free spirit. Someone who could be convincing as an eccentric Southerner with a flair for the dramatic. Someone who would think nothing of sitting on the back seat of a speeding convertible and whipping off her shirt in a show of solidarity with the other Ya-Yas.

Khouri knew Ashley would be perfect for the part. She was the last missing piece in a cinematic puzzle that had taken four years to assemble. That is the reason she went after Ashley with such a passion, playing off their common Kentucky roots, Nashville experiences, and shared viewpoints on movie making.

Khouri's e-mails to Ashley were downright shameless.

"She kept sending me these impassioned letters," Ashley told *Premiere* magazine, "at the end of which she made me vow never to show anybody how sappy they were."

Ashley had not set foot in her Nashville farmhouse for four months, and she desperately wanted to go there to recuperate after making *High Crimes*, but how could she possibly say no to Khouri after she had opened up her heart in the e-mails?

Finally, Ashley said yes. She was no dream buster.

The third film that Ashley released in 2002 was *Frida*, a look at the life of Mexican artist Frida Kahlo, who is known mostly for her paintings of women with organs outside their bodies. Ashley accepted a supporting role in the film primarily as a favor to her friend Salma Hayek, one of sixteen producers involved with the film. Hayek, a Mexican-born actress best known for *Wild Wild West* (1999) and *Desperado* (1995), also played the starring role of Frida.

Ashley Judd as Catwoman? It makes sense if you think about it. Selina Kyle, the Catwoman known to tradition-bound fans of the comic book character, was orphaned as a young girl by a suicidal mother and alcoholic father. As an adult, she vowed never to be hurt again, choosing a life in which she could use her catlike skills to walk the thin line between good and evil. She was no villain, but neither was she a saint. On those occasions when she worked on the side of truth, justice, and the American way, it was because it suited her own whims and needs.

When Warner Brothers signed Ashley to play the role of Catwoman, there were those who disparaged the choice. Could a Southerner play Catwoman? Critics have seldom been kind to Southerners who step outside the box. Could Ashley successfully reprise the role played so effectively by Michelle Pfeiffer in the 1992 sequel *Batman Returns*? Was Ashley enough of a seductress? She had used her sexuality often enough in films, but would she be able to effectively use the promise of sexuality as Pfeiffer had done so well? Was Ashley athletic enough? She was impressive in *Double Jeopardy,* but she was playing an ordinary woman who did extraordinary things. In *Catwoman,* she would play a heroic figure who audiences would expect to be larger than life.

Of course, anyone familiar with the full range of Ashley's work would have no problem answering yes to all the above questions. Even so, it took a certain amount of corporate courage for Warner Brothers to sign Ashley for the role, especially since all that was in place was a screenplay written by John Rogers, the cowriter of *American Outlaws.* With a projected release date of 2003, there was no production company, no director, no costars—nothing but a thirty-four-year-old actress who would be thirty-five (and thus middle-aged) by the time the film was released.

In some ways it was a stroke of genius. The one movie that Ashley had made that was universally praised by critics was *Ruby in Paradise.* It was perhaps the only role that she had ever played that depended entirely on her ability to be convincing as the character she portrayed. She did a brilliant job.

There are those who think that *Catwoman* may allow her, for the first time since *Ruby in Paradise,* to truly get inside a character's personality. Is it possible for her to duplicate the artistry of *Ruby* with a fictional character that will be targeting a mass audience? "It's possible, if she gets a good director," said *Ruby in Paradise* director Victor Nunez. "There is no reason why that depth cannot be there."

The biggest hurdle will be the reluctance of critics to accept a Southern Catwoman. Although the Civil War has been over for nearly 140 years, there remains a strong bias against Southerners in the media. Producer Lynda Obst's comment that she originally did not feel Ashley could play a big-city television assistant and magazine columnist because she is from the South is reflective of that.

The effect of that prejudice on Ashley's sensibilities should not be underestimated. It has been an obstacle that she has had to overcome, just as African-Americans have had to overcome similar indignities (it is one reason why she works so well with Morgan Freeman; they share an intuitive appreciation of the obstacles associated with achieving success in films).

It is a form of racism that Ashley sometimes eyes with wonderment. "Sometimes people are surprised to find I have an urban, sophisticated side to me, as if I'm well-rounded in ways they didn't expect, either as an actress or as a Southerner or both," she told the Kentucky-based *Ace Weekly*. "I can walk into someone's office and after five minutes they'll tell me, 'You're so CULTIVATED.' I feel like they're just waiting for me to say something like, 'Aw shucks.'"

Each time Ashley makes a film she knows it will be greeted by reviewers who dislike her because she is a woman (most movie critics are male) and by reviewers who dislike her because she is a Southerner (most movie critics live outside the South) and by reviewers who resent the success of her mother and sister (most movie critics, Roger Ebert excluded, have never experienced success firsthand).

Yet, she plows ahead, averaging two or three films a year. She still reads everything that is written about her, but the words of her detractors, even when bitter and unkind, no longer bring her to tears, because it is no longer about *them*—it is now about her and what she wants to do with her life.

"One thing that's important to me is to be just impervious to what people have to say," Ashley told the *Boston Globe*. "I mean, certainly I enjoy critical acclaim. But in regard to what I've seen [fame] do to others, my friends and my family, my position is to just live my life.... I just think it's so important to have your inner peace and your quality friendships and to love what you do. That's what my life is about."

Movies and albums come and go, but life continues in Leiper's Fork, where the Judds have helped define the character of the community. "Gosh, it seems like they have been here forever," said Marty Hunt, owner of Leiper's Fork Antiques. "They're part of the landscape, you know. I might add that all of us in Leiper's Fork try to protect them as much as we can. I told my husband one day that I am going to get hit by lightning for lying, because when all these people come here and chase them [Judds] around, I tell them they all live together in another house, which is in the opposite direction. They are important to us and we want to help protect their privacy."

The feeling is mutual. There is only one grocery in town and the Judds shop there like everyone else. Sometimes when Naomi or Wynonna or Ashley shop in the store, they ask if anyone is having a problem paying their grocery bills. If the answer is yes, they pay off that individual's debt on the spot.

Leiper's Fork may be small (population 400), but it has a huge heart, aided in no small degree by the generosity of the Judds. In the aftermath of the September 11, 2001, terrorist attack on New York, Naomi and Wynonna (Ashley was out of town) volunteered for a community fundraiser for the victims. Wynonna performed from a makeshift stage on a front porch and Naomi gave a heartwarming speech to the crowd of about two thousand. When the money in the collection till was totaled there was enough to send a check for over forty thousand dollars to New York.

For Ashley's first (and only) acting coach, Robert Carnegie, it is difficult to consider Ashley's life apart from the relationship she has with her mother and sister. That is because it was that relationship that convinced him to take Ashley under his wing. Once it became apparent that Ashley was going to become a successful actress, he had only one thought: "When the mother was still sick and trying to recuperate and Ashley had done *Ruby in Paradise*, I was just thrilled for the mother. I knew she could now relax and know that both daughters were going to be OK. Ashley has gone on to excel in her field beyond the way they excelled in theirs and they excelled tremendously—you like to see your students do well."

Ashley's story is far from over, but in some areas of her life there has been resolution, however tentative. Her relationship with Wynonna, always loving but not always healthy, has evolved into a mature emotional partnership in which each sister plays a well-defined role. Ashley truly enjoys the company of her niece and nephew, and through the children she has found a way to cement her new relationship with her sister.

Naomi is a different story. Ashley's relationship with her mother is still evolving and may never find the level of self-realization that defines her relationship with her sister, but that is probably to be expected. Healthy living is about adjusting to the reality of the moment and not about the atonement of past injustices, unintentional or otherwise. In a 2001 article written for *Redbook* magazine, Naomi said what everyone else had known all along. "You see, I bear a lot of guilt about the way I raised Ashley," she wrote.

Later, she continued: "While I was trying to keep Wynonna out of the juvenile detention center, I had a powerful feeling that Ashley was OK. I've found in these last few years that I overestimated that—that Ashley was, in fact, suffering and lonely."

Today, Ashley wants an adjustment that will allow her to move on, while Naomi still seems haunted by the past. That is why there always will be a *feeling* of tension between them. Most of Naomi's life is in the past, while most of Ashley's life is in the future. The two women have little in common as adults, except their shared past.

"Ashley is not a thing like her mother and sister, except the drive to succeed," observed Ashley's high school English teacher, Louise Curnutte. "I have never seen anyone with so much confidence. She just exudes it. I don't know where she got it. She was tossed around from pillar to post for a while. She submersed herself in books and ended up being this self-confident, beautiful creature."

As dominant as her relationship with her mother and sister has been—and as influential as that sometimes-tortured relationship has been on her career choices—Ashley's immediate future is with Dario and that will shake up all the priorities in her life. She has talked of having children and there is every reason to think she will do so at the earliest opportunity. Her personal life in the years ahead is certain to be filled with surprises and tests of her deepest held beliefs about family.

Professionally, she may be at a crossroads. "I think [her career] is still very much in her hands," said Victor Nunez. "She has certainly been successful—and how can you deny her success?—but I do think she is capable of doing much more than she has already. I think it is going to depend on her—how shall I put this—knowing that the craft of acting is not simply about being a star. The audience comes to see a star be themselves over and over. You don't want to see a star be different. But an actor, on the other hand, you want them to be different...how they choose in terms of their speech and body movements, so that you come to believe and you forget that they are actors. This country values being a star more than it values being an actor, and I'm not sure you can do both."

In Ashley's case, life may be imitating art. Nunez, who has devoted a lifetime making what some people call "small films" and what others call works of art, knows and understands the dilemma Ashley faces with her career.

"Remember the scene on the pier [in *Ruby in Paradise*], where Mike McCaslin scolds Ruby for going back to her job?" Nunez asked. "He says, 'There's got to be more than that.' She chews him out. She says he doesn't know what he's talking about. At the time, that was good enough for Ruby. She was just thrilled to be engaged and connected. I felt this was a scene in which Ruby comes as close to being Ashley as anywhere in the film, where she states that he can say that she should do more, but she was working and making her own choices and that's what matters."

Nunez laughed, perhaps feeling that he had said more than he intended. "For me to say anything beyond that," he continued, "is to become Mike McCaslin and I don't want to be Mike McCaslin." He gave it a few more moments of thought, the silence washing over his words like the Florida surf that cleansed Ruby of her past. Finally, he said, "Somehow we all have to find our own way."

# *Filmography*

**KUFFS** (1992)
> Director: Bruce A. Evans
> Writers: Bruce A. Evans and Raynold Gideon
> Producer: Raynold Gideon

> Cast
>> Christian Slater (George Kuffs)
>> Milla Jovovich (Maya Carlton)
>> Ric Roman Waugh (Gangster)
>> Steve Holladay (Gangster)
>> Chad Randall (Gangster)
>> Clarke Coleman (Gangster)
>> Leon Rippy (Kane)
>> Craig Benton (paint store owner)
>> Ashley Judd (wife of paint store owner)
>> Bruce Boxleitner (Brad Kuffs)
>> Joshua Cadman (Bill Donnelly)
>> Mary Ellen Trainor (Nikki Allyn)
>> Aki Aleong (Mr. Chang)

**Summary:**

George Kuffs is a twenty-one-year-old unemployed dropout who abandons his pregnant girlfriend and flees to San Francisco, where he hopes to get money from his big brother, a cop who heads up a special adjunct to the police department that is organized to provide private protection to paying citizens. Before he can talk his brother out of the money, the brother is killed by a criminal syndicate that wants to control the district. Kuffs inherits the district from his brother and tries to keep it going as a business while hunting down his brother's killers. Ashley Judd has a nonspeaking role in the movie and only appears for a few seconds. Many people consider this movie to be one of the worst of 1992.

## TILL DEATH US DO PART (1992)
Director: Yves Simoneau
Writer: Vincent Bugliosi, Ken Hurwitz

### Cast
Treat Williams (Alan Palliko)
Arliss Howard (Vincent Bugliosi)
Rebecca Jenkins (Sandra Stockton)
J. E. Freeman (Detective Robert Guy)
Pruitt Taylor Vince (Michael Brockington)
Embeth Davidtz (Katherine Palliko)
John Schuck (William Lang)
Ashley Judd (Gwen Fox)

### Summary:
This made-for-television movie is about a Los Angeles district attorney who becomes obsessed with prosecuting a renegade police officer. The movie was released on video on August 5, 1992.

## RUBY IN PARADISE (1993)
Director: Victor Nunez
Writer: Victor Nunez
Producer: Keith Crofford

### Cast
Ashley Judd (Ruby Lee Gissing)
Todd Field (Mike McCaslin)
Bentley Mitchum (Ricky Chambers)
Allison Dean (Rochelle Bridges)
Dorothy Lyman (Mildred Chambers)
Betsy Douds (Debrah Ann)
Felicia Hernandez (Persefina)
Divya Satia (Indian singer)
Bobby Barnes II (Wanda)
Sharon M. Lewis (TV Weather Anchor)
Paul E. Mills (TV Evangelist)
Brik Berkes (Jimmy)
Abigail McKelvey (Canadian tourist)

### Summary:
Ruby Lee Gissing is a young woman in her early twenties who bolts from her Tennessee home and flees to Florida, where she hopes

to discover the meaning of life. Instead, she goes through a series of relationships and experiences that allow her to discover, for the first time, her own strengths and weaknesses. That, she learns after a heartbreak or two, is the true meaning of life. The script is beautifully written and masterfully directed by Victor Nunez, an effort matched only by Ashley Judd's stunning performance. This is a quiet film, one with little action; its power is derived solely from its ability to touch the emotions of those who view it. As of 2002, *Ruby in Paradise* remained Judd's strongest creative effort.

## NATURAL BORN KILLERS (1994)
Director: Oliver Stone
Writer: Quentin Tarantino and David Veloz
Producers: Jane Hamsher, Don Murphy III, Clayton Townsend

Cast
Woody Harrelson (Mickey Knox)
Juliette Lewis (Mallory Wilson Knox)
Robert Downey Jr. (Wayne Gale)
Tommy Lee Jones (Dwight McClusky)
O-Lan Jones (Mabel, Waitress in Diner)
Ed White II (Pinball Cowboy)
Richard Lineback (Sonny)
Lanny Flaherty (Early Hickey)
Carol-Renee Modrall (Short Order Cook)
Rodney Dangerfield (Ed Wilson)
Ashley Judd (Grace Mulberry)

Summary:
Mickey and Mallory Knox are a Bonnie-and-Clyde-type couple who go on a killing spree that is so violent, so unconscionable in its brutality, that it makes them media celebrities. This dark comedy takes a look at the way violence has been glamorized in America, often to the point of making superstars out of mass murderers. Ashley Judd plays the role of the only living witness to the killings. Her part was cut from the original release, but it was restored for the director's cut when it was issued in video and DVD.

## HEAT (1995)
Director: Michael Mann
Writer: Michael Mann
Producers: Art Linson, Michael Mann

### Cast

Al Pacino (Vincent Hanna)
Robert De Niro (Neil McCauley)
Val Kilmer (Chris Shiherlis)
Jon Voight (Nate)
Tom Sizemore (Michael Cheritto)
Diane Venora (Justine Hanna)
Amy Brenneman (Easy)
Ashley Judd (Charlene Shiherlis)
Mykelti Williamson (Sergeant Drucker)
Wes Studi (Detective Casals)
Ted Levine (Bosko)
Dennis Haysbert (Breedan)
William Fichtner (Roger Van Zant)
Natalie Portman (Lauren)

### Summary:

Neil McCauley is a master thief who puts together a team of crooks to pull off a heist on a bond-bearing armored car. Assigned to the case is Detective Vincent Hanna, a streetwise cop who is McCauley's equal as a strategist. Actually, the men are similar in the way they approach their work. Both men are perfectionists who put their work ahead of their personal relationships. It is the interplay between the two men, even though they are only in the same scene twice, that qualifies this film as a psychological thriller. Ashley Judd plays the wife of one of the gang members.

## THE PASSION OF DARKLY NOON (1995)

Director: Philip Ridley
Writer: Philip Ridley
Producers: Dominic Anciano, Frank Henschke, Alain Kleitsman

### Cast

Brendan Fraser (Darkly Noon)
Ashley Judd (Callie)
Viggo Mortensen (Clay)
Loren Dean (Jude)
Grace Zabriskie (Roxy)
Lou Myers (Quincy)
Kate Harper (Ma)
Mel Cobb (Pa)

**Summary:**

Callie is a young woman who lives on a farm located deep in the forest. Also living on the farm with her is her boyfriend, Clay, a mute who has a propensity for wandering off in the forest for days at a time. One day, while Clay is away from the farm, a stranger named Darkly Noon shows up. He explains that his parents were killed by townspeople who were fearful of their cultlike religious views. Callie allows him to sleep in the barn and tells him that he can stay as long as he wishes. Psychotic to the core, he soon becomes obsessed with Callie and turns on her and her boyfriend in an attempt to destroy them. Hampered by a weak script, this was one of the worst movies of 1995.

## SMOKE (1995)

Director: Wayne Wang
Writer: Paul Auster
Producers: Kenzo Horikoshi, Greg Johnson II, Hisami Kuroiwa,
        Peter Newman

Cast

William Hurt (Paul Benjamin
Harvey Keitel (Auggie Wren)
Jared Harris (Jimmy Rose)
Forest Whitaker (Cyrus Cole)
Ashley Judd (Felicity)
Victor Argo (Vinnie)
Mary B. Ward (April Lee)

**Summary:**

Auggie Wren is the owner of a Brooklyn cigar store that becomes the focal point for a series of neighborhood stories that run parallel to each other and sometimes overlap. One of the stories involves a former lover who shows up at the cigar store to inform Auggie that he has a daughter he does not know about who needs help to escape a life of drug abuse. Ashley Judd plays the role of the daughter. Although she is only on screen for a few minutes, she delivers an emotionally explosive performance.

## A TIME TO KILL (1996)

Director: Joel Schumacher
Writer: Akiva Goldsman, based on the John Grisham novel
Producers: Arnon Milchan, Michael Nathanson, Hunt Lowry

### Cast

Matthew McConaughey (Jake Tyler Brigance)
Sandra Bullock (Ellen Roark)
Samuel L. Jackson (Carl Lee Hailey)
Kevin Spacey (District Attorney Rufus Buckley)
Oliver Platt (Harry Rex Vonner)
Charles Dutton (Sheriff Ozzie Walls)
Donald Sutherland (Lucien Wilbanks)
Kiefer Sutherland (Freddie Lee Cobb)
Ashley Judd (Carla Brigance)
Tonea Stewart (Gwen Hailey)

### Summary:

Carl Lee Hailey is a black Mississippi factory worker who takes the law into his hands after his ten-year-old daughter is raped and beaten by two white thugs. When the men are arrested, he lies in wait and guns them down. Coming to his rescue is Jake Brigance, a conservative white lawyer who sympathizes with Hailey because he has a daughter of his own. He knows in his heart that he would have done the same thing if the situation had been reversed. The situation grows complicated when the Ku Klux Klan intervenes on behalf of the slain white men. From that point on, the story revolves around the tension between the battling mindsets of compassionate conservatives and ultra-right-wing ideologues. A liberal law student who volunteers to assist Brigance in his defense of Hailey injects an element of liberalism into the story, but it seems to get lost in the prevailing question asked by the movie: Is it all right to take another person's life if the cause is perceived to be just? Ashley Judd plays the part of Brigance's wife, who offers the only refuge of higher ground in the story, though that is not obvious until the end of the movie.

## NORMA JEAN AND MARILYN (1996)

Director: Tim Fywell
Writer: Jill Isaacs, based on Anthony Summers's book
Producer: Guy Riedel

### Cast

Ashley Judd (Norma Jean Dougherty)
Mira Sorvino (Marilyn Monroe)
Josh Charles (Eddie Jordan)
Ron Rifkin (Johnny Hyde)
David Dukes (Arthur Miller)

Peter Dobson (Joe DiMaggio)
John Rubinstein (Darryl Zanuck)
Dana Goldstone (Lee Strasberg)

**Summary:**

*Norma Jean and Marilyn* takes the view that there were two different Marilyn Monroes: the one who grew up in a dysfunctional family and had a passion for becoming a movie star, and the one who achieved stardom but was forever trying to reclaim her past. To tell this story, director Tim Fywell used two actresses. Ashley Judd played the young Norma Jean and Mira Sorvino played the star Marilyn Monroe. The film strays into unintentional farce each time it puts the two Marilyn together to converse with each other, but the acting by both actresses is solid throughout.

**NORMAL LIFE (1996)**
Director: John McNaughton
Writer: Peg Haller and Bob Schneider
Producer: Richard Maynard

**Cast**
Ashley Judd (Pam Anderson)
Luke Perry (Chris Anderson)
Bruce A. Young (Agent Parker)
Jim True (Mike Anderson)
Edmund Wyson (Darren)
Michael Skewes (Swift)
Scott Cummins (Hank Chilton)
Kate Walsh (Cindy Anderson)
Tom Towles (Frank Anderson)
Penelope Milford (Adele Anderson)

**Summary:**

*Normal Life* is an extraordinary drama about a seemingly ordinary couple. Chris Anderson, played by Luke Perry, is a cop who has lived his entire life as a straight arrow. His world is turned upside down when he meets Pam, an alcoholic, dope-smoking woman who has turned to drugs for a reason: she is, at her core, a psychotic personality who has progressed into early adulthood by self-medicating herself. Beautifully played by Ashley Judd, Pam pushes Chris to the edge—then jumps into the abyss with him. Many critics found the film disturbing. Others found it to be a fascinating study in madness. Either way, most people seemed to agree that Ashley gave a dazzling performance.

## THE LOCUSTS (1997)
Director: John Patrick Kelley
Writer: John Patrick Kelley
Producers: Bruce Franklin, Marc Ezralow

### Cast
Kate Capshaw (Delilah)
Jeremy Davies (Flyboy)
Vince Vaughn (Clay Hewitt)
Ashley Judd (Kitty)

### Summary:
*The Locusts* is about a drifter (played by Vince Vaughn) who shows up in a small town looking for work. He ends up at a ranch operated by a middle-aged widow (played by Kate Capshaw) who has a passion for young men. Although the drifter soon discovers a love interest (played by Ashley Judd), it is the widow's mentally challenged son who becomes the object of his obsession. Tension arises when the drifter attempts to free the son from his mother's control. The movie attempts to deal with a range of serious subjects, including mental illness, incest, and homosexuality, but without much success.

## KISS THE GIRLS (1997)
Director: Gary Fleder
Writer: David Klass, based on the James Patterson novel
Producers: David Brown, Joe Wizan

### Cast
Morgan Freeman (Dr. Alex Cross)
Ashley Judd (Dr. Kate McTiernan)
Cary Elwes (Nick Ruskin)
Alex McArthur (Davey Sikes)
Tony Goldwyn (William "Will" Rudolph)
Jay O. Sanders (Kyle Craig)
Bill Nunn (John Sampson)
Brian Cox (Chief Hatfield)
Gina Ravera (Naomi Cross)
Helen Martin (Nana Cross)

Tatyana Ali (Janell Cross)
Mena Suvari (Coty Pierce)

## Summary:

*Kiss the Girls* is the movie that established Ashley Judd as a star. It is about a police forensic psychologist, Alex Cross (played by Morgan Freeman), whose niece is kidnapped by a serial killer who keeps his victims imprisoned until he decides what to do with them. There are no clues in the case until one of his victims, Dr. Kate McTierenan (played by Ashley Judd), manages to escape and provide the police with important clues. On the case as a consultant, Cross teams up with McTierenan to solve the crime.

## SIMON BIRCH (1998)

Director: Mark Steven Johnson
Writer: Mark Steven Johnson, based on a novel by John Irving
Producers: Laurence Mark, Roger Birnbaum

### Cast

Ian Michael Smith (Simon Birch)
Joseph Mazzello (Joe Wenteworth)
Ashley Judd (Rebecca Wenteworth)
Oliver Platt (Ben Goodrich)
David Strathairn (Rev. Russell)
Dana Ivey (Grandmother Wenteworth)
Beatrice Winde (Hilde Grove)
Jan Hooks (Miss Leavey)
Cecilley Carroll (Marjorie)
Sumela Kay (Ann)
Sam Morton (Stuart)
Jim Carrey (adult Joe Wenteworth)
John Mazzello (Simon Wenteworth)

## Summary:

*Simon Birch* is about a little boy who grows up thinking he was put on earth for a special purpose. The fact that Simon Birch (played by Ian Michael Smith) is a dwarf makes that easier for him to believe, for why else would God do that to a child without a good reason? Simon Birch's best friend, Joe Wenteworth (played by Jospeh Mazzello), is on a mission of his own: his unmarried mother, Rebecca (played by Ashley Judd), has never disclosed the name of his father and he thinks that life will not be complete until he knows his father's identity. In a plot that sometimes seems a little too perfect, the missions of the two friends merge to provide resolution to the story. Ashley has little screen time in this movie, but her performance is memorable. This movie is based on John Irving's novel *A Prayer for Owen Meany*.

## EYE OF THE BEHOLDER (1999)

Director: Stephan Elliott
Writer: Stephan Elliott, based on the Marc Behm novel
Producers: Tony Smith, Nicolas Clermont, Al Clark

Cast
Ewan McGregor (Eye)
Ashley Judd (Joanna Eris)
Patrick Bergin (Alexander Leonard)
Genevieve Bujold (Dr. Jeanne Brault)
k. d. lang (Hilary)
Jason Priestley (Gary)
Anne-Marie Brown (Lucy Wilson)
David Nerman (Mike)
Maria Revelins (Miss Keenan)
Lisa Forget (nurse)

Summary:

*Eye of the Beholder* is about a British intelligence agent called Eye (played by Ewan McGregor) who uses electronic surveillance to spy on his targets. Assigned to the Washington embassy, it is his job to both protect and investigate British officials living in America. It is while he is investigating a case in which a British official is being blackmailed that Eye stumbles across a crime committed by Joanna Eris (played by Ashley Judd). He quickly becomes obsessed with her and follows her across the country as she flees from both her actions and her past. The fact that she is a serial killer, seemingly without redeeming qualities, seems to have little impact on him. He is a voyeur and her life is like a drug that threatens to destroy his life.

## DOUBLE JEOPARDY (1999)

Director: Bruce Beresford
Writer: David Weisberg, Douglas Cook
Producer: Leonard Goldberg

**Cast**
Tommy Lee Jones (Travis Lehman)
Ashley Judd (Elizabeth Parsons)
Benjamin Weir (Matty Parsons)
Jay Brazeau (Bobby Long)
Bruce Greenwood (Nick Parsons/Simon Ryder/Jonathan Devereaux)
John MacLaren (Rudy)
Ed Evanko (Warren)
Annabeth Gish (Angela Green/Angela Ryder)

**Summary:**
*Double Jeopardy* is Ashley Judd's biggest box-office success. It is about a housewife and mother, Libby Parsons (played by Ashley), who is framed for her husband's murder and sent to prison. While serving her time, she entrusts the care of her young son to her best friend, Angie Green (played by Annabeth Gish). One day, quite by accident, she learns that her husband is very much alive and living with Angie. Convinced by a jailhouse lawyer that she has the legal right (not true) to kill her husband once she gets out of prison, she begins a search for him shortly after being paroled from prison. Participating in this search, although for opposite reasons, is her parole officer Travis Lehman (played by Tommy Lee Jones). Although the critics gave this movie mixed reviews, moviegoers seemed to love it.

## WHERE THE HEART IS (2000)
Director: Matt Williams
Writer: Lowell Ganz, Babaloo Mandel
Producers: Susan Cartsonis, David McFadzean, Patricia Whitcher

**Cast**
Natalie Portman (Novalee Nation)
Ashley Judd (Lexie Coop)
Stockard Channing (Thelma "Sister" Husband)
Joan Cusack (Ruth Meyers)
James Frain (Forney Hull)
Dylan Bruno (Willy Jack Pickens)
Ray Prewitt (Tim)

## Summary:

*Where the Heart Is* is about a seventeen-year-old pregnant girl (played by Natalie Portman) who is abandoned in a small Oklahoma town by her boyfriend. For a time, the girl lives in the local Wal-Mart, living off the store like an explorer living off the land, but her secret life becomes public knowledge when she delivers a baby on the floor of the store. When she is taken to the hospital, he meets a nurse (played by Ashley Judd) who befriends her and helps her put her life in order. As time goes by, it is apparent that it is the friend who really needs the help. This movie is notable for several reasons, but especially for a monologue that Ashley delivers about the molestation of her children.

## SOMEONE LIKE YOU (2001)

Director: Tony Goldwyn
Writer: Elizabeth Chandler, based on Laura Zigman's novel
Producers: Lynda Obst

### Cast

Ashley Judd (Jane Goodale)
Greg Kinnear (Ray Brown)
Hugh Jackman (Eddie Alden)
Marisa Tomei (Liz)
Ellen Barkin (Diane Roberts)
Catherine Dent (Alice)
Peter Friedman (Stephen)
Laura Regan (Evelyn)

## Summary:

*Someone Like You* was Ashley Judd's first romantic comedy. Ashley plays Jane Goodale, a talk-show staffer who has problems with the male relationships in her life. When she gives up her apartment to move in with Ray Brown (played by Greg Kinnear), another staffer on the talk show, she realizes she has made yet another mistake when after only six weeks he tells her it just isn't working out. Frustrated by her failures, she secretly writes a sexist column for a men's magazine that accuses all men of being cheaters. The column brings her national fame and complicates her life further when she discovers that she is in love with a man (played by Hugh Jackman) who has invited her into his apartment to live on a platonic basis.

## HIGH CRIMES (2001)
Director: Carl Franklin
Writer: Yuri Zeltser, based on Joseph Finder's novel
Producer: Jesse Beaton, Lisa Henson, Arnon Milchan, Janet Yang
Cast
    Ashley Judd (Claire Kubik)
    Morgan Freeman (Charles Grimes)
    James Caviezel (Tom Chapman)
    Adam Scott (Lt. Terrence Embry)
    Amanda Peet (Jackie Grimaldi)
    Michael Gaston (Major Waldron)

**Summary:**
*High Crimes* was Ashley Judd's second film with Morgan Freeman. She plays a Harvard law professor who defends her husband in a military court after he has been charged with participating in a massacre in El Salvador. Assisting her in the case is Charles Grimes (played by Freeman), a former military officer with military court experience.

## DIVINE SECRETS OF THE YA-YA SISTERHOOD (2002)
Director: Callie Khouri
Writer: Mark Andrus, Callie Khouri
Producer: Bonnie Bruckheimer, Hunt Lowry

Cast
    Sandra Bullock (Sidda Lee Walker)
    Ellen Burstyn (Vivi Abbott Walker)
    James Garner (Shep Walker)
    Ashley Judd (young Vivi)

**Summary:**
Based on the best-selling novel by Rebecca Wells, *Divine Secrets of the Ya-Ya Sisterhood* is about a successful playwright, Sidda Lee Walker (played by Sandra Bullock), who moves to New York from the South, partially to escape her oppressive mother, Vivi (played by Ellen Burstyn). When a national magazine profiles Sidda Lee, Vivi is outraged by comments made about her in the article. A pitched battle between mother and daughter ensues, broken up only by the Ya-Ya Sisterhood, a group of Vivi's lifelong friends. Because this film depicts Sidda Lee and Vivi at three stages in their life—as children, young adults, and at the present time—three different groups of actress had

to be assembled. Ashley Judd plays Vivi as a wild and carefree young adult.

## FRIDA (2002)

Director: Julie Taymor
Writer: Rodrigo Garcia, Gregory Nava
Producer: Salma Hayek and others

### Cast

Salma Hayek (Frida Kahlo)
Alfred Molina (Diego Rivera)
Geoffrey Rush (Leon Trotsky)
Ashley Judd (Tina Modotti)
Edward Norton (Nelson Rockefeller)
Antonio Banderas (David Siqueiros)
Mia Maestro (Cristina Kahlo)
Valeria Golino (Lupe Marin)

### Summary:

*Frida* is about the Mexican artist Frida Kahlo, who made a name for herself by doing paintings of women in which their organs were shown outside their bodies. Ashley Judd took a supporting role in this film, primarily as a favor to Salma Hayek, a coproducer of the film who also plays the lead role.

# Select Bibliography

Cader, Michael, John Jusino, and others. *People Almanac*. New York: Cader Books, 1999.

Dickerson, James L. *Natalie Portman: Queen of Hearts*. Toronto, Canada: ECW Press, 2002.

——————————— *Goin' Back to Memphis: A Century of Blues, Rock 'n' Roll, and Glorious Soul*. New York: Schirmer Books, 1996.

Feiler, Bruce. *Dreaming Out Loud: Garth Brooks, Wynonna Judd, Wade Hayes, and the Changing Face of Nashville*. New York: Avon Books, 1998.

Judd, Naomi, with Bud Schaetzle. *Love Can Build a Bridge*. New York: Fawcett Crest, 1993.

Leamer, Laurence. *Three Chords and the Truth*. New York: HarperCollins, 1997.

Mansfield, Brian, and Gary Graff, editors. *MusicHound Country: The Essential Album Guide*. Detroit, Michigan: Visible Ink Press, 1997.

Moses, Robert, Alicia Pottere, and Beth Rowen, editors. *A&E Entertainment Almanac*. Boston and New York: Houghton Mifflin Company, 1996.

Stambler, Irwin, and Grelun Landon. *Country Music: The Encyclopedia*. New York: St. Martin's Griffin, 1997.

## Magazines and Newspapers

Addiego, Walter. "Revenge of the wronged woman." *San Francisco Examiner*, September 24, 1999.

Ballard, Steve. "Recovering Franchitti hopes to race in CART opener." *USA Today*, January 3, 2000.

Bellafante, Ginia. "Sybil in a Wonderbra." *Time*, May 20, 1996.

Biddle, Frederic M. "Judd's Norma Jean Shines Through Bad Script." *Boston Globe*, May 18, 1996.

Brennan, Patricia. "Sibling Rivalry: An Only Child Who Found Her 'Sisters.'" *Washington Post*, February 20, 1994.

Bruni, Frank. "On the way to paradise Ashley Judd draws raves in her first starring role." *Detroit Free Press*, November 17, 1993.

Burr, Ty. "Out of Focus." *Entertainment Weekly*, February 4, 2000.

——————— "Seeing 'Double.'" *Entertainment Weekly*, February 25, 2000.

Camp, Todd. "Southern charm & despair." *Ft. Worth Star-Telegram*, April 28, 2000.

Cannon, Damian. "The Passion of Darkly Noon." *Movie Reviews UK, 1997.*

Clark, Mike. "Pacino, De Niro spark red-hot 'Heat.'" *USA Today*, date unavailable.

——————— "Grisham's 'Kill' works overtime." *USA Today*, date unavailable.

——————— "'Kiss the Girls' is serial overkill." *USA Today*, date unavailable.

Clehane, Diane. "Ashley Judd: Smart and Sexy." *Biography Magazine*, April 2001.

Cote, Simon. "Heat." *Austin Chronicle*, September 22, 1997.

Crane, Robert. "20 Questions." *Playboy*, May 1999.

DeVault, Russ. "The Judds." *Atlanta Constitution*, January 27, 1994.

DeVries, Hilary. "Unabashedly Ashley." *TV Guide*, May 18–24, 1996.

Crawford, Julie. "Eye of the Beholder director." *North Shore News*, February 7, 2000.

Dickerson, James L. "There's nothing wrong with being country." *Nine-O-One Network*, January/February 1987.

——————— "RCA Records/Nashville chief Joe Galante." *Nine-O-One Network*, February 1988.

——————— "Rocking Into the Sun Set." *Mid-South Magazine*, October 20, 1985.

Dollar, Rob. "Judd sister dances to different drummer." *Kentucky New Era*, August 1986.

——————— "Hollywood Actress remembers that 'crazy' encounter." *Kentucky New Era*, spring 1994.

Dowling, Chuck. "Normal Life (1996)." *Jacksonville Film Journal*, date unavailable.

East, Jim. "Wynonna's ex stays free if 'Star' repaid." *Nashville Tennessean*, January 20, 2000.

Ebert, Roger. "Heat." *Chicago Sun-Times*, December 15, 1995.

——————— "Normal Life." *Chicago Sun-Times*, October 10, 1996.

——————— "The Locusts." *Chicago Sun-Times*, 1997.

——————— "Double Jeopardy." *Chicago Sun-Times*, date unavailable.

————————— "Where the Heart Is." *Chicago Sun-Times*, April 4, 2000.

————————— "Someone Like You." *Chicago Sun-Times*, March 30, 2001.

Ebner, Mark. "Hep-C Generation." *Details*, October 1999.

Fine, Marshall. "School Daze: An Interview with actress Natalie Portman." *Drdrew.com.*

Fuller, Graham. "Mira Sorvino." *Interview*, November 1995.

Gleiberman, Owen. "Don't Have a Cow." *Entertainment Weekly*, April 6, 2001.

Griffiths, John. "Driving Miss Ashley." *McCall's*, September 2000.

Guthmann, Edward. "In the 'Heat' of Violence De Niro, Pacino— spiritual brothers." *San Francisco Chronicle*, December 15, 1995.

————————— "'Normal Life' Is Neither." *San Francisco Chronicle*, January 24, 1997.

Hayek, Salma. "Ashley alight." *Interview*, September 1998.

Hochman, David. "She's a little bit country/she's a little bit Hollywood." *Us Magazine*, January 1996.

Jensen, Jeff. "Queen of Heart." *Entertainment Weekly*, April 21, 2000.

King, Susan. "Act of Faith: Naomi Judd reveals why she decided to cooperate with a TV biopic." *Los Angeles Times (TV Times)*, May 14–20, 1995.

Hairston, Gail. "Star Found in Rain Forest." *Arts & Sciences* (University of Kentucky), date unavailable.

Hilburn, Robert. "Wondrous Wynonna." *Los Angeles Times*, March 18, 1996.

———————— "Reunited...for Now." *Los Angeles Times*, March 2, 2000.

Hinson, Hal. "Natural Born Killers." *Washington Post*, August 26, 1994.

———————— "Heat." *Washington Post*, December 15, 1995.

Hobson, Louis B. "Dumb luck." *Calgary Sun*, April 23, 1997.

———————— "Ashley Judd is loving life." *Calgary Sun*, September 28, 1997.

Hochman, David. "She's a Little Bit Country, She's a Little Bit Hollywood, The Youngest Judd Heats Up." *Us Magazine*, January 1996.

Holden, Stephen. "Casanova Complex: Collecting For the Kill." *New York Times*, October 3, 1997.

———————— "Tiny Boy with an Enormously Consuming Quest." *New York Times*, September 11, 1998.

Hong, Neil Chue. "The Passion of Darkly Noon." *Edinburgh University Film Society Programme*, 1997–98.

Hosier, Annie. "Wynonna Puts the Bad Times Behind Her." *Las Vegas Sun*, May 15, 1998.

Iwasaki, Scott. "Sassy Wynonna steals show from Bolton." *Deseret News*, June 30, 1998.

James, Caryn. "2 Bodies for the 2 Marilyn Monroes." *New York Times*, May 18, 1996.

Johnson, Kevin. "Bolton's Over the Top/Judd's Restrained." *St. Louis Post-Dispatch*, June 20, 1998.

Johnson, Mark Steven. "Simon Birch." *Nashville Scene*, September 28, 1998.

Johnson, G. Allen. "Sweat, smoke and Southern decay." *San Francisco Examiner*, October 3, 1997.

Judd, Ashley. "The Life I Might Have Lived." *Marie Claire*, May 1999.

Judd, Naomi. "Why we all want to know someone like Ashley." *Redbook*, May 2001.

Kaplan, Michael. "Ashley Judd." *Us Magazine*, March 1997.

Keel, Beverly. "The Man Nobody Knows." *Nashville Scene*, October 2, 1997.

King, Randall. "Judd, jury & executioner." *Winnipeg Sun*, date unavailable.

LaSalle, Mick. "Turning a Blind 'Eye' to Plain Badness." *San Francisco Chronicle*, January 28, 2000.

———————— "'Someone' Isn't Especially Likable/Talent Wasted in romantic comedy." *San Francisco Chronicle*, March 30, 2001.

Longino, Miriam. "Revelations." *Atlanta Constitution*, February 15, 1996.

Lovell, Glenn. "Ashley Judd: Nashville Goes Hollywood Whole Hog." *San Jose Mercury News*, November 8, 1993.

Maslin, Janet. "From Dainty Little Wife to One Reckless Avenger." *New York Times*, September 24, 1999.

Mathews, Jake. "Simon Birch." *Los Angeles Times*, September 11, 1998.

———————— "The Locusts." *Los Angeles Times*, October 3, 1997.

McKinney, Melonee. "Fans shell out for Judd's junk." *Nashville Tennessean*, August 26, 2000.

Mendoza, N. F. "'Sisters' Star Thrives on Loud-Mouth Roles." *Arizona Republic*, December 9, 1995.

Mitchell, Pamela. "Homecoming candidate disqualified." *Kentucky Kernel*, October 16, 1989.

Morden, Darryl. "Crossing Over." *Hollywood Reporter, April 21, 1998*

————— "Women Rule." *Hollywood Reporter*, September 19, 1997.

Morice, Laura. "Southern Comforts." *Premiere*, October 2001.

Morse, Steve. "Wynonna experiences 'revelations.'" *Boston Globe* February 14, 1996.

Morris, Bob. "Ashley's World." *Elle Magazine*, September 1999.

Murray, Steve. "Movies: Judd knows who she is—even if you don't." *Atlanta Constitution*, November 12, 1993.

Nance, Kevin. "Ashley in Paradise." *Lexington Herald-Leader*, May 1, 1994.

————— "Ashley in paradise 'respectable'/Judd not fazed by fame of mother." *Lexington Herald-Leader*, May 1, 1994.

Nash, Alanna. "Mother, May I?" *Entertainment Weekly*, February 4, 2000.

Osborne, Bert. "Kentucky's Sweetheart." *Ace Weekly*, March 29, 2001.

Perkins, Ken Parish. "Here Come the Judd." *Orbit*, May 1996.

Perry, Cassandra. "Ground Zero." *Delta Democrat-Times*, June 3, 2001.

Pogrebin, Robin. "Behold! A Hot New Star! But Who Said It First?" *New York Times*, August 12, 1996.

Portman, Janie. "School Is Where Her Heart Is." *Ottawa Citizen*, April 21, 2000.

Rabin, Nathan. "In Henry's wake." *The Onion*, date unavailable.

Rainer, Peter. "Movie Review: Smoke." *Los Angeles Times*, June 9, 1995.

Rea, Steven X. "Mother and Daughter." *Philadelphia Inquirer*, December 11, 1984.

Rebello, Stephen. "Greg Kinnear." *Maxim*, December 2000.

Rochlin, Margy. "Tough Guy Finds His Warm and Fuzzy Side." *The New York Times*, November 2, 1997.

Roland, Tom. "Wynonna expecting 2nd child, plans to wed." *Nashville Tennessean*, January 5, 1996.

——————————— "Judds reunite with new energy." *Nashville Tennessean*, January 1, 2000.

Rowe, Douglas J. "Ashley Judd's Public, Private Life." *Associated Press*, October 6, 2000.

Sasfy, Joe. "The Judds: Rural Urbanity." *The Washington Post*, November 30, 1984.

Schaefer, Stephen. "The non-singing daughter of country music's first family plays to win in Double Jeopardy." *Mr. Showbiz, 2000.*

Schickel, Richard. "Summons to Justice." *Time*, July 29, 1996.

Schmitt, Brad. "Naomi speaks about her stripper run-in." *Nashville Tennessean*, January 30, 2001.

——————————— "Stripper wants Naomi charged with assault." *Nashville Tennessean*, January 27, 2001.

——————————— "A male stripper, Naomi Judd and teen-age kids." *Nashville Tennessean*, January 26, 2001.

Schoemer, Karen. "Big Hair, Big Heart." *Newsweek*, February 12, 1996.

Scott, A. O. "So Are All Men Dogs or Are They Really Bulls?" *New York Times*, March 30, 2001.

Seiler, Andy. "Crawling 'Locusts' leaves lust in the dust." *USA Today*, December 1, 1998.

Shiffman, John. "Wynonna's ex faces jail for gabbing." *Nashville Tennessean*, December 18, 1999.

Shulgasser, Barbara. "Giving direction to 'Normal Life.'" *San Francisco Examiner*, January 24, 1997.

Sischy, Ingrid. "Interview." *Interview*, August 1996.

Smith, Sandy. "Being stars tests, and strengthens, the bonds between Judds." *Nashville Tennessean*, date unavailable.

Spanjian, Marilee. "Wynonna's sale a gold mine for shoe fanatics." *Nashville Tennessean*, August 25, 2000.

Stack, Peter. "Freeman, Judd Save the 'Girls.'" *San Francisco Chronicle*, October 3, 1997.

——————— "This 'Heart Misses a Beat." *San Francisco Chronicle*, April 28, 2000.

Statne, Vince. "Blue Blood: UK basketball's most famous fan." *Kentucky Monthly*, November 1998.

Stein, Jeannine. "Dressed to Present." *Los Angeles Times*, March 19, 1998.

Strauss, Bob. "Actress Ashley Judd stays true to herself." *Boston Globe*, September 28, 1997.

Svetkey, Benjamin. "Making His Case." *Entertainment Weekly*, February 11, 2000.

Svokos, Heather. "Judd the not-so obscure Ashley does the lecture circuit." *Lexington Herald-Leader*, April 9, 1999.

———————— "She got fame: Ashley Judd makes starring lineup in the acting game." *Lexington Herald-Leader*, February 23, 1995.

———————— "'Eye of the Beholder' no easy ride for Ashley Judd." *Lexington Herald-Leader*, February 1, 2000.

———————— "'Birch' was work of love for Judd." *Lexington Herald-Leader*, September 18, 1998.

———————— "For Ashley Judd, A New Role Is Murder." *Lexington Herald-Leader*, February 3, 2000.

———————— "A change of pace for Ashley Judd." *Lexington Herald-Leader*, March 30, 2001.

Teasdale, Barbara. "Ashley Judd Emerges from the Shadow of Her Famous Family." *Reel.com*.

Thompson, Bob. "Catering to the gypsy in Judd." *Toronto Sun*, September 30, 1997.

———————— "Judd in Jeopardy." *Toronto Sun*, September 19, 1999.

Travers, Peter. "A Time to Kill." *Rolling Stone*, August 8, 1996.

———————— "Eye of the Beholder." *Rolling Stone*, 1999.

———————— "Someone Like You." *Rolling Stone*, issue 866.

Tucker, Ken. "The Show." *Entertainment Weekly*, April 6, 2001.

Van Wyk, Anika. "Wynonna lives up to family's risk-taking ways." *Calgary Sun*, February 12, 2000.

Vincent, Mal. "Ashley Judd Makes Own Kind of Music on Screen." *Arizona Republic*, October 3, 1997.

Weintraub, Bernard. "Psst. The One with the Third Billing is the Star." *New York Times*, July 21, 1996.

——————————————— "Playing Two Marilyns, The Iconic, the Unloved." *New York Times*, May 15, 1996.

——————————————— "The fabulous Judd no one knows." *Redbook*, November 1997.

Williams, Jeannie. "'Simon' says Judd ready to take off." *USA Today*, August 28, 1998.

Winer, Linda. "'Picnic' Hampered." *Newsday*, April 22, 1994.

Wolley, John. "A Mother & Child Reunion." *Tulsa World*, February 11, 2000.

Wyatt, Gene. "'Kiss the Girls' takes her one step closer to being an acting force." *Nashville Tennessean*, date unavailable.

——————————— "Guess who we spotted at Wal-Mart." *Nashville Tennessean*, April 28, 2000.

——————————— "Three cheers for Ashley." *Nashville Tennessean*, March 30, 2001.

Young, Josh. "Devil's Advocate." *Entertainment Weekly*, August 6, 1999.

Unsigned. "Judds: We're Just Paupers to 'The King.'" *Associated Press*, March 11, 1987.

——————————— "Judge Throws Out Movie Lawsuit." *Associated Press*, March 12, 2001.

——————————— "Ashley Judd Dating Michael Bolton." *Mr. Showbiz*, October 29, 1996.

——————————— "Rather, Grisham hobnob on set of 'Time to Kill.'" *Associated Press*, October 29, 1995.

——————— "Hurricane Wynonna Shakes Up Nashville." *Boston Globe*, February 10, 1996.

——————— "Wynonna's marriage hits the skids after 2 months." *National Enquirer, April 16, 1996.*

——————— "Ashley Judd's Oscar Tease." *Mr. Showbiz*, March 26, 1998.

——————— "Interview with Ashley Judd." *Ampersand* (University of Kentucky), date unavailable.

——————— "Vince Vaughn Interview." *Cosmopolitan*, date unavailable.

——————— "Intruder found at Judd's has bail set at $50,000." *Associated Press*, September 30, 1999.

——————— "Judd fan arrested." *Nashville Tennessean*, September 28, 1999.

——————— "Ashley Judd Snags 'Catwoman' Role." *Associated Press*, April 3, 2001.

——————— "Judd Gets Pay Hike for 'Animal Husbandry.'" *Mr. Showbiz*, January 7, 2000.

——————— "Wynonna: Singing With Mom is Trying." *Associated Press*, July 10, 2001, first published by the *Macomb Daily*.

——————— "The Blues Comes Back to the Delta." *Rolling Stone*, July 19, 2001.

——————— "Judd, ET Settle Lawsuit by Journalist." *Associated Press*, June 18, 2001.

——————— "Wynonna Judd to Marry Road Manager." *Associated Press*, August 23, 2001.

——————— "Celebrities Arrive for Judd Wedding." *Associated Press*, December 10, 2001.

——————— "Ashley Judd Marries Race Car Driver." *Associated Press*, December 13, 2001.

——————— "Ashley Judd." *Internet Movie Database*, date unavailable.

——————— "Great Scot: Dario Franchitti." *Talk*, June/July 2001.

## Court Documents
State of Tennessee v. Thomas G. Beard, Circuit Court of Williamson County, Tennessee, No. S-82-253.

State of Tennessee v. Guy Paul Dukes, General Sessions Court of Williamson County, Tennessee, No. WCSD 99-9379.

## Television
Pauley, Jane. "Naomi and Wynonna Judd together again." *NBC Dateline*, December 3, 1999.

Rose, Charlie. "Interview with Natalie Portman." *The Charlie Rose Show*, May 4, 2000.

*CNN Showbiz Weekend*, the Academy Awards, March 2001.

# Index